EDWARD ABBEY, a self-proclaimed "agrarian anarchist," has been hailed as the "Thoreau of the American West." Known nationally as a champion of the individual and one of this country's foremost defenders of the natural environment, he was the author of twenty books, both fiction and nonfiction, including *Desert Solitaire, The Monkey Wrench Gang,* and *The Journey Home*. In 1989, at the age of sixty-two, Edward Abbey died in Oracle, Arizona.

BY EDWARD ABBEY

The Journey Home

*Some Words in Defense
of the American West*

Edward Abbey

Illustrations by

JIM STILES

Ⓟ

A PLUME BOOK

PLUME
Published by the Penguin Group
Penguin Books USA Inc., 375 Hudson St., New York, N.Y. 10014, U.S.A.
Penguin Books Ltd, 27 Wrights Lane, London W8 5TZ, England
Penguin Books Australia Ltd, Ringwood, Victoria, Australia
Penguin Books Canada Ltd, 10 Alcorn Avenue, Toronto, Ontario, Canada
M4V 3B2
Penguin Books (N.Z.) Ltd, 182-190 Wairau Road, Auckland 10, New Zealand

Penguin Books Ltd, Registered Offices: Harmondsworth, Middlesex, England

Published by Plume, an imprint of Dutton Signet, a division of Penguin
Books USA Inc. Previously published in a Dutton edition.

First Plume Printing, January, 1991

The author wishes to thank the trustees of the Guggenheim Foundation
for a fellowship award given during the preparation of this book.

Grateful acknowledgment is also made to the publishers of the following
periodicals and books for permission to reprint portions of *The Journey
Home*, which appeared originally, in somewhat different form, in their
pages: *American West, Audubon Magazine, High Country News, Mountain Gazette,
National Geographic Society, Not Man Apart Magazine, Plateau Magazine,
Playboy, Sierra Club Books, Time, Inc.*

 REGISTERED TRADEMARK—MARCA REGISTRADA

LIBRARY OF CONGRESS CATALOGING-IN-PUBLICATION DATA

Abbey, Edward, 1927-1989
    The journey home : some words in defense of the American West /
Edward Abbey ; illustrations by Jim Stiles.
        p.   cm.
    Reprint. Originally published: New York : Dutton, c1977.
    ISBN 0-525-48396-9
    ISBN 978-0-452-26562-2 (international)

    1. Abbey, Edward, 1927-1989—Homes and haunts—West (U.S.)
2. West (U.S.)—Description and travel—1951-1980. 3. Authors,
American—20th century—Bibliography. 4. Wilderness areas—West
(U.S.) I. Title.
[PS3551.B2Z468   1991]
813'.54—dc20
[B]   90-45182
                                                       CIP

Set in ITC New Baskerville
Original edition designed by Dorothea von Elbe

This book is for Mildred Postlewaite Abbey, my wise, enduring and beautiful mother; and for Paul Revere Abbey, my father, who taught me to hate injustice, to defy the powerful, and to speak for the voiceless.

"The earth, like the sun, like the air,
belongs to everyone—and to no one."

Contents

Introduction

I am not a naturalist. I never was and never will be a naturalist. I'm not even sure what a naturalist is except that I'm
not one. I'm not even an amateur naturalist. The only Latin
I know is *omnia vincit amor*—and *in vino veritas*. In boyhood I
thought *cave canem* meant "beware the cane." I never studied
botany or zoology or ecology or any other branch of natural
science. Like most war veterans I went to college but mainly
because that seemed easier than working. While in school I
majored in philosophy, not biology, and my intellectual
heroes were Democritus (who died laughing—laughing at

Plato) and Bertrand Russell (who died fighting) and Lao-tse (who wrote one small best-selling book) and Beethoven (who will never die). The subject of my master's thesis was politics—the morality of violence. I failed journalism, not once but twice. During my long erratic seasonal career with the National Park Service I was employed never as a naturalist but as a ranger and sometimes as a fire lookout, the latter role an ideal one for the amateur philosopher. Today I consider myself a working novelist (one of the few in America who works for a living) and my highest ambition is to compose one good, very long novel—*The Fat Masterpiece*. That accomplished, I shall retire to my hut in the heart of the desert and spend the remainder of my days in meditation, contemplating my novel. I hope to become a rock. I plan to return in future incarnations as a large and lazy soaring bird.

The aim of this preamble is not to indulge a foolish vanity, as might appear, but to assist those reviewers and critics who persist in attempting to read my work as studies in natural history. Led wildly astray by this misunderstanding, they are puzzled and exasperated by such books as *Black Sun* and *The Monkey Wrench Gang,* the former a romance and the other a sort of comic extravaganza, which fail to meet their predetermined specifications. Unless revised, the critics' expectations will likewise be disappointed in this book.

Much as I admire the work of Thoreau, Muir, Leopold, Beston, Krutch, Eiseley and others, I have not tried to write in their tradition. I don't know how. I've done plenty of plain living, out of necessity, but don't know how to maintain a constant level of high thinking. It's beyond me. Some itch in the lower parts is always dragging me back to mundane earth, down to my own level, among all you other common denominators out there in the howling wilderness we call modern American life. My literary idols anyway have always been people like Rabelais, Knut Hamsun, B. Traven, Theodore Dreiser, Celine, Steinbeck—the unloved.

Several years ago I published a book called *Desert Solitaire,* followed closely by *Cactus Country, Appalachian Wilderness* and *Slickrock.* Although classified by librarians as "nature books," they belong to the category of personal history rather than natural history. Since they deal ostensibly with actual places, they do contain descriptions of certain flora and fauna, bushes and bugs, rocks and snakes and the weather. All the technical information was stolen from reliable sources and I am happy to stand behind it. But as people who may have read them should know, those four books are in the main simple narrative accounts of travel and adventure, with philosophical commentary added here and there to give the prose a high-toned surface gleam. They have little to do with biological science.

For I am not a naturalist. Hardly even a sportsman. True, I bagged my first robin at the age of seven, with a BB gun back on the farm in Home, Pennsylvania, but the only birds I can recognize without hesitation are the turkey vulture, the fried chicken, and the rosy-bottomed skinny-dipper. My favorite animal is the crocodile. I'll never make it as a naturalist. If a label is required say that I am one who loves unfenced country. *The open range.* Call me a ranger. Though I've hardly earned the title I claim it anyway. The only higher honor I've ever heard of is to be called a man.

So much for the mantle and britches of Thoreau and Muir. Let Annie Dillard wear them now. As I see it my problem here is to explain what this book is about. Not to classify it but to introduce it. This is the kind of book that needs an introduction and to make sure it's done right I'm doing it myself.

The Journey Home, like its predecessors *Desert Solitaire* and the others, is partly a book of personal history, one man's odyssey in search of Ithaca. Like so many others in this century I found myself a displaced person shortly after birth and have been looking half my life for a place to take my stand. Now that I think I've found it, I must defend it. My home is the American West. All of it. This book is in part the story of how I discovered my home, in part a description of it, and in its emphasis an effort to defend that home against alien invaders—as will be shown—from another world. Most of the book was written during the past five years in the form of adversary essays and assays, polemics, visions and hallucinations, and published piece by piece in various odd places from *Audubon* to the *Vulgarian Digest*. Fragments of autobiography, journalistic battle debris, nightmares and daydreams, bits and butts of outdoors philosophizing, all stirred together in a blackened iron pot over a smoking fire of juniper, passionflower and thorny mesquite. *Agitate.* Redneck slumgullion, like any stew, makes a tasty, nutritious and coherent whole. And why not? Society too, human society, is like a stew—if you don't keep it stirred up you get a lot of *scum* on top. Coherent or not, these chunks of words share one common theme: the need to make sense of private experience by exploring the connections and contradictions among wildness and wilderness, community and anarchy; between civilization and human freedom. Eat hearty, mates.

Final note. If certain ideas and emotions are expressed in these pages with what seems an extreme intransigence, it is not merely because I love an argument and wish to provoke (though I do), but because I am—really am—an extremist, one who lives and loves by choice far out on the very verge of things, on the edge of the abyss, where this world falls off into the depths of another. That's the way I like it.

E. A.

Wolf Hole, Arizona

Hallelujah on the Bum

In the summer of 1944, the year before the year I fell in love, I hitchhiked from Pennsylvania to Seattle by way of Chicago and Yellowstone National Park; from Seattle down the coast to San Francisco; and from there by way of Barstow and Needles via boxcar, thumb, and bus through the Southwest back home to the old farm, three months later. I started out with twenty dollars in my pocket and a piece of advice, cryptic I'd say, from my old man: "Don't let anybody take you for a punk." I didn't know what he meant. I was seventeen: wise, brown, ugly, shy, poetical; a bold, stupid, sun-dazzled kid, out to see the country before giving his life in the war against Japan. A kind of hero, by God! Terrified but willing.

Chicago. A good truck driver took me through the core of the city, right through the Loop, and even in summer it seemed to me the bleakest, hardest, coldest town I'd ever seen; I've never been back. In Minnesota I was picked up by a kindly middle-aged shoe salesman who tried to seduce me; I didn't understand what he wanted and resisted his timid advances. I was so innocent, so ignorant, I had never even heard of homosexuality. Maybe that is what saved me. Meantime I was scribbling, scribbling, keeping a log all the way, suffering already the first pangs of the making of books.

South Dakota. Broke. I stacked wheat for ten days under the summer sun, huge sheaves heavy with dew, and got sick drinking the hard artesian water. In a little town named Pierre I stopped in a drugstore near the capitol for a thin wartime vanilla milkshake. A group of giant plainsmen in gabardine suits and big hats sat near me drinking coffee, talking politics. One introduced himself to me, said he was the governor of South Dakota. I believed him. He was.

Through the Badlands. Another milkshake at Wall's. On to Wyoming, where near Greybull I saw for the first time something I had dreamed of seeing for ten years. There on the western horizon, under a hot, clear sky, sixty miles away, crowned with snow (in July), was a magical vision, a legend come true: the front range of the Rocky Mountains. An impossible beauty, like a boy's first sight of an undressed girl, the image of those mountains struck a fundamental chord in my imagination that has sounded ever since.

Among the forests, bears, paint pots, boiling pools, and gushing geysers of Yellowstone. Traffic was getting mighty scarce. Picked up and then left at a side road in the Idaho Panhandle, I walked all afternoon, all evening, all through the night, along the deserted highway, through a dark forest in the high country, and heard a cougar scream. I stopped once and slept for a while in a deep, dry, grassy ditch until the cold drove me up and onward.

In the morning a rancher picked me up, took me along for another fifty miles. He offered me a job for the summer, said he'd teach me to be a cowboy. My God, but I was tempted; yet the westering urge was too strong in me. I thought I couldn't wait to see the Pacific Ocean and declined his offer. A mistake.

Seattle was just another big city. All cities tend to look pretty much alike from the hitchhiker's point of view. I didn't even see the ocean. Going south to Portland, I got a ride with a long, lean fellow from Oklahoma, who said his name was Fern. He was a hard, tough, rambling hombre, and he looked like Gary Cooper; I liked him at once, especially when he stopped in the woods and let me fire his revolver at some whiskey bottles. He said he was a wounded veteran, not a draft dodger. He showed me his tattoos: on his left arm a mermaid, on his right the motto Semper Fidelis.

He had no money; I bought the food and was also privileged to stand guard at night while Fern, with his rubber hose (Okie credit card), siphoned gas from cars parked on dark streets in small Oregon towns.

One evening I sat alone in the car for half an hour, on a side street, while Fern went off with his gun to see a friend, he said. He came back in a hurry, breathing heavily, giggling, and we roared into the night, out of that town. Driving south, he pulled a bottle from a brown paper sack, opened it, drank, offered me a swig. My first taste of hard liquor. After another drink, grinning, he showed me a wad of greenbacks. I was scared, but impressed. He said he was going to get him a big fat woman that night. And he did. . . .

Next day we drove into northern California, to Sacramento. We stopped at a gas station, where I went to the toilet; when I came back outside, Fern and his car were gone. With him went my coat, my hat, my satchel containing everything else I possessed except the shirt, pants, and shoes I was wearing. My wallet and some twenty dollars were also gone, since Fern had advised me to keep my money and papers locked in the glove compartment of the car. Safer, he'd explained.

I had ten cents in my pocket and a jackknife. I was hungry. The first thing I did was put to good use one of the few useful things Fern had taught me: how to make a meal from a cup of coffee. Entering a drugstore and taking a counter stool, I ordered one cup of coffee and pulled the cream pitcher and the sugar bowl close. As I slowly drank the coffee, I kept adding as much sugar and cream as the mug would hold, making a thick, sweet sludge, highly nourishing, which I scooped up with the spoon. Fortified, I walked out. And I still had a nickel in my pocket.

The following day I was knocking pecans out of a tree for pay. There was this pecan tree and a tarp spread out on the ground beneath it and a wooden mallet in my hands. Every time I whacked the trunk a shower of pecans, leaves, dust, twigs, bugs, caterpillars and birds' nests fell out of the tree and into my hair and down inside my shirt. After one afternoon of pecan knocking, I took my pay and thumbed a ride to Stockton, where I'd been told they needed hands for the peach canneries.

For two weeks I worked in the cannery, slopping around over the juicy floors, the squashed and quartered peaches. The air, hot and steamy, reeked with the sweet stink of rotten fruit. I carried crates of peaches off the loading dock and up to the women on the line, whose work was to skin and slice the peaches. Since they were paid by the crate, they preferred large peaches—less work, same money—and whenever I brought one of these ladies a crate of small peaches she would scream at me in language I shudder to remember and sometimes fling a few hard green ones at me as I retreated fast, ducking down behind the stacks of empties. They were all sick, those women, sick with fury and insult, overwork and boredom, abandoned by their menfolk, fighting one another, penned up all day in that foul shed. They worked with sharp little knives; one day I saw a woman running down the aisle with her hands over her face, blood streaming between her fingers.

Taking my pay, I left them there, those poor women in their outrage and misery, and took off afoot for Yosemite Valley. I wanted to see the big trees, the high waterfalls, and the granite face of El Capitan. Made it too, by God, after a couple of days' trudging through the golden hills, past the manzanita and Emory oaks, along the narrow asphalt road that led into John Muir's range of light.

Later. . . . Back into the flat and sweltering Central Valley, south through Fresno—where I saw Saroyan's home—to Bakersfield, up over the Tehachapi Pass and into the desert. At once I felt as if I had left California behind and was mighty glad of it. A long, windy night on the back of a flatbed truck, under the new moon, brought me at dawn to the town of Needles and my first view of the Colorado River.

Needles in August must be one of the two or three hottest inhabited places on earth. A fearful, scalding heat that makes you hurry from shade to shade. With forty dollars in my shoe and hope in my heart, I stood all day on the eastern edge of town, thumb out, begging for a lift. Nobody stopped. Across the river waited a land that filled me with strange excitement: crags and pinnacles of naked rock, the dark cores of ancient volcanoes, a vast and silent emptiness smoldering with heat, color, and indecipherable significance, above which floated a small number of pure, clear, hard-edged clouds. For the first time I felt I was getting close to the West of my deepest imaginings—the place where the tangible and the mythical become the same.

All day long I waited at the side of the highway, sheltering in the scant shade of a mesquite tree, cocking my thumb at the few cars and trucks that approached. They were very few; this was wartime and not many people had business in the backlands of Arizona. I would have walked, but had sense enough to perceive that the desert sun could make walking not merely unpleasant but hazardous—even suicidal. I did not have sense enough, however, to understand that most southwesterners, in those years before the advent of air-conditioning, stayed passive and shaded up during the summer days and did their driving at night. And nobody in Needles cared to take the enormous trouble of telling me about it. Nearby, across the broken glass, the weeds, the junkyard, the ditch, ran the tracks of the Atchison, Topeka, and Santa Fe ("Holy Faith") Railroad. Now and then I could see a freight train forming up in the yards, brakemen hanging one-handed to the ladders, some old hog in bib overalls, blue-striped cap, and necktie peering out of the engine cab. I waved; they waved back like all good railroaders.

At evening time, drinking my third quart of milk that day, still stranded, I became aware of a black man standing in the brush between me and the tracks. He was watching me with care. There's something in my face that never fails to catch the eye of panhandlers. I've never been missed by a bum yet. And so, when the white-haired old black man came close and mumbled a few words at my ear, I had to go into the café across the highway and buy a couple of hamburgers and another quart of milk and bring them back to him. He tried to explain why he didn't want to go into the café himself, but at the time I couldn't quite figure it out.

We had supper together under the mesquite tree at the edge of the quiet highway. Exchanged intelligence. His name I no longer recollect, but his destination was Chicago. Mine was Home—Home, Pennsylvania. He offered to show me how to get there.

After sundown, in the lavender loveliness of the desert twilight, we crept through the junk and creosote bushes toward the railway and squatted down in a comfortable ditch within spitting distance of the rails. From the division yards to the west came the clash and shock of coupling iron, the screech of hot metal, the rumble of switch engines. We waited, smoking my companion's hand-rolled Bull Durham cigarettes.

We heard two sharp whistles—the highball signal. Presently the train came slowly through the gloom, three big diesels pulling a string of boxcars so long we couldn't see the caboose. Ponderously the cars rolled by, slowly picking up speed; I could see the wooden ties sinking under the wheels, rising between them. Sealed boxcars passed us bearing brands from all over the nation: Southern Pacific, Great Northern, New York Central, Denver and Rio Grande, Union Pacific, Baltimore and Ohio, Pennsy, Santa Fe, Wabash, Lackawanna, Eastern Seaboard (Route of Phoebe Snow). . . . The first empty appeared, doors open; we stood up, stepped into the cinders and gravel of the roadbed, began to trot along beside the train. As the empty came abreast of us, my new friend threw his bundle in, grabbed hold of the edge of the doorway, pulled himself up and half into the car. He turned to give me assistance as I ran along. I was clutching at the edge of the sliding door with one hand, holding my pack and bedroll with the other, reluctant to toss them inside because now I wasn't certain I could get aboard. The floor of the boxcar was chest high and the train was gaining speed. As I hesitated, the old black man grappled me at the wrist with both his big paws and hauled me halfway in; I danced along the ties on tiptoe at twenty miles per hour. "Come on, boy," he hollered, "pitch your roll up and get in here." I made it.

We rattled half the night up and out of the valley of the Colorado, up into the highlands of western Arizona. We sat in the corner of the boxcar, forward out of the wind, on piles of moldy straw, jounced and jolted by the iron wheels, the hard boards, the shaking, swaying car. Nevertheless, I slept. Missed the moonlight on the mesas. Awoke as the train slowed down outside Kingman, pulling into the division. We decided to stay aboard, though it meant chancing capture by the yard bulls. The train stopped in the center of the yards, surrounded by floodlights, other trains, the cyclone fences. An express roared through in a blast of iron, whistle blaring away and off into the distance. We huddled in the darkest corner of our boxcar, waiting, and heard the brakemen pass swinging their lanterns and talking. Nobody looked in. Our train backed off the siding, detached or attached a few more cars, lurched forward onto the mainline. Again we were rolling eastward, climbing in wide arcs toward the summit of the Colorado Plateau, into the yellow pine forests of the high country. Though it was still August, the night became very cold; the old bum and I squeezed together for warmth.

At Flagstaff I got caught. Not by the railroad men, but by the city cops. We'd jumped off the train as it was pulling into the yard and taken a detour around the station, intending to catch another freight on the east side of town. Half frozen, we also needed something hot to eat and drink. While my buddy skulked in the shadows, I walked toward the center of town to find a café that might still be open. It must've been after midnight. The cops picked me up. I still had forty dollars in my left shoe, but I wasn't going to tell them about it. They drove me to City Hall, booked me for vagrancy, and threw me into the drunk tank for the rest of the night.

Cold steel, cold cement, a rabble of coughing, drunken, sick bums sprawled on the floor, curled up in the corners. The smell of vomit and urine, the fumes of sweet wine, the peculiar stale and bitter odor of old sweat-soaked rags. There were no benches, no bunks, no tables, nothing but this tank of steel and concrete and in the center of the ceiling, protected by wire mesh, one yellow light bulb.

Ah, one other thing, most weird and marvelous, like something out of a dream. Did I really see it? Perhaps it was a dream. As I write these words a quarter of a century later, I am no longer certain what was real, what was unreal.

There was a cage within the cage. Yes. And the bars of this inner cage were painted yellow. And inside the inner cage—alone—was one giant, gleaming, half-naked Negro, mad as the moon, who howled and bellowed and sang and jabbered all night long.

In the morning the guards marched us into a courtroom. The judge kept us waiting half an hour, to teach us respect for the law, then came shuffling in, black gown and all. The guards made us stand up. The judge sat down. We sat down. Justice moved swiftly. The drunks pleaded guilty—most of them Indians—and received their sentences on the spot. Which they had already served. When my turn came, I pleaded not guilty, creating a small sensation behind the bench. The judge and the clerk held a consultation; then the judge informed me that my trial was scheduled for December 10, about three and a half months hence, and that I would be confined in the city jail until that time unless I was prepared to post bond in the amount of fifty dollars. I said I didn't have fifty dollars. He asked me how much I had. After a moment's hesitation I said a dollar and forty cents, which was the amount the police had confiscated, along with my pocketknife, pack, and bedroll, when they locked me up. The judge asked me if I was a draft dodger. I said no. He asked to see my draft card. I told him I was only seventeen and therefore not registered. He reduced the bail to one dollar and told me to get the hell out of Flagstaff and never come back.

The cops gave me back my possessions, including the balance of my apparent funds, the forty cents. One of them took me into a restaurant and bought me a good lunch and returned my dollar and then drove me to the eastern edge of town and dropped me by the highway. He warned me to stay off the trains because some of them carried military equipment and armed guards who were dying for an opportunity to shoot a potential saboteur. This seemed like good advice; during the day before, at Needles, I had noticed the tanks, trucks, and artillery pieces chained to the flatbeds, although I had not seen any guards on the trains. I spent the remainder of the day hitchhiking, but got exactly nowhere. After sundown and supper I slunk into the forest, spread my sleeping bag under the pines, and shivered through a second bitter night. Early in the morning I caught an eastbound freight, alone this time, pulling myself into another empty boxcar just as the train was beginning to roll out of the yards.

A magnificent day—warm, clear, brilliant with sunshine. All through the morning we rumbled, rattled, and roared across the great plateau of northern Arizona, stopping now and then to let more important trains pass, but making good time all the same. Through the wide-open door of my sidedoor Pullman I saw for the first time in my life the high rangelands of the Navajos, the fringes of the Painted Desert, the faraway buttes and mesas of Hopi country. Sometimes I would catch a glimpse of a hogan under a scarp of sandstone, a team and wagon hitched by the door, a couple of Indians sprawled in the shade of a juniper tree. It all looked good to me. And then we came to New Mexico.

Brightest New Mexico. The sharp, red cliffs of Gallup. Mesas and mountains in the distance. Lava beds baking under the sun. Old volcanoes. Indian villages, cornfields, antique adobe churches, children splashing in a stream, an enchanted mesa. And over all a golden light, a golden stillness, a sweet but awesome loneliness—one old white horse browsing on a slope miles away from any sign of man; no fences; one solitary windmill standing by a grove of junipers, cowpaths radiating toward the horizon; a single cottonwood tree, green as life, in the hot red sand of a dry riverbed.

Proud of my freedom and hobohood I stood in the doorway of the boxcar, rocking with the motion of the train, ears full of the rushing wind and the clattering wheels, and stared and stared and stared, like a starving man, at the burnt, barren, bold, bright landscape passing before my eyes. Telegraph poles flashed by close to the tracks, the shining wires dipped and rose, dipped and rose; but beyond the line and the road and the nearby ridges, the queer foreign shapes of mesa and butte seemed barely to move at all; they revolved slowly at an immense distance, strange right-angled promontories of rose-colored rock that remained in view, from my slowly altering perspective, for an hour, for two hours, at a time. And all of it there, simply *there,* neither hostile nor friendly, but full of a powerful, mysterious promise.

In the evening we came to a town of 35,000 souls that lay in a shallow valley in the desert between volcanoes on the west and—on the east—a mountain range pink as the heart of a watermelon.

Albuquerque. Through the middle of this small dusty city ran a wide but shallow river the color of mud, shining like polished brass under the cloud-reflected light of sunset.

The train slowed, approaching the yards, I jumped off and rolled in the cinders, tumbleweeds, and broken wine bottles of the ditch. Dragging my gear I crawled to my feet and limped along the street toward the heart of town. Great golden spokes of light streamed across the sky. Blue herons croaked in the willows by the water. Three rough-looking toughs in blue jeans and straw cowboy hats followed me up the road, laughing, welcoming me to New Mexico. *"Chinga tu madre, cabrón."* Sons of Pancho Villa. I said nothing. They lost interest in me and turned away. I entered the city, up First Street into Albuquerque's skid row. It looked familiar.

After three months of wandering I was homesick. I longed for the warm green hills of Pennsylvania, for the little wooden baseball towns, the sulfurous creeks and covered bridges, the smoky evenings rich with fireflies; I thought of the winding red-dog road that led under oak and maple trees toward the creaking old farmhouse that was our home, where the dogs waited on the front porch, where my sister and my brothers played in the twilight under the giant sugar maple, where my father and mother sat inside in the amber light of kerosene lamps, listening to their battery-powered Zenith radio, waiting for me. I was sick for home.

Safe in the Greyhound bus depot, I took off my shoe and bought a ticket straight through to Pennsylvania.

2

The Great American Desert

In my case it was love at first sight. This desert, all deserts,
any desert. No matter where my head and feet may go, my
heart and my entrails stay behind, here on the clean, true,
comfortable rock, under the black sun of God's forsaken
country. When I take on my next incarnation, my bones will
remain bleaching nicely in a stone gulch under the rim of
some faraway plateau, way out there in the back of beyond.
An unrequited and excessive love, inhuman no doubt but
painful anyhow, especially when I see my desert under attack. "The one death I cannot bear," said the Sonoran-

Arizonan poet Richard Shelton. The kind of love that makes
a man selfish, possessive, irritable. If you're thinking of a
visit, my natural reaction is like a rattlesnake's—to warn you
off. What I want to say goes something like this.

Survival Hint #1: Stay out of there. Don't go. Stay home
and read a good book, this one for example. The Great
American Desert is an awful place. People get hurt, get sick,
get lost out there. Even if you survive, which is not certain,
you will have a miserable time. The desert is for movies and
God-intoxicated mystics, not for family recreation.

Let me enumerate the hazards. First the Walapai tiger,
also known as conenose kissing bug. *Triatoma protracta* is a
true bug, black as sin, and it flies through the night quiet as
an assassin. It does not attack directly like a mosquito or
deerfly, but alights at a discreet distance, undetected, and
creeps upon you, its hairy little feet making not the slightest
noise. The kissing bug is fond of warmth and like Dracula
requires mammalian blood for sustenance. When it reaches
you the bug crawls onto your skin so gently, so softly that
unless your senses are hyperacute you feel nothing. Select-
ing a tender point, the bug slips its conical proboscis into
your flesh, injecting a poisonous anesthetic. If you are asleep
you will feel nothing. If you happen to be awake you may
notice the faintest of pinpricks, hardly more than a brief
ticklish sensation, which you will probably disregard. But the
bug is already at work. Having numbed the nerves near the
point of entry the bug proceeds (with a sigh of satisfaction,
no doubt) to withdraw blood. When its belly is filled, it pulls
out, backs off, and waddles away, so drunk and gorged it
cannot fly.

At about this time the victim awakes, scratching at a
furious itch. If you recognize the symptoms at once, you can
sometimes find the bug in your vicinity and destroy it. But
revenge will be your only satisfaction. Your night is ruined.
If you are of average sensitivity to a kissing bug's poison,
your entire body breaks out in hives, skin aflame from head

to toe. Some people become seriously ill, in many cases requiring hospitalization. Others recover fully after five or six hours except for a hard and itchy swelling, which may endure for a week.

After the kissing bug, you should beware of rattlesnakes; we have half a dozen species, all offensive and dangerous, plus centipedes, millipedes, tarantulas, black widows, brown recluses, Gila monsters, the deadly poisonous coral snakes, and giant hairy desert scorpions. Plus an immense variety and near-infinite number of ants, midges, gnats, bloodsucking flies, and blood-guzzling mosquitoes. (You might think the desert would be spared at least mosquitoes? Not so. Peer in any water hole by day: swarming with mosquito larvae. Venture out on a summer's eve: The air vibrates with their mournful keening.) Finally, where the desert meets the sea, as on the coasts of Sonora and Baja California, we have the usual assortment of obnoxious marine life: sandflies, ghost crabs, stingrays, electric jellyfish, spiny sea urchins, man-eating sharks, and other creatures so distasteful one prefers not even to name them.

It has been said, and truly, that everything in the desert either stings, stabs, stinks, or sticks. You will find the flora here as venomous, hooked, barbed, thorny, prickly, needled, saw-toothed, hairy, stickered, mean, bitter, sharp, wiry, and fierce as the animals. Something about the desert inclines all living things to harshness and acerbity. The soft evolve out. Except for sleek and oily growths like the poison ivy—oh yes, indeed—that flourish in sinister profusion on the dank walls above the quicksand down in those corridors of gloom and labyrinthine monotony that men call canyons.

We come now to the third major hazard, which is sunshine. Too much of a good thing can be fatal. Sunstroke, heatstroke, and dehydration are common misfortunes in the bright American Southwest. If you can avoid the insects, reptiles, and arachnids, the cactus and the ivy, the smog of the southwestern cities, and the lung fungus of the desert valleys (carried by dust in the air), you cannot escape the desert sun. Too much exposure to it eventually causes, quite literally, not merely sunburn but skin cancer.

Much sun, little rain also means an arid climate. Compared with the high humidity of more hospitable regions, the dry heat of the desert seems at first not terribly uncomfortable—sometimes even pleasant. But that sensation of comfort is false, a deception, and therefore all the more dangerous, for it induces overexertion and an insufficient consumption of water, even when water is available. This leads to various internal complications, some immediate—sunstroke, for example—and some not apparent until much later. Mild but prolonged dehydration, continued over a span of months or years, leads to the crystallization of mineral solutions in the urinary tract, that is, to what urologists call urinary calculi or kidney stones. A disability common in all the world's arid regions. Kidney stones, in case you haven't met one, come in many shapes and sizes, from pellets smooth as BB shot to highly irregular calcifications resembling asteroids, Vietcong shrapnel, and crown-of-thorns starfish. Some of these objects may be "passed" naturally; others can be removed only by means of the Davis stone basket or by surgery. Me—I was lucky; I passed mine with only a groan, my forehead pressed against the wall of a pissoir in the rear of a Tucson bar that I cannot recommend.

You may be getting the impression by now that the desert is not the most suitable of environments for human habitation. Correct. Of all the Earth's climatic zones, excepting only the Antarctic, the deserts are the least inhabited, the least "developed," for reasons that should now be clear.

You may wish to ask, Yes, okay, but among North American deserts which is the *worst*? A good question—and I am happy to attempt an answer.

Geographers generally divide the North American desert—what was once termed "the Great American Desert"—into four distinct regions or subdeserts. These are the

Sonoran Desert, which comprises southern Arizona, Baja California, and the state of Sonora in Mexico; the Chihuahuan Desert, which includes west Texas, southern New Mexico, and the states of Chihuahua and Coahuila in Mexico; the Mojave Desert, which includes southeastern California and small portions of Nevada, Utah, and Arizona; and the Great Basin Desert, which includes most of Utah and Nevada, northern Arizona, northwestern New Mexico, and much of Idaho and eastern Oregon.

Privately, I prefer my own categories. Up north in Utah somewhere is the canyon country—places like Zeke's Hole, Death Hollow, Pucker Pass, Buckskin Gulch, Nausea Crick, Wolf Hole, Mollie's Nipple, Dirty Devil River, Horse Canyon, Horseshoe Canyon, Lost Horse Canyon, Horsethief Canyon, and Horseshit Canyon, to name only the more classic places. Down in Arizona and Sonora there's the cactus country; if you have nothing better to do, you might take a look at High Tanks, Salome Creek, Tortilla Flat, Esperero ("Hoper") Canyon, Holy Joe Peak, Depression Canyon, Painted Cave, Hell Hole Canyon, Hell's Half Acre, Iceberg Canyon, Tiburon (Shark) Island, Pinacate Peak, Infernal Valley, Sykes Crater, Montezuma's Head, Gu Oidak, Kuakatch, Pisinimo, and Baboquivari Mountain, for example.

Then there's The Canyon. *The* Canyon. The Grand. That's one world. And North Rim—that's another. And Death Valley, still another, where I lived one winter near Furnace Creek and climbed the Funeral Mountains, tasted Badwater, looked into the Devil's Hole, hollered up Echo Canyon, searched for and never did find Seldom Seen Slim. Looked for *satori* near Vana, Nevada, and found a ghost town named Bonnie Claire. Never made it to Winnemucca. Drove through the Smoke Creek Desert and down through Big Pine and Lone Pine and home across the Panamints to Death Valley again—home sweet home that winter.

And which of these deserts is the worst? I find it hard to judge. They're all bad—not half bad but all bad. In the Sonoran Desert, Phoenix will get you if the sun, snakes, bugs, and arthropods don't. In the Mojave Desert, it's Las Vegas, more sickening by far than the Glauber's salt in the Death Valley sinkholes. Go to Chihuahua and you're liable to get busted in El Paso and sandbagged in Ciudad Juárez—where all old whores go to die. Up north in the Great Basin Desert, on the Plateau Province, in the canyon country, your heart will break, seeing the strip mines open up and the power plants rise where only cowboys and Indians and J. Wesley Powell ever roamed before.

Nevertheless, all is not lost; much remains, and I welcome the prospect of an army of lug-soled hiker's boots on the desert trails. To save what wilderness is left in the American Southwest—and in the American Southwest only the wilderness is worth saving—we are going to need all the recruits we can get. All the hands, heads, bodies, time, money, effort we can find. Presumably—and the Sierra Club, the Wilderness Society, the Friends of the Earth, the Audubon Society, the Defenders of Wildlife operate on this theory—those who learn to love what is spare, rough, wild, undeveloped, and unbroken will be willing to fight for it, will help resist the strip miners, highway builders, land developers, weapons testers, power producers, tree chainers, clear cutters, oil drillers, dam beavers, subdividers—the list goes on and on—before that zinc-hearted, termite-brained, squint-eyed, nearsighted, greedy crew succeeds in completely californicating what still survives of the Great American Desert.

So much for the Good Cause. Now what about desert hiking itself, you may ask. I'm glad you asked that question. I firmly believe that one should never—I repeat *never*—go out into that formidable wasteland of cactus, heat, serpents, rock, scrub, and thorn without careful planning, thorough and cautious preparation, and complete—never mind the expense!—*complete* equipment. My motto is: Be Prepared.

That is my belief and that is my motto. My practice, however, is a little different. I tend to go off in a more or less random direction myself, half-baked, half-assed, half-cocked, and half-ripped. Why? Well, because I have an indolent and melancholy nature and don't care to be bothered getting all those *things* together—all that bloody *gear*—maps, compass, binoculars, poncho, pup tent, shoes, first-aid kit, rope, flashlight, inspirational poetry, water, food—and because anyhow I approach nature with a certain surly ill-will, daring Her to make trouble. Later when I'm deep into Natural Bridges Natural Moneymint or Zion National Parkinglot or say General Shithead National Forest Land of Many Abuses why then, of course, when it's a bit late, then I may wish I had packed that something extra: matches perhaps, to mention one useful item, or maybe a spoon to eat my gruel with.

If I hike with another person it's usually the same; most of my friends have indolent and melancholy natures too. A cursed lot, all of them. I think of my comrade John De Puy, for example, sloping along for mile after mile like a goddamned camel—indefatigable—with those J. C. Penny hightops on his feet and that plastic pack on his back he got with five books of Green Stamps and nothing inside it but a sketchbook, some homemade jerky and a few cans of green chiles. Or Douglas Peacock, ex-Green Beret, just the opposite. Built like a buffalo, he loads a ninety-pound canvas pannier on his back at trailhead, loaded with guns, ammunition, bayonet, pitons and carabiners, cameras, field books, a 150-foot rope, geologist's sledge, rock samples, assay kit, field glasses, two gallons of water in steel canteens, jungle boots, a case of C-rations, rope hammock, pharmaceuticals in a pig-iron box, raincoat, overcoat, two-man mountain tent, Dutch oven, hibachi, shovel, ax, inflatable boat, and near the top of the load and distributed through side and back pockets, easily accessible, a case of beer. Not because he enjoys or needs all that weight—he may never get to the bottom of that cargo on a ten-day outing—but simply because Douglas uses his packbag for general storage both at home and on the trail and prefers not to have to rearrange everything from time to time merely for the purposes of a hike. Thus my friends De Puy and Peacock; you may wish to avoid such extremes.

A few tips on desert etiquette:

1. Carry a cooking stove, if you must cook. Do not burn desert wood, which is rare and beautiful and required ages for its creation (an ironwood tree lives for over 1,000 years and juniper almost as long).

2. If you must, out of need, build a fire, then for God's sake allow it to burn itself out before you leave—do not bury it, as Boy Scouts and Campfire Girls do, under a heap of mud or sand. Scatter the ashes; replace any rocks you may have used in constructing a fireplace; do all you can to obliterate the evidence that you camped here. (The Search & Rescue Team may be looking for you.)

3. Do not bury garbage—the wildlife will only dig it up again. Burn what will burn and pack out the rest. The same goes for toilet paper: Don't bury it, *burn it.*

4. Do not bathe in desert pools, natural tanks, *tinajas,* potholes. Drink what water you need, take what you need, and leave the rest for the next hiker and more important for the bees, birds, and animals—bighorn sheep, coyotes, lions, foxes, badgers, deer, wild pigs, wild horses—whose *lives* depend on that water.

5. Always remove and destroy survey stakes, flagging, advertising signboards, mining claim markers, animal traps, poisoned bait, seismic exploration geophones, and other such artifacts of industrialism. The men who put those things there are up to no good and it is our duty to confound them. Keep America Beautiful. Grow a Beard. Take a Bath. Burn a Billboard.

Anyway—why go into the desert? Really, why do it? That sun, roaring at you all day long. The fetid, tepid, vapid little water holes slowly evaporating under a scum of grease, full of cannibal beetles, spotted toads, horsehair worms, liver flukes, and down at the bottom, inevitably, the pale cadaver of a ten-inch centipede. Those pink rattlesnakes down in The Canyon, those diamondback monsters thick as a truck driver's wrist that lurk in shady places along the trail, those unpleasant solpugids and unnecessary Jerusalem crickets that scurry on dirty claws across your face at night. Why? The rain that comes down like lead shot and wrecks the trail, those sudden rockfalls of obscure origin that crash like thunder ten feet behind you in the heart of a dead-still afternoon. The ubiquitous buzzard, so patient—but only so patient. The sullen and hostile Indians, all on welfare. The ragweed, the tumbleweed, the Jimson weed, the snakeweed. The scorpion in your shoe at dawn. The dreary wind that blows all spring, the psychedelic Joshua trees waving their arms at you on moonlight nights. Sand in the soup du jour. Halazone tablets in your canteen. The barren hills that always go up, which is bad, or down, which is worse. Those canyons like catacombs with quicksand lapping at your crotch. Hollow, mummified horses with forelegs casually crossed, dead for ten years, leaning against the corner of a barbed-wire fence. Packhorses at night, iron-shod, clattering over the slickrock through your camp. The last tin of tuna, two flat tires, not enough water and a forty-mile trek to Tule Well. An osprey on a cardón cactus, snatching the head off a living fish—always the best part first. The hawk sailing by at 200 feet, a squirming snake in its talons. Salt in the drinking water. Salt, selenium, arsenic, radon and radium in the water, in the gravel, in your bones. Water so hard it bends light, drills holes in rock and chokes up your radiator. Why go there? Those places with the hardcase names: Starvation Creek, Poverty Knoll, Hungry Valley, Bitter Springs, Last Chance Canyon, Dungeon Canyon, Whipsaw Flat, Dead Horse Point, Scorpion Flat, Dead Man Draw, Stinking Spring, Camino del Diablo, Jornado del Muerto . . . Death Valley.

Well then, why indeed go walking into the desert, that grim ground, that bleak and lonesome land where, as

Genghis Khan said of India, "the heat is bad and the water makes men sick"?

Why the desert, when you could be strolling along the golden beaches of California? Camping by a stream of pure Rocky Mountain spring water in colorful Colorado? Loafing through a laurel slick in the misty hills of North Carolina? Or getting your head mashed in the greasy alley behind the Elysium Bar and Grill in Hoboken, New Jersey? Why the desert, given a world of such splendor and variety?

A friend and I took a walk around the base of a mountain up beyond Coconino County, Arizona. This was a mountain we'd been planning to circumambulate for years. Finally we put on our walking shoes and did it. About halfway around this mountain, on the third or fourth day, we paused for a while—two days—by the side of a stream, which the Navajos call Nasja because of the amber color of the water. (Caused perhaps by juniper roots—the water seems safe enough to drink.) On our second day there I walked down the stream, alone, to look at the canyon beyond. I entered the canyon and followed it for half the afternoon, for three or four miles, maybe, until it became a gorge so deep, narrow and dark, full of water and the inevitable quagmires of quicksand, that I turned around and looked for a way out. A route other than the way I'd come, which was crooked and uncomfortable and buried—I wanted to see what was up on top of this world. I found a sort of chimney flue on the east wall, which looked plausible, and sweated and cursed my way up through that until I reached a point where I could walk upright, like a human being. Another 300 feet of scrambling brought me to the rim of the canyon. No one, I felt certain, had ever before departed Nasja Canyon by that route.

But someone had. Near the summit I found an arrow sign, three feet long, formed of stones and pointing off into the north toward those same old purple vistas, so grand, immense, and mysterious, of more canyons, more mesas and plateaus, more mountains, more cloud-dappled sun-spangled leagues of desert sand and desert rock, under the same old wide and aching sky.

The arrow pointed into the north. But what was it pointing *at?* I looked at the sign closely and saw that those dark, desert-varnished stones had been in place for a long, long, time; they rested in compacted dust. They must have been there for a century at least. I followed the direction indicated and came promptly to the rim of another canyon and a drop-off straight down of a good 500 feet. Not that way, surely. Across this canyon was nothing of any unusual interest that I could see—only the familiar sun-blasted sandstone, a few scrubby clumps of blackbrush and prickly pear, a few acres of nothing where only a lizard could graze, surrounded by a few square miles of more nothingness interesting chiefly to horned toads. I returned to the arrow and checked again, this time with field glasses, looking away for as far as my aided eyes could see toward the north, for ten, twenty, forty miles into the distance. I studied the scene with care, looking for an ancient Indian ruin, a significant cairn, perhaps an abandoned mine, a hidden treasure of some inconceivable wealth, the mother of all mother lodes. . . .

But there was nothing out there. Nothing at all. Nothing but the desert. Nothing but the silent world.

That's why.

3

Disorder and Early Sorrow

The first time I investigated Big Bend National Park was a long time ago, way back in '52 during my student days at the University of New Mexico. My fiancée and I drove there from Albuquerque in her brand-new Ford convertible, a gift from her father. We were planning a sort of premature, premarital honeymoon, a week in the wilderness to cement, as it were, our permanent relationship. Things began well. With all the other tourists (few enough in those days), we followed the paved road down from Marathon and into the park at Persimmon Gap, paused at the entrance station for instruction and guidance, as per regulations, and drove up into the Chisos Mountains that form the heart of this rough, rude, arid national park. We camped for a few days in the Chisos Basin, hiking the trails to Lost Mine, to the Window, to Emory Peak and Casa Grande. Some of the things I saw from those high points, looking south, attracted me. Down in those blue, magenta, and purplish desert wastes are odd configurations of rock with names like Mule Ear Peaks and Cow Heaven Anticline. I was interested; my fiancée was satisfied with long-distance photographs.

When I inquired of a ranger how to get down there, he told me we'd have to backpack it; there was, he said, "no road." I showed him my 1948 Texaco map; according to the map there was a road—unpaved, ungraded, primitive to be sure, but a road all the same—leading from the hamlet of Castolon near the southwest corner of the park to Rio Grande Village at the east-central edge of the park. Fifty miles of desert road.

"That road is closed," the ranger told me.

"Closed?"

"Not fit for travel," he explained. "Permanently washed out. Not patrolled. Not safe. Absolutely not recommended."

My sweetheart listened carefully.

I thanked him and departed, knowing at once where I wanted to go. Had to go. Since we were not equipped for backpacking, it would have to be on wheels. My fiancée expressed doubts; I reassured her. We drove down the old road along Alamo Creek—the only road at that time—to the mouth of Santa Elena Canyon. We contemplated the mouth of Santa Elena Canyon for a day, then headed east to Castolon, where we stocked up on water and food. I made no further inquiries about the desert road; I did not wish to expose myself to any arguments.

A short distance beyond Castolon we came to a fork in the road. The left-hand fork was marked by a crude, hand-painted wooden sign that said:

Staked in the middle of the right-hand fork was a somewhat more official-looking board that said:

The left-hand fork led northeasterly, up a rocky ravine into a jumble of desert hills. The other fork led southeasterly, following the course of the Rio Grande into the wastelands of southern Big Bend. One would have liked to meet Mr. Hartung but his road was not our road.

I pulled up the No Road sign, drove through, stopped, replaced the sign. Our tire tracks in the dust showed clearly on each side of the warning sign, as if some bodiless, incorporeal ghost of a car had passed through. That should confuse the park rangers, I thought, if they ever came this way. My fiancée meanwhile was objecting to the whole procedure; she felt it was time to turn back. Gently but firmly I overruled her. We advanced, cautiously but steadily, over the rocks and through the sand, bound for Rio Grande Village—an easy fifty-mile drive somewhere beyond those mountains and buttes, mesas and ridges and anticlines on the east.

All went well for half a mile. Then we came to the first of a hundred gulches that lie transverse to the road, formed by the rare flash floods that drain from the hills to the river. The gulch was deep, narrow and dry but filled with sand and cobbles. The drop-off from bank to streambed was two feet high. Time to build road. I got out the shovel, beveled off the edge of the cut bank on either side, removed a few of the larger rocks, logs, and other obstacles. Revving the Ford's hearty V-8 engine, I put her in low and charged down, across the rocks, and up the other side. A good little car, and it made a game effort, hanging to the lip of the far embankment while the rear wheels spun furiously in the sand and gravel. Not quite sufficient traction; we failed to make it. I backed down into the bottom of the gulch, opened the trunk, took out the luggage and filled the trunk with rocks. That helped. Gunning the engine, we made a second lunge for the top and this time succeeded, though not without cost. I could smell already the odor of burning clutch plate.

Onward, though my fiancée continued to demur. We plunged into and up out of another dozen ravines, some of them deeper and rougher than the first, sometimes requiring repeated charges before we could climb out. Although the car had less than 5,000 miles to its career, some parts began to give under the strain. The right-hand door, for example, would no longer latch. Evidently the frame or body had been forced a trifle askew, springing the door. I wired it shut with a coat hanger. My sweetheart, in a grim mood by this time, suggested again that we turn around. I pointed out that the road ahead could hardly be as bad as what we had come through already and that the only sensible course lay in a resolute advance. She was doubtful; I was wrong, but forceful. I added water to the boiling radiator, diluting the manufacturer's coolant, and drove on.

There seemed no choice. After all, I reasoned, we had already disregarded a park ranger's instructions and a clear warning sign. Our path was littered not only with bolts, nuts, cotter pins, and shreds of rubber but with broken law as well. Furthermore, I had to see what lay beyond the next ridge.

In the afternoon we bogged down halfway through a stretch of sand. I spent two hours shoveling sand, cutting brush and laying it on the roadway, and repeatedly jacking up the rear of the car as it advanced, sank, stopped. I could have partially deflated the tires and got through more easily but we had no tire pump, and ahead lay many miles of stony trail.

By sundown of the first day we had accomplished twenty miles. The car still ran but lacked some of its youthful élan. The bright enamel finish was scarred and scoriated, dulled by a film of dust. We made camp and ate our meal in silence. Coyotes howled like banshees from the foothills of Backbone Ridge, gaunt Mexican cattle bellowed down in the river bottom, and across the western sky hung the lurid, smoldering fires of sunset, a spectacle grim and ghastly as the announcement of the end of the world. A scorpion scuttled out of the shadows past our mesquite fire, hunting its evening meal. I made our bed in a dusty clearing in the cactus, but my beloved refused to sleep with me, preferring, she said, to curl up in the back seat of her car. The omens multiplied and all were dark. I slept alone under the shooting stars of Texas, dreaming of rocks and shovels.

Dawn, and a dusty desert wind, and one hoot owl hooting back in the bush. I crawled out of my sack and shook my boots out (in case of arachnids), made breakfast and prepared for another struggle through the heat, the cactus, the rock, and, hardest of all, the unspeaking enmity of my betrothed.

The second day was different from the first. Worse. The washouts rougher than before, the ravines deeper, the sandy washes broader, the stones sharper, the brush thornier. In the morning we had our first flat. No repair kit, of course; no pump, no tire irons. I bolted on the spare tire, which meant that for the next thirty miles we would have no spare. Onward. We thrashed in and out of more gullies and gulches, burning up the pressure plate, overheating the engine, bending things. Now the other door, the one on the driver's side, had to be secured with coat-hanger wire. Sprung doors were always a problem with those old Ford convertibles.

We clattered on. Detouring an unnecessarily bad place on the road, I veered through the cactus and slammed into a concealed rock. Bent the tie-rod. Taking out the lug wrench, I hammered the tie-rod as straight as I could. We drove on with the front wheels toed in at a cockeyed angle. Hard to steer and not good for the tires, which were compelled, now one, now the other, or both at once, to slide as well as roll, forward. They might or might not endure for the twenty miles or so that, according to my Texaco road map and the record of the odometer, we still had to cover.

As in any medical disorder, one malady aggravates another. Because of the friction in the front end I found it harder to negotiate the car across the washes and up out of ravines. It was no longer sufficient merely to gear down into low, pop the clutch, and *charge!* up the far side. I had to charge *down* as well as *up*. The clutch still functioned, but it was going. I prayed for the clutch, but it was the oil pan I worried about. My fiancée, clutching at the dashboard with both hands, jaw set and eyes shut, said nothing. I thought of iron seizures, bleeding crankcases, a cracked block.

Nevertheless: forward. Determination is what counts.

Cactus, sand pits, shock-busting chuckholes, axle-breaking washouts, rocks. And more rocks. Embedded like teeth in the roadway, points upward, they presented a constant nagging threat to my peace of mind. No matter how slowly I drove forward, lurching over the ruts at one mile an hour, there was no way I could avoid them all. I missed a few, but one of them got us, five miles short of the goal, late in the afternoon of the second day. A sharp report rang out, like a gunshot, followed by the squeal of hot air, the sigh of an expiring tire, and I knew we were in difficulty.

I stopped to inspect the damage, for form's sake, but there was really nothing I could do. Nothing practical, that is, except maybe pull the wheel and roll it on to Rio Grande Village by hand where, possibly, I could have it fitted with a new tire, and roll it back here to the stricken Ford. I suggested this procedure to my one and only. She objected to being left alone in this scorching wilderness full of animals and Mexicans while I disappeared to the east. Did she wish to walk with me? No, she didn't want to do that either.

That helped make up my mind. I got back in the car, started the engine and drove on, flat tire thumping on the roadway, radiator steaming, clutch smoking, oil burning, front wheels squealing, the frame and all moving parts a shuddering mass of mechanical indignation. The car clanked forward on an oblique axis, crabwise, humping up and down on the eccentric camber of the flat. Scraps of hot, smoking rubber from the shredded tire marked our progress. Late in the evening, on scalloped wheel rim and broken heart, we rumbled painfully into Rio Grande Village, pop. 22 counting dogs.

My fiancée took the first bus out of town. She had most of our money. I was left behind to hitchhike through west Texas with two dollars and forty-seven cents in my pocket. The car, as I later heard, was salvaged by my sweetheart and her friends, but never recovered its original *esprit de Ford*. Nor did I ever see my fiancée again. Our permanent relationship had been wrecked, permanently. Not that I could blame her one bit. She was fully justified. Who could question that statement? All the same it hurt; the pain lingered for weeks. Small consolation to me was the homely wisdom of the philosopher, to wit:

> A woman is only a woman
> But a good Ford is a car.

4

Fire Lookout: Numa Ridge

July 12, Glacier National Park

We've been here ten days before I overcome initial inertia sufficient to begin this record. And keeping a record is one of the things the Park Service is paying us to do up here. The other, of course, is to keep our eyeballs peeled, alert for smoke. We are being paid a generous wage (about $3.25 an hour) to stay awake for at least eight hours a day. Some people might think that sounds like a pretty easy job. And they're right, it is an easy job, for some people. But not for all. When I mentioned to one young fellow down at park headquarters, a couple of weeks ago, that I was spending the summer on this fire lookout he shuddered with horror. "I'd go nuts in a place like that," he said, thinking of solitary confinement. I didn't tell him I was cheating, taking my wife along. But that can be risky too; many a good marriage has been shattered on the rock of isolation.

Renée and I walked up here on July 2, packs on our backs, two hours ahead of the packer with his string of mules. The mules carried the heavier gear, such as our bedrolls, enough food and water for the first two weeks, seven volumes of Marcel Proust, and Robert Burton's *Anatomy of Melancholy.* Light summer reading. Renée had never worked a fire lookout before, but I had, and I knew that if I was ever going to get through the classics of world lit it could only be on a mountain top, far above the trashy plains of *Rolling Stone, Playboy,* the *New York Times,* and *Mizz* magazine.

The trail is about six miles long from Bowman Lake and climbs 3,000 feet. We made good time, much better time than we wished because we were hustled along, all the way, by hordes of bloodthirsty mosquitoes. We had prepared ourselves, of course, with a heavy treatment of government-issue insect repellent on our faces, necks, arms, but that did not prevent the mosquitoes from whining in our ears and hovering close to eye, nostril, and mouth.

We also had the grizzly on our mind. Fresh bear scat on the trail, unpleasant crashing noises back in the dark of the woods and brush, reminded us that we were intruding, uninvited, into the territory of *Ursus horribilis,* known locally as G-bear or simply (always in caps) as GRIZ. It was in Glacier, of course, only a few years ago, that two young women had been killed on the same night by grizzlies. We clattered our tin cups now and then, as advised, to warn the bears we were coming. I was naturally eager to see a GRIZ in the wild, something I'd never done, but not while climbing up a mountain with a pack on my back, tired, sweaty, and bedeviled by bugs. Such an encounter, in such condition, could only mean a good-natured surrender on my part; I wasn't *about* to climb a tree.

Bear stories. My friend Doug Peacock was soaking one time in a hot spring in Yellowstone's back country. Surprised by a grizzly sow and her two cubs, he scrambled naked as a newt up the nearest pine; the bear kept him there, freezing in the breeze, for two hours. Another: Riley McClelland, former park naturalist at Glacier, and a friend were treed by a GRIZ. Remembering that he had an opened sardine can in his pack, Riley watched with sinking heart as the bear sniffed at it. Disdaining the sardine lure, however, the bear tore up the other man's pack to get at a pair of old tennis shoes.

Sacrifice, that may be the key to coexistence with the GRIZ. If we surprise one on the trail, I'll offer up first my sweat-soaked hat. If that won't do, then cheese and salami out of the pack. And if that's not enough, well, then nothing else to do, I guess, but push my wife his way. *Droit du seigneur à la montagne*, etc.

We reach the lookout without fulfilling any fantasies. The lookout is a two-room, two-story wood frame cabin at timberline, 7,000 feet above sea level. On the north, east, and southeast stand great peaks—Reuter, Kintla, Numa, Chapman, Rainbow, Vulture. Northwest we can see a bit of the Canadian Rockies. West and southwest lie the North Fork of the Flathead River, a vast expanse of Flathead National Forest, and on the horizon the Whitefish Range. Nice view: 360 degrees of snow-capped scenic splendor, lakes, forest, river, fearsome peaks, and sheltering sky.

We remove the wooden shutters from the lookout windows, shovel snow from the stairway, unlock the doors. The pack string arrives. The packer and I unload the mules, the packer departs, Renée and I unpack our goods and move in. Except for a golden-mantled ground squirrel watching us from the rocks, a few Clark's nutcrackers in the subalpine firs, we seem to be absolutely alone.

July 14 (Bastille Day!)

The Great Revolution was a failure, they say. All revolutions have been failures, they say. To which I reply: All the more reason to make another one. Knocking off "work" at five o'clock (the transition from work to nonwork being here discernible by a subtle reshading in the colors of the rock on Rainbow Peak), my wife and I honor this day by uncorking a bottle of genuine Beaujolais. With Renée's home-baked crusty French bread and some real longhorn cheese from the country store down at the hamlet of Polebridge, it makes a fitting celebration.

A golden eagle soars by *below us*, pursued by—a sparrow hawk? My wife the bird-watcher is uncertain; but it must have been. Looking unhurried but pursuing a straight course, the eagle disappears into the vast glacial cirque above Akakola Lake, followed steadily, slightly above, by the smaller bird. More Clark's nutcrackers. Chipping sparrows. Mountain chickadees. Oregon juncoes. Clouds of mosquitoes whining at the windows, greedy for blood. A doe, a fawn, a yearling buck with velvet horns jostling one another at our salt deposits on the rocks outside. The doe is dominant; the young buck retreats. Women's Lib has reached out even here, for God's sake, all the way from Washington Square to Numa Ridge. Depressing thought. Striving to uphold the natural superiority of the male, I have beaten my wife—at chess—five games straight. Now she refuses to play with me. You can't win.

What *do* people do on a lookout tower when, as now, the season is wet and there are no fires? Aside from the obvious, and reading Proust and *The Anatomy of Melancholy*, we spend hours just gazing at the world through binoculars. For example, I enjoy climbing the local mountains, scaling the most hideous bare rock pitches step by step, hand by hand, without aids, without rope or partners, clinging to fragments of loose shale, a clump of bear grass, the edge of an overhanging snow cornice, above a nightmarish abyss, picking a route toward even higher and more precarious perches—through these U.S. Navy 7 × 50 lenses. The effortless, angelic, and supine approach to danger.

It's not all dreaming. There are some daily chores. Ever since arrival I've been packing snow to the lookout from a big drift a hundred yards below, carrying it up in buckets, dumping it into steel garbage cans, letting it melt in the sun. Now we've got 120 gallons of snow water in addition to the drinking water brought up by muleback. Then there's firewood. Although we have a propane stove for cooking, the only heat in the lookout comes from an old cast-iron cookstove. And with the kind of rainy, windy weather we've been having, heat is a necessity. Even in July. So a couple of times a week I go down the trail with ax and saw, fell one of the many dead trees in the area—fir, whitebark pine—buck the log into eighteen-inch lengths, tote it up the hill armload by armload.

Three times a day we take weather observations—wind speed and direction, temperature, relative humidity—or my wife does, since she is the scientist in this family. We wash windows, occasionally. We patch and repair things. We listen to the Park Service radio and the Forest Service radio, ready to relay messages if necessary. I entertain the deer and the squirrels with my flute. Renée bakes things, studies the maps, memorizes the terrain. But mostly we sit quietly out on the catwalk, reading about aristocratic life in *fin-de-siècle* Paris and looking at northwestern Montana in the summer of '75.

This is a remote place indeed, far from the center of the world, far away from all that's going on. Or is it? Who says so? Wherever two human beings are alive, together, and happy, there is the center of the world. You out there, brother, sister, you too live in the center of the world, no matter where or what you think you are.

July 16

Heavy cloud buildup in northwest. Lightning likely, fire danger rising, humidity dropping. The haze lies heavy over yonder Whitefish Range, obscuring the farther peaks. Looks like smog, but is only water vapor, dust, the smoke from many campfires along the North Fork. They tell us.

One longs for a nice little forest fire. We need some excitement around this joint. Nothing healthier for the forests than a good brisk fire now and then to clear out the undergrowth, give the moose and bear some living room. Besides we need the overtime pay. If that idiot Smokey the Bear (the noted ursine bore) had *his* way all us fire fighters would starve to death.

We see a Townsend's solitaire, abundant here. Hermit thrush. Swallowtail butterflies. Little spiders hanging on threads from the attic trapdoor. A six-legged spider (war veteran) on the outside of the windowpane chewing on a mosquito. Good show! mate. One snowshoe hare loping into the brush.

Gordon the Garbage Man, one of the park's seasonal employees, comes up the mountain for a visit, leaves us two big Dolly Vardens fresh from the lake. Fried by my frau, filleted and anointed with lemon, they make a delicately delicious supper. If I weren't so corrupt and lazy, I'd take hook and line myself, drop down to Lake Akakola 1,200 feet below, and catch a similar supper every evening. According to the old logbooks here, at least some of the previous lookouts used to do that.

Officially, all measurements at Glacier National Park are now given in meters. All road and trail signs, all park maps, show distances and heights in meters and kilometers, without their Anglo-American equivalents. The Park Service, no doubt at the instigation of the Commerce Department, is trying to jam the metric system down our throats whether we want it or not. We can be sure this is merely the foot in the door, the bare beginning of a concerted effort by Big Business–Big Government (the two being largely the same these days) to force the metric system upon the American people. Why? Obviously for the convenience of world trade, technicians, and technology, to impose on the entire planet a common system of order. All men must march to the beat of the same drum, like it or not.

July 17

Still no real fires, aside from a few trivial lightning-storm flare-ups in the forest across the river, soon drowned by rain. But we are ready. Perhaps I should describe the equipment and operations of a lookout.

We live and work in the second story of the cabin. The ground-floor room, dark and dank, is used only for storage. Our room is light, airy, and bright, with windows running the length of all four walls. Closable louvred vents above each window admit fresh air while keeping out rain. In the center of this twelve-foot by twelve-foot room, oriented squarely with the four directions, stands the chest-high fire finder. The Osborne Fire Finder consists essentially of a rotating metal ring about two feet in diameter with a handle to turn it by and a pair of sights, analogous to the front and rear sights of a rifle, mounted upright on opposite sides. When the lookout spots a fire, he aims this device at the base and center of the smoke (or flame, if discovered at night) and obtains an azimuth reading from the fixed base of the fire finder, which is marked off into 360 degrees. By use of the vernier scale attached to the rotating ring, the lookout can get a reading not only in degrees but precisely to the nearest minute, or one-sixtieth of a degree.

Having determined the compass direction of the fire from his own location, the lookout must still establish the location of the fire. To do that he must be able to recognize and identify the place where the fire is burning and to report its distance from his lookout station. A metal tape stretched between front and rear sights of the fire finder, across a circular map inside the rotating ring, gives the distance in kilometers. Another aid is the sliding peep sight on the rear sight, by means of which the lookout can obtain a vertical angle on his fire. Through a bit of basic trigonometry the vertical angle can be translated into distance. Or if another lookout, at a different station, can see the same fire, the line of his azimuth reading extended across a map of the area intersects the line of the first lookout's reading to give the exact point of the fire. Assuming both lookouts are awake, fairly competent, and on duty at the same time.

If these procedures sound complicated, that is an illusion. The technical aspects of a lookout's job can be mastered by any literate anthropoid with an IQ of not less than seventy in about two hours. It's the attitude that's difficult: Unless you have an indolent, melancholy nature, as I do, you will not be happy as an official United States government fire lookout.

Anyway, having determined the location of his fire, and being reasonably certain it is a fire and not a smoking garbage dump, a controlled slash burn, a busy campground, floating vapors, or traffic dust rising from a dirt road, the lookout picks up his radio microphone or telephone and reports his discovery to fire-control headquarters. After that his main task becomes one of assisting the smoke-chasers in finding the fire, relaying messages, looking for new and better fires.

July 20

Bear claw scratches on the wooden walls of the ground-floor storage room. Last thing before retiring each night I set the bear barrier in place on the stairway leading to our quarters. The bear barrier is a wooden panel with many nails driven through it, the points all sticking out. Supposed to discourage *Ursus stairiensis* from climbing up to our catwalk balcony. In a previous lookout's log we had read this entry:

> Woke up this morning to see a big black bear staring at me
> thru window, about six inches from my face. Chased him
> off with a Pulaski.

The Pulaski is a fire-fighting tool, a combination ax and
pickax. I keep one handy too, right under the bed where I
can reach it easy. I'd keep it under the pillow if my old lady
would let me.

Thinking about GRIZ. Almost every day, on the park or
forest radio, we hear some ranger report a bear sighting,
sometimes of grizzly. Campers molested, packs destroyed by
hungry and questing bears. Somebody was recently attacked
and mauled by a GRIZ north of the line, in Waterton Lakes.
Bear jams on the park highway, though not so common here
as they used to be in Yellowstone, before so many of Yellowstone's bears mysteriously disappeared, do occur in Glacier
from time to time.

No doubt about it, the presence of bear, especially grizzly
bear, adds a spicy titillation to a stroll in the woods. My bear-
loving friend Peacock goes so far as to define wilderness as a
place and only a place where one enjoys the opportunity of
being attacked by a dangerous wild animal. Any place that
lacks GRIZ, or lions or tigers, or a rhino or two, is not, in his
opinion, worthy of the name "wilderness." A good definition, worthy of serious consideration. A wild place without
dangers is an absurdity, although I realize that danger
creates administrative problems for park and forest man-
agers. But we must not allow our national parks and national
forests to be degraded to the status of mere public playgrounds. Open to all, yes of course. But—*enter at your own
risk.*

Enter Glacier National Park and you enter the homeland
of the grizzly bear. We are uninvited guests here, intruders,
the bear our reluctant host. If he chooses, now and then, to
chase somebody up a tree, or all the way to the hospital, that
is the bear's prerogative. Those who prefer, quite reason-

ably, not to take such chances should stick to Disneyland in all its many forms and guises.

July 22

Bowman Lake 3,000 feet below looks more like clear Pennzoil than water. A milky turquoise green color, strange to my eyes. The North Fork even more so. The cause is not man-made pollution of any sort, but what is called "glacier milk," a solution of powdered rock washed down from under the bellies of the glaciers hanging all around us under the high peaks.

Toy boats glide up and down the lake, trailing languorous wakes that spread across the oil-smooth water in slow-subsiding ripples. Anglers at work. The fishing is poor this summer, they say; weather too wet, too much insect life in the air and floating down the streams.

Too wet? You can say that again. This is the foggiest, boggiest, buggiest country I have ever seen in my life. Everywhere I look, below timberline, the land is clothed in solid unbroken greenery. Damp, humid green all over the place— gives the country an unhealthy look. I guess I really am a desert rat. The sound of all these verdant leafy things breathing and sweating and photosynthesizing around me all the time makes me nervous. Trees, I believe (in the ardor of my prejudice), like men, should be well spaced off from one another, not more than one to a square mile. Space and scarcity give us dignity. And liberty. And thereby beauty.

Oyster stew for lunch. Out of tin can. Had buckwheat cakes for breakfast, with wild huckleberry syrup by Eva Gates, Bigfork, Montana.

Enormous clouds with evil black bottoms floating in from the Pacific, great sailing cities of cumulo-nimbus. Lightning plays among their massy depths. Will it bring us fire? God, one hopes so. What are we up here for, perched like condors on this mighty mountain, if not to conjure up a storm? The children need shoes. All those fire fighters down at headquarters need overtime. The forest needs a rebirth, a renascence, a weeding out.

July 23

Down the mountain I go, returning same day with mail, wine, cheese, other essentials. I sing, as I march along, songs I hope will warn the GRIZ of my approach. But what kind of music does the GRIZ like? Suppose he *hates* old cowboy songs? Or Puccini?

All the way up the mountain, under a dark and grumbling sky, a personal cloud of hungry mosquitoes envelopes my head. I am relieved and glad when the first lightning strikes begin to bounce off the crags above. Am less glad when I reach the open ridge at timberline with jagged high-voltage bolts crashing all around. No place to hide now; I keep going for the relative safety of the lookout cabin and reach it just as the storm bursts out in all its awful grandeur.

We cower inside in the dark, Renée and I, trying to stay away from all metal objects, as instructed. But, of course, the lookout is crowded with metallic objects—iron stoves, fire finder, steel cots, water cans, buckets, ax, dishpan. We can feel the next charge building up; we stand on the negative terminal of a high-powered electrical system, the positive pole directly overhead. Our skin prickles, our hair stands up. We hear a fizzing noise above us, on the roof of the cabin where the lightning rod sticks up. A crackling sound, like a burning fuse. I know what's coming now, and an instant later it comes, a flash that fills the room with blue-white light, accompanied simultaneously by a jarring crash, as if the entire cabin had been dropped from the sky upon our rocky ridge. No harm done. The building is thoroughly grounded, top and sides, and Thor's hammer blow passes on safely into the heart of the mountain. Lightning strikes many times in the same place. As every lookout learns.

That evening we spot a couple of small flare-ups across the river in the national forest. But both are soon drowned out by rain and never go anywhere.

July 27

The bird list grows slowly. Add barn swallow, cliff swallow, water pipit, raven, blue grouse, white-tailed ptarmigan, rufous hummingbird, brown creeper, gray jay, evening grosbeak, red-shafted flicker, loon. *Loon!*—heard from the lake far below—that wild, lorn, romantic cry, one of the most thrilling sounds in all North America. Sound of the ancient wilderness, lakes, forest, moonlight, birchbark canoes.

We have also seen two cow moose, one with calf, romping through the fields below the lookout, and a badger, several black bear (but no GRIZ yet), elk droppings, mountain goat tracks, least chipmunks, ground squirrels, pikas, hoary marmots, many deer. And there's a big wood rat living downstairs among the water cans, firewood, tools, and boxes. Met him the other day.

The flowers have been blooming, on and off, ever since we got here. We've identified the following so far: purple-eyed mariposa, false asphodel, valerium, harebell, blue penstemon, arnica, fleabane, mountain penstemon, bear grass, sulfur flower, stonecrop, Indian paintbrush, alum root, glacier lily, prince's pine, mountain gentian, forget-me-not, bluebonnet, alpine buttercup, yellow columbine, elephant head, blanket flower, alpine aster, swamp laurel, fireweed.

The bear grass, with its showy panicle of flowers on a two- or three-foot stalk, is the most striking flower in Glacier. It reminds me of pictures of the giant lobelia on the slopes of Mount Kilimanjaro. The deer eat the flower stalks.

Bear sighting reported on park radio: A ranger reports one grizzly sow with two cubs in "Moose Country," along the Going-to-the-Sun Highway. The bear, he says, is reared up on her hind legs, roaring and waving her arms at tourists as they surround her, their cameras clicking. He breaks it up. Nobody hurt. This time.

The park radio is our chief amusement. Over a million people visited the park last summer, most of them driving through by way of the Going-to-the-Sun. Many traffic problems every day, much police work.

Exempli gratia 1: 1961 converted schoolbus at Logan Pass, brakes burned out, driver thinks he can bring bus down mountain by driving in low gear, requests ranger escort. Not allowed. Tow truck dispatched.

E.g. 2: Ranger reports distraught wife and children at Lake McDonald campground. "Woman is very upset," he says. Cause? Her husband, the children's father, went off on a hike with a fifteen-year-old baby-sitter, been gone for hours. (Family is reunited later in evening.)

E.g. 3: Rookie ranger reports five bikers camping under highway bridge and smoking a controlled substance. "I think they're smoking dope," he says, "although, of course, I don't know what dope smells like."

Our friend Gus Chambers up on Swiftcurrent Lookout in the center of the park spots the first genuine park fire of the season. (And the only one, as it turns out.) He gives his azimuth reading, the UTM (Universal Transverse Mercator) coordinates, locates it one kilometer south-southeast of Redhorn Lake. No one can see the fire but Gus; we other lookouts are sick with envy and rage. One snag burning in a small valley, remote from any trail; too windy for smoke jumpers, fire fighters are flown to scene by helicopter.

Fire caused by lightning. When Smokey Bear says that only *You* can prevent forest fires, Smokey is speaking an untruth. A falsehood. Ninety percent of the fires in the American West are lightning-caused, as they have been for the last 20,000 years, or ever since the glaciers retreated. Yet the forests survived. And thrived. Hard to explain this to some old-time foresters, who often feel the same passionate hatred for fire that sheepmen feel for coyotes. Now, after fifty years of arduous fire-suppression effort, the useful role of natural fire in the forest ecosystem is becoming recognized among foresters. But the public, indoctrinated for so long in the Smokey Bear ethic, may not be easy to reeducate.

No one disputes the fact that it will always be necessary to quell forest fires that threaten lives, homes, business establishments, or valuable stands of timber scheduled for logging.

July 30

Renée bakes a prune pie. An experiment. I read Burton on "Heroical Love." The days sail by with alarming speed; why this headlong descent into *oblivion*? What's the rush? Sinking comfortably into the sloth and decay of my middle middle age, I am brought up short nevertheless, now and then, by the alarming realization that all men, so far, have proved mortal. Me too? Each day seems more beautiful than the last. Every moment becomes precious. Thus are we driven to the solitary pleasures of philosophy, the furtive consolations of thought.

Gus's fire is out. Burnt only five acres. Snow slides in Logan Pass again, traffic halted. Hiker killed on Snyder Lake trail, trying to climb cliff. Child lost and found. Woman, sixty-seven, lost for three hours near Bowman Lake. Found. GRIZ trees three hikers at Trout Lake.

More bugs. Mosquitoes as numerous as ever, soon to be augmented by swarms of flying ants. And now another enemy, the moose fly, appears, the bloodsucking *Muscas horribilis sangria*. Mean, vicious Draculas with wings. About the size of bats. We stay inside when the wind dies and all these flying plagues come forth together.

I read the old lookout logs. First of all Numa Ridge lookouts was Scotty Beaton, who worked here twenty-two summers, beginning in 1928. Unlike all succeeding lookouts, whose logbook entries tend (like mine) to rant and ramble, Scotty kept his notations terse, laconic, to the point. Viz.:

Aug. 2, 1945: hot & dry done my usual chores

July 28, 1946: Very warm—Hugh Buchanan the ranger came up with a Paper to have me Pledge I wouldn't overthrow the government that never entered my mind in the fifty five years I been in this country

July 5, 1948: Moved up today the bears had moved into the lower part of the Lookout & took a few bites out of the upper story. The lower part a hell of a mess.

July 22, 1949: Done usual chores

Sept. 11, 1950: Found mud in bottom of water barrel put there by youngster from McFarland's dude ranch. Same kid who broke crosshairs on firefinder, tramped down nails in bear board and set my binoculars on the hot stove.

According to the logbooks, every lookout since Scotty found Numa Ridge a delightful place—but only one of the twenty-four (including many couples) came back for a second season, and the second was enough for him. In the fire lookout's vocation many are called, few chosen. The isolation is too much for most. This is my seventh summer as a lookout; I guess I like it.

Down on Loneman Peak in the southern part of Glacier sits Leonard Stittman. This is his fourteenth summer on Loneman. In all those summers he has had a total of eight visitors, all of them rangers.

We've had a ranger-visitor too–Art Sedlack, the man who shot the snowmobile.

It happened one night in December 1974. Sedlack, on duty at Walton Ranger Station in Glacier, caught a snowmobiler buzzing around in an area where snowmobiles are not supposed to be. This sort of thing had been going on for a long time, and the operator of this particular snowmobile was a repeat offender. Suddenly inspired, Sedlack drew his trusty .38 Ranger Special and shot the snowmobile right through the head. "One snowmobile, immobilized," he reported by radio. Sensation! For a while Sedlack's rear end was in a sling as the owner of the slain snowmobile and other local motorized recreationists demanded blood, a head for a head. Sedlack might have lost his job but for an outpouring of public support, phone calls and letters from all over western Montana. Reconsidering, the park administration suspended him for one week without pay, then sent him to the service's police-training school in Washington, D.C. Now he is back in Glacier, an unrepentant and even better ranger.

Art talks about the bear problem in the national parks. Really a human problem. Too many humans crowding the roads and trails, conflict inevitable. Solution: Reduce population. Which population? Ah yes, indeed, that is the question.

A bear, when caught in mischief, is tranquilized and tagged on the ear. Caught again, it is tagged on the other ear. A bear with both ears tagged is in trouble. It may be transported to a locality remote from human activity, but this is not a solution. There are no vacant areas in nature. The newcomer bear is not welcome among established inhabitants, is harried, fought, driven out by native bears, becomes a loner, an outlaw, a rogue—doomed. If caught in trouble a third time he or she will likely be "taken away" for good. That is, shot dead.

August 2

Fog and rain. Foul is fair and fair is foul. Cut more wood, keeping bin full. When I go down the hill to the john in the morning I find the mosquitoes huddled inside, waiting for me as usual. As usual I light up a Roi-Tan, a good cheap workingman's cigar, and the moquitoes flee, choking and swearing. I sit there and contemplate, through the smoke, the dim shapes of fir tree and mule deer through the mists. On clear mornings, sunshine on my lap, I can look right down on the pearly, oily, iridescent surface of Bowman Lake in all its incredible rich blueness. I think, if I think at all, about simplicity, convenience, the advantages of what I call Positive Poverty.

There is of course no flush toilet on a fire lookout. But the pit toilet is a perfectly adequate, comfortable and even pleasant substitute for the elaborate bathrooms of the modern home. A little lime or wood ashes keep down the odors, discourage flies. In cold weather one kerosene or Coleman lamp keeps the outhouse warm enough. What more does one need? And no freezing pipes, no water pump, no septic tank to worry about, no awful plumber's bills. And the basic good sense of it: Instead of flushing our bodily wastes into the public water supply, we plant them back in the good earth where they belong. Where our bodies must go as well, in due course, if we are to keep the good earth productive.

Nor is there running water up here. Or electricity. I carry the water by the bucketful up from the barrels in the cellar. We heat the water on the wood stove, wash and scald-rinse the dishes in a pair of dishpans, bathe (when we feel like it) in a small galvanized tub set on the floor or out on the catwalk when the sun is shining. Before the big drifts melted, Renée and I sometimes scrubbed ourselves with handfuls of snow, standing naked on the dazzling snowbanks, in the heat of the sun.

Hauling water, cutting firewood, using a pit toilet seem like only normalcy to me, raised as I was on a backwoods Pennsylvania farm. For Renée, a city girl, these methods are new, but she adapts at once, without difficulty, to such minor deprivations. No problem at all. Most of what we call modern conveniences are no more than that at best. They are far from being necessities. And what a terrible price most of us have to pay for our tract homes, our fancy plumbing, our automobiles, our "labor-saving" appliances, the luxuriously packaged ersatz food in the supermarkets, all that mountain of metal junk and plastic garbage under which our lives are smothered. Men *and* women trapped in the drudgery and tedium of meaningless jobs (see Studs Terkel's *Working* if you don't believe me), and the despoliation of a continent, the gray skies, the ruined rivers, the ravaged hills, the clearcut forests, the industrialized farms, all to keep that Gross National Product growing ever grosser. Madness and folly. Untouched by human hands. Unguided by human minds.

Not that technology and industrialism are evil in themselves. The problem is to get them down to human scale, to keep them under human control, to prevent them from ever again becoming the self-perpetuating, ever-expanding monsters we have allowed them to become. What we need is an optimum industrialism, neither too much nor too little, a truly sophisticated, unobtrusive, below-ground technology. For certainly science, technology, industrialism have given us a number of good things. Not many, but some. My list begins with the steel ax. Matches. Nails, hammer, handsaw. Writing paper and pen and ink. The birth-control pill. Or the condom. (Forget-me-not.) Galvanized bucket—no, strike that item; the old oaken bucket is good enough. The cast-iron stove. Electricity. And solar heating. Windmills and suction pumps. Candles, Aladdin lamps, pianos, and platinum flutes. The coal-burning locomotive, transcontinental train service, the horse collar, the pneumatic-tired wagon, bicycles, the rocket-powered spaceship. But not automobiles. (What? Spaceships! Yes. Why not? I believe space exploration is a worthy human adventure.) Radios and record players, but not television. Anesthetics and aspirin, but not BHT, sodium nitrite, monosodium glutamate, or artificial coloring. The democratic rifle and the egalitarian revolver, but not the authoritarian B-52. And so on.

But we cannot pick and choose this way, some technophiles may insist—it's the entire package, plagues and all, or nothing. To which one must reply: If that is true then we have indeed lost control and had better dismantle the whole structure. But it is not true: We *can* pick and choose, we can learn to select this and reject that. Discrimination is a basic function of the human intelligence. Are we to be masters or slaves of the techno-industrial machine?

My cigar has gone out. The mosquitoes come sneaking back. They whine around my ears like the sirens of commerce, like bill collectors, like the National Association of Manufacturers. The sound of greed.

Time to sharpen the old ax. A chill wind is blowing and the fog rolls in again. Dark birds flap through the mist, croaking for blood.

August 3
Done usual lookout chores.

August 4

Done usual lookout chores. To wit: woke, ate, answered radio check, looked, chopped wood, carried water, read Burton ("Of all causes of this affliction," he writes, meaning romantic love, "the most remote are the stars"), looked, re-leveled fire finder, washed dishes, played chess then flute, watched sun go down, went to bed.

In the evening after sundown an owl flies round and round the lookout, swooping silent as a moth through the fog and gloom, checking out our chipmunks. Barred owl? Short-eared owl? Hard to tell in this darkness. A spooky bird of ill import.

August 5

My wife looks prettier every day. By God, a man begins to get ideas in a place like this.

August 7

High winds all day, clear sky, scudding clouds. The surface of the lake below, stirred by the wind, looks like brushed aluminum, has the color of my knife blade. The peaks round about stand forth in startling, blazing, preter-natural brilliance. A cold, immaculate clarity. Shall we climb Rainbow Peak one of these days? Ever see Goat Haunt? Belly River? Mount Despair? Loneman? Gunsight Pass? Rising Wolf Mountain? Spirit Lake? Two Medicine Mountain? Almost A Dog Mountain? Vulture Peak?

August 11

Storms. Fog and drizzle, brief blaze of sun—a rainbow floats in the fog below.

Lightning again, flashing through the mist; the thunder rumbles in at a thousand feet per second. Pink lightning. Heaven and earth link nerves in illuminated ecstasy—or is it pain? Once, in another place, I saw lightning score a direct hit on a juniper tree. The tree exploded in a burst of flame.

Now comes another direct hit on our lookout. First the buzzing sound, the eerie *hiss* and *fizz* directly overhead. That sinister touch, God's fingertip upon our roof. Light, deadly, an almost dainty touch, you might say. Followed by the flash of light and the *crack!* of a great whip. The building vibrates.

When the hard winds blow the cabin creaks and groans, tugging at the cables that keep it anchored to the rock. On our east side the ridge drops off at fifty degrees down a tree-less slope to the bottom of the cirque 600 feet blow.

In the evening things settle down a bit. We go for a walk down the trail, down through the drifting fog. The huckleberries are ripening now, but it looks like a poor crop. The bears will be roaming and irritable. Mushrooms bulge through the damp duff under the pines—fat, brown, speckled domes of fungoid flesh. Delicacies for the deer. The mushrooms remind me of bitter days at another lookout post, 2,000 miles away and a decade in the past. I was enduring the agonies of unrequited love, exactly as Burton describes them, and in my misery I contemplated with interest some of the mushrooms growing all about the tower of that other lookout; the rosy hoods of *Amanita muscaria* suggested the possibility of flight beyond the sorrows of this sublunar sphere. But I refrained, not from fear of hallucination or death, but because I was becoming accustomed to the realization that I enjoyed my sufferings more. So the girl I loved had betrayed me by running off with her husband. What of it? I survived.

> Men have died and worms have eaten them, but not for love.

August 15

Been gone three days, leaving Renée to man the lookout on her own. She was willing and ready and is in fact a better

fire lookout than I. Much more conscientious, not so cor-
rupted by subversive notions of fire ecology, etc.

Down from Numa Ridge, the first thing I did was go to
Logan Pass, hike the Highline Trail to Granite Park and up
Swiftcurrent Peak to visit Gus at his fire lookout. Late in the
evening I returned to Logan Pass. Nineteen miles round
trip. On the way I had passed a group of mountain goats, six
of them, grazing not fifty feet from the trail, indifferent to
my presence. Returning at twilight, I encountered five bighorn rams bunched up right on the trail, blocking my way.
They showed no inclination to move and I wasn't going to
climb around them. I approached to within twenty feet,
waved my arms and whistled; grudgingly they got up and let
me through. That's the way it is in the Peaceable Kingdom,
the wildlife so accustomed to hikers they won't even get out
of your way.

I had timed my walk badly. The dark settled in while I was
still five miles from Logan Pass, the road, and my car. The
trail wound through thickets of alder brush, with a cliff on
my left and a drop-off on my right. A cloudy, starless night.
Hard to see more than ten, fifteen feet ahead. Odd noises
off in the thickets. I began to think about GRIZ again. What
to do if I met one now? No climbable trees in sight and my
only weapon a pocketknife. Words of wisdom, often heard
at Glacier, whispered through my brain: "Anyone who hikes
alone, after dark, is asking for trouble." Bears are omnivorous, have no pride at all, will eat anything, even authors.
Even if the GRIZ hears me coming, I realized, he will have
difficulty getting out of my way on this mountain trail. We'd
have to sidle past one another, smiling apologetically, like
strangers in a narrow doorway. I walked on, singing loudly,
feeling foolish, half amused by my own fear. Yes, I did want
to meet a grizzly in the wild—but not just yet. Nothing happened that night. I saw nothing but shadows, heard nothing
but the wind and those obscure crashing sounds, now and
then, below the trail.

August 16

Old magazines on the shelves under the fire finder, left here by former lookouts. I leaf through *Field and Stream, Outdoor Life, Hook & Bullet News.* Here's an interesting item:

> *Stock taking.* California has a new procedure for scattering the trout it stocks in streams in an attempt to foil hatchery-truck chasers. The fish are not released until dusk or after dark and are placed in one spot rather than in several. Wardens report that the fish are well scattered by daylight and the night stocking stymies the truck followers.

And another:

> *Pump Priming.* In an effort to stimulate the lagging fishing and subsequent business decline caused by the ban on keeping fish caught in Lake St. Clair, the Michigan Marine and Snowmobile Dealers Association is trying to raise $50,000 to $100,000 to finance the tagging of thousands of fish that would be worth anywhere from $100 to $10,000 apiece to the anglers catching them. The ban resulted from mercury contamination tests run on some of the lake's fish.

So it goes, sportsmen.

Reflections on hunting. My father was a hunter. During the Great Depression and the war years, he killed dozens of deer, hundreds of cottontail rabbits, in order to put meat on the table for his hungry family. My mother would can the extra rabbit, putting it up in jars. During the fifties and sixties, as the times got better, my father gradually gave up hunting. Never in his life has he killed another living thing for sport. Except, that is, during his boyhood. Before he grew up. Hunters, he would explain, never kill for sport.

All those red-coated men we see out in the field during deer season—what are they up to? Well, some of them are hunters, engaged in the ancient, honorable, and serious business of providing meat for kith and kin. The majority, however, outnumbering the hunters and the deer as well by ninety-nine to one, are not hunters but merely gunners. Sportsmen.

The sportsman's pursuit of game is incidental to his primary purposes, which can be defined as follows, in descending order of importance:

1. Get away from wife and kids for a few days
2. Get drunk and play poker with cronies by the light of a Coleman lamp in tent, lodge, or Winnebago
3. Swap lies with same
4. Maybe shoot some legal game
5. Failing that, shoot some illegal game—cow, horse, chicken, game warden, etc.
6. Failing that, shoot *something*—side of barn, road sign, his own foot, whatever's handy.

How do I know about this? Because I was there. I too was once a sportsman. But I grew up. In that one respect anyhow. Like my old man, Paul, who beat me to it.

August 18

Somebody falls into McDonald Falls again. "Bring the wagon," radios ranger. The hurry-up wagon. Happens every year. As at North Rim, Grand Canyon, where somebody disappears every summer.

Whole family mauled by a grizzly on Grinnel Glacier trail. Father, mother, two children. Apparently the children had been walking far ahead of their parents, got between a sow and her cub. Children attacked. Their screams bring father running to the scene, who attempts to fight off the GRIZ with his bare hands. Reinforced by mother, the bear knocks them both about, then wanders off. Entire family hospitalized with serious injuries. Rangers close trail to further hiking for time being.

Might be hard to explain to those people why the grizzly bear is a vital part of the Glacier wilderness. But it is. The parks are for people? Certainly. And for bears also? Absolutely. How do we resolve the inevitable conflict? Are we going to ration the wilderness experience? Probably; that process has already begun at Glacier National Park, where back-country camping is restricted to certain sites, requiring written permits and advance reservations. A sad and ominous but unavoidable expedient.

One calamity after another. One mishap after another. A ranger's work is never done. And more and more, in every national park, that work consists largely of police work. The urbanization of our national parks. All through the summer bumper-to-bumper auto traffic crawls up and down the Going-to-the-Sun Highway. I've said it before and I'll say it again, we've got to close the parks to private cars if we want to keep them as parks. The parks are for people, not machines. Let the machines find their own parks. Most of America has been surrendered to them already, anyway. New Jersey, for example. Southern California.

On the forest radio, the weather report concludes as usual with the daily fire-fighting capability report: "We have available in Missoula today fifty-two smoke jumpers, two B-16s, one Neptune, two twin Beechcraft, two helicopters, four DC-7s, etc." All on standby, in readiness.

There used to be ten active fire-lookout stations in Glacier. Now there are only four. My old lookout tower on North Rim was deactivated five years ago. More and more lookouts are superseded by aircraft patrols. Part of the national industrializing pattern, human beings put out of work by machines. Labor-intensive jobs (so to speak) made obsolete by capital-intensive substitutes. One hour of an airplane's time costs more than two or three days' pay for a human lookout on a mountaintop. But no doubt it is, as they say, more efficient. And what happens to all the displaced fire lookouts? They swell the ranks of the unemployed. They wander the streets of small western towns, kicking beer cans around, getting in trouble.

Who cares? Most fire lookouts are crazy anyhow. Once from a peak in southern Arizona, at sundown, with the west-

ern sky full of smoke, dust, and clouds, I looked straight at
the sun with my lookout's binoculars. I knew it was a foolish
thing to do. Could have ruined my eyes forever. At the very
least might have impaired my night vision. But the haze
seemed so extremely dense, the sun so blood-red behind it,
that I thought it might be safe, just this once. All I wanted
was one quick glimpse of those plasmic bonfires 10,000 miles
high leaping into space from the rim of the roaring sun. So I
looked. And I saw them. It was a sublime and terrifying
spectacle, which I can never forget. And my eyes survived,
apparently unharmed, although a few years later I began to
have trouble reading the numbers in a phone book, and my
arms seemed too short to hold a newspaper far enough away
from my eyes to make it readable.

"You need glasses," the eye doctor said. "You're far-
sighted."

"Why?"

"Middle age."

I told him about the time I stared at the sun face to face.

"You were lucky," he said.

August 22

Renée takes off for a three- or four-day tour of the park,
leaving me here alone with my dirty dishes and the unswept
floor. Two old-time park naturalists arrive, sit around drinking my coffee and telling what they call North Dakota jokes.

"Why won't a North Dakotan eat pickles?"

"Can't get his head in the jar."

"What does it say on the bottom of Coke bottles in North
Dakota?"

"Open other end."

Etc. They do all the laughing.

Fog and rain, rain and fog. The fire season is shot to hell.
Word from headquarters is that we're to be "terminated"
(without prejudice) on September 5. Lookout completely
socked in. Black bear with two cubs seen near Moose Wallow

during my evening walk. Huckleberries, whortleberries, raspberries all ripening, but few of them.

The short-eared owl comes back at dusk, circling my glass-walled home. Perhaps it is me that silent bird is looking for. All my superstitions rise to the surface. At midnight under the full moon, dip your hand in the punky water of a hollow stump if you want to rid it of warts. Etc.

Cut and stack wood, refilling bin. Install new stovepipe. Caulk window frames. Repair broken shutters. Won't be here much longer.

One young punk showed up at nine-thirty this morning, jogging up the trail. Gasping for breath, before he even said hello he asked what time it was. So he could time his hike. A goggle-eyed bore with hairy legs, wearing track shorts and tennis shoes. Outward Bound type. He hung around for a few minutes, saw little of interest in me or the lookout, and trotted down the trail again, vanishing into the clouds below.

Days now getting perceptibly shorter. Full moon rising over Rainbow Peak. Grand, gorgeous, shocking-pink sunset. Feel of autumn in the air. In August! Two golden eagles hovering on the sky, high above my cabin. God Bless America—Let's Save Some of It. Long live the weeds and the wilderness yet.

August 23

Rain, wind, rain, and fog. When the storm clears I see fresh snow on Kintla, Rainbow, and Reuter peaks, down to the 8,000-foot line. Temperature was 34° F this morning at 0630. Everything wet and slimy. Expect to see snails and other Mollusca crawling up the windowpanes. Horny octopi. . . .

August 24

Awoke this morning, after a long cold night, to find two inches of snow on the catwalk railing, on the pines, on everything in sight. Wet, fat snow, clinging to every twig and needle.

Renée returns, but only briefly. Has to leave at once for Vancouver. Her grandfather's dying. I am alone for the final week on this cold, dismal, rain- and snow-soaked mountain. I get so lonesome I wash the dishes for diversion. Loneliness. Mount Despair. Wintertime in August.

August 26

Termination date has now been advanced to August 28.

I go for long walks in the evening, hoping for one clear sight of GRIZ. The silence of the woods. No birds speak except one woodpecker, far below, hammering on a snag. But 1,000 feet below, under the snowline, the weather is late summer. Tufts of moss, like scalp locks, dangle from the branches of the lodgepole pine, the larch, the spruce. This is the forest primeval. Elaborate spiderwebs hang face-high across the trail, each with a tiny golden spider waiting at the center. Damp smells of fern and pine bark, the distant drumming of the woodpecker. Sounds like Red Norvo at the vibraphone. Bluebells still in bloom down here, wild roses covered with dew. Running water across the stones of the trail. I pause on the way back up to drink a handful; the sweet, cold, piney flavor reminds me of boyhood, the Allegheny Mountains back in old Pennsylvania. Lost at twilight in the green depths of the Big Woods.

Back to the cold darkness of the lookout cabin. I build a fire in the stove, sit with my feet on the open oven door and play the flute. The deer outside lift their heads to listen for a moment, then resume their feeding. Down in Arizona I used to rouse the coyotes at dawn, playing certain high notes on this silver-plated instrument. I'd play our tune and wait and after a few moments their wild cries came floating back to me across the desert, mimicking my song.

August 27

Last full day on the mountain. Sun shining for a change. Many deer hang about, fighting over my various urine-supplied salt deposits. Obvious pecking order among them: One old battle-scarred six-point buck is clearly dominant; the others keep their distance from him but jostle one another roughly.

Always looking and listening, these deer. Even the fawns have that wary look. Danger everywhere. Nor do they look well-fed, even now in late summer. Gaunt and ganted, lean and bony deer, how will they ever get through the coming winter? A tough life. Always hard times for deer. The struggle for existence. All their energy goes into survival—and reproduction. The only point of it all—to go on. On and on and on. What else is there? Sometimes I am appalled by the brutality, the horror of this planetary spawning and scheming and striving and dying. One no longer searches for any ulterior significance in all this; as in the finest music, the meaning is in the music itself, not in anything beyond it. All we have, it seems to me, is the beauty of art and nature and life, and the love which that beauty inspires.

Smell of cooking rubber. I withdraw my booted feet from the oven.

August 28

Raining again. Storm predicted. The packer with his mules is coming up the mountain this morning. I clean the lookout, put everything away, bolt the shutters back on the windows, pack our baggage, sign off on the radios. "This is Numa Ridge Fire Lookout going ten-seven [out of service] for about ten months. Have a good winter, everybody."

The packer arrives. Followed by the wind. We load the mules in a driving rain and start down the mountain.

5
_____

Snow Canyon

Snow Canyon near the town of Saint George in the extreme
southwestern corner of Utah is a broad gorge about three
miles long, ranging in elevation from 2,000 feet above sea
level on the canyon floor to 3,500 feet at the summit of the
volcanic cinder cones near its head. The walls of the canyon,
formed of red and buff-colored Navajo sandstone, are 500
to 750 feet high. This is low desert country, like the Mojave
to the southwest, pleasant in winter but fiercely hot in summer, with such characteristic plants of the lower Sonoran life

zone as creosote and mesquite. You would seldom see snow in Snow Canyon; the name was given by pioneer Mormon settlers Lorenzo and Erastus Snow.

Snow Canyon is dry, virtually waterless, containing but one remote year-round stream. The stream that largely formed the canyon through corrasion and erosion was blocked and diverted by recent volcanic activity. About 1,000 years ago, molten magma found a weak point in the crustal structure and poured forth, cooling and solidifying as it moved into the head of what is now Snow Canyon. At the same time two cinder cones, each 800 to 900 feet high, formed above the volcanic vents. The cinder cones and the rough, jagged basaltic lava flows resemble those of Sunset Crater National Monument near Flagstaff, Arizona. In the background at both places stands a great volcanic mountain of a far more ancient period. At Sunset Crater this is the collapsed remnant (12,650 feet high) called the San Francisco Peaks; at Snow Canyon the old-timer that looms beyond is known as the Pine Valley Mountain, 10,360 feet high, a caldera of vast dimensions from which issued in Triassic times the many flows of lava that can now be seen in the Virgin River Valley between Saint George and Zion National Park.

The combination of sandstone and ancient and modern lava formations gives Snow Canyon more than routine geologic interest. But in a land where spectacular scenery is commonplace, a little corner of it like Snow Canyon does not attract much attention. Most of the people in Utah have never heard of it. The first time I drove through, several years ago, I didn't even bother to stop.

In truth Snow Canyon is not a spectacular place. Small in area (65,000 acres), it contains no waterfalls or geysers, no tremendous cliffs such as those of Zion, no deep and narrow canyons. However, like any portion of the earth's surface that has not been engulfed by industry, there is much of great interest and beauty if you take the time and make the effort to see it. But you must get out of your car. You've got to be willing to walk.

Out of our shells and into the air (what machine can match a pair of legs?), we see that Snow Canyon is more than a museumlike panorama of pinkish cliffs, blue-black lava, and photogenic sky. There is an amazing variety of plant life here. No crowded thickets, no rank jungles of anything, but a cool, spare spacing of many things, all ancient, all important—if not to us, then certainly to whatever it was that seeded, nursed, and cradled them into existence. Manzanita, for example, with its bright green leaves and glowing red skin, growing in a clump twenty feet across, right next to a shaggy piñon pine with porcupine-girdled trunk. (Too many porcupines here—not enough coyotes, lions, eagles, or badgers.) Hedgehog cactus, prickly pear, buckhorn cholla, and nearby such fantastic lilies as the yucca and Schott's agave. Rabbitbrush, sand sage, big sagebrush, green ephedra (Mormon tea), juniper, desert holly, singleleaf ash, saltbush.

On the shady northern side of sandstone and lava we find green, gold, black, and auburn lichens in symbiotic clusters, patiently dissolving the rock of ages into sand and soil. Down in the bottom of the canyon are stands of creosote shrubs; along the edge of the sandy wash is desert hackberry, ordinarily a shrub but here grown to arboreal size, big enough to shade a cow, which it does. Tumbleweeds and cheatgrass— signs of overgrazing. A number of other grasses I cannot identify. In spring and fall appears a wide range of flowers, perennial and annual.

The animal and bird life is not numerous, but it's here: kit fox, coyote, desert mule deer, bobcat, badger, chipmunk, ground squirrel, skunk, and porcupine. Among the reptiles and lizards are diamondbacks, sidewinders, chuckwallas, and even, maybe, a few Gila monsters. As in any lower Sonoran desert area, you can turn up scorpions and centipedes without much trouble.

If you're fond of rock, as I am, you will find much that is

fascinating here. The sandstone, rich in iron oxides, is not only full of color but cross-bedded and checkered, seamed by old fault lines, elaborately sculptured by weathering and erosion. Despite the dryness of Snow Canyon, lovely pot-holes full of rainwater remain, as big as thirty feet long, twenty feet wide, and six inches deep, alive with tadpoles and algae. According to park ranger Michael Eager, there are bigger, deeper, better such natural tanks among the sandstone domes high on the west side of the canyon.

The basalt formations are also interesting, with caves and lava tubes and highly polished scoops, chutes, and potholes in the drainage channels. In places you will find the ancient Triassic lava and the recent Holocene lava sprawled in mighty chunks side by side on the underlying red beds of sandstone.

Like everything else in America, including America, Snow Canyon was discovered by the Indians. Until a century ago it was part of the hunting preserve of the Shivwits tribe, who still survive, though confined to a tiny reservation on the Utah-Nevada border. Exactly how this canyon and some 10,000 square miles of other territory in southwest Utah and northwest Arizona passed from possession of the Shivwits to a few contemporary cattle ranchers (supported and sub-sidized by the Bureau of Land Management, Department of the Interior, United States Government), is not explained in detail or with much clarity by official school history books. I suppose the Indians, if we asked them, could tell us the full story. I'd rather not ask.

6

Desert Places

Big Bend, Texas
The biggest centipedes I've ever seen—eight inches long.
With yellow fangs, a pair of jaws in front that look like the
horns of a bull. On the tip of each leg a sharp claw. But the
centipede, despite its name, does not have 100 feet. I con-
vinced myself of this by trapping one upside down beneath a
flat piece of glass; I counted twenty-one pairs of legs. I re-
leased the creature and it scurried off like a toy train, all
those legs in synchromesh transmission. Tonight, perhaps, it
will return and crawl into my sleeping bag.

The bite of the centipede is slightly poisonous, but then so is that of most humans. This does not justify the centipede. It is a fierce and vigorous myriopod with a single-minded devotion to only three ideas: capturing, killing, devouring. Product of a hostile environment, it knows no higher law.

The scorpions are plentiful—in the woodwork, under logs, under the stones near the river's shore. The giant desert hairy scorpion, the striped-tail scorpion, the deadly yellow scorpion. Most ancient of all land-dwelling animals, they have adapted with optimum efficiency to the varied demands of their surroundings. As predators they are classic in design: eight strong legs for pursuit; a pair of lobsterlike pincers for grasping prey; and the famous tail curving forward over the head, with the stinger on its tip for injecting poison. With his victim disabled, the scorpion proceeds to dine fastidiously, taking hours for the meal. He does not tear apart and chew his captive in the vulgar fashion of the centipede, or swallow it whole in the manner of fishes and birds. Instead he draws it firmly against his mouth opening—the scorpion hardly appears to have a recognizable head—and patiently, efficiently, thoroughly sucks all the bodily juices and living tissue from the inside of his prey, leaving only the empty shell, the chitinous exoskeleton. Daintily wiping the fringe of hairs surrounding the mouth, the scorpion backs away, rather like a crab—to which he is related—and retires into his dungeon. Of low metabolism and phlegmatic temperament, the scorpion may go days and weeks before venturing forth to seek his next meal.

The scorpion's kindred are here too. The vinegaroon or whiptail scorpion, running about with its hairlike tail pointing straight up like the antenna of a radio; the sand cricket or *niña de la tierra* (in Navajo *woh-seh-tsinni,* "Old Man Baldy"); the solpugid or sun spider, another arachnid of grotesque appearance and, like the vinegaroon and the sand cricket, harmless. The tarantula, the brown recluse spider, and *hic et ubique* the black widow. All perfectly harmless to man, unless disturbed or handled roughly. Why these various little animals, who wish nothing from us but the right to pursue happiness in their own manner, should seem so loathsome and malignant I do not fully understand. The honeybee is more poisonous, dangerous, and common than most of these, and yet the bee we accept. No doubt it can be explained. But why should I, regarding them with the best of intentions, a certain understanding, and a sympathetic ideology, also feel that twinge of repulsion when I see the fragile scorpion with its slim translucent limbs, its elegant carriage, its solitary devotion, come out of the shadows and into the light of my campfire?

New Mexico

Of all the western states I love New Mexico best, though I first saw it going the wrong way, east, in that side-door Pullman bound from Needles, California to Amarillo, Texas. I was on my way home to Pennsylvania to feed the pigs for the last time and join the United States Army. We came at evening to a shining river, a smoky and jeweled city, with a mountain wall beyond. Albuquerque. I liked the tone of that big ugly rowdy town and three years later, free of the army, came back and went to school there. My roommate was a huge red-eyed cowboy from Colorado. A breeder of horses and tamer of broncs, he was a shy sensitive fellow when sober but a demonic giant when drunk. And he was almost always drunk. We lived in a cinder-block hut twenty miles from campus, commuting the distance via a hairy-scary mountain road in his black Lincoln convertible in never more than twenty minutes. Until then I had never known who it was that shot up all the road signs around Albuquerque. In return I taught him how to burn down billboards. He taught me how to subdue a bad horse. It was simple. While he sat on the corral gate throwing beer cans at us I sat on the bronc trying to hit its head with a lead pipe every time it bucked. But I could never even see let alone reach

that animal's head always down there between its forelegs.
The method was to keep falling off and climbing back on
until the horse became bored. My friend knew other games.
On the day before the season opened we went deer hunting
with handguns; I quit when I realized he was stalking not
deer but me. Of all gun-happy people I have ever known, he
was the happiest. For example, target practice: He owned a
field full of brown weeds; he fenced it with chickenwire and
stocked it with clean white rabbits. In one beautiful all-night
poker game I cleaned him of $240, but lost it all at dawn
when he proved on a final bet that he could break a cinder
block over his head. One day he got married and I had to
move out. For wedding present I gave the bride my stolen
U.S. Army chrome-plated .45 automatic, loaded. Brightest
New Mexico, fairest of them all. I live elsewhere now.

Arizona

The arboreal desert and the desert mountains, where the
superstitious search for Apache gold. For the Dutchman's
lost mine. For whatever it is they lost a long time ago and
have been hunting ever since.

For myself, all my life a prospector, I was prospecting for
revelation. For a blinding light illuminating everything. On
the trail to Weaver's Needle. But what I found, what I stumbled onto, was a family of wild pigs. Also known as peccaries
or javelinas. I heard them before I saw them, a grunting and
snuffling and squealing in the brush up ahead. All around
us was the lilac twilight, the barren and savage crags
softened by evening, while from a damp place somewhere
down in La Barge Canyon came the melancholy chorus of
red-spotted toads.

The javelinas, nearsighted and hard-of-hearing, did not
notice my approach until I was almost upon them. Then
they stampeded off in all directions, two of them nearly running me down. A musky odor hung in the air. They must
have been more startled than I was. Whimsical little beasts

they are, with bristling coats and oversize heads half as big as their whole bodies—a far evolutionary cry from the domestic hogs I had known in boyhood, those Berkshires and Poland Chinas with bodies of lard wallowing on stubby legs, midget red eyes squinting from faces of smug complacency.

There's little pork on the javelina. Nothing but hide and hair, bone, blood, muscle, nerves, and gristle, and within the physiological assembly, completing the composition, the passionate appetites of the wild beast. Pure drive, rudimentary brains, raw, concentrated vigor. A simple personality but vital, vivid. Crashing through the cholla. I can hear them still.

Superstition Mountain stands gaunt and grim above the desert floor, resembling a titanic altar, ancient, corroded, rotten with the blood of gods. Or like the crumbling ruin of a castle, a fortress left over from some prehuman age of giants. No, this is all rhetoric. The mountain looks like what it is: the eroded remains of a volcanic pile, limestone sediments, igneous intrusions. Which is mystery enough. The truth always more difficult to imagine than fantasy.

The suburbs of Phoenix have crept to the foot of the mountain. Around its base floats a haze of smoke and dust. Rich in lung fungus. But the mountain stands above these passing phenomena, taking its coloration and much of its character from greater events. At night it appears as a colossal bulk looming against the stars; in the dawn it acquires a magenta tone, soft and livid, glowing in rust-red porphyry when the sun comes up; during the day it turns brown or golden above the shimmering heatwaves, or bleak gray beneath the shadows of drifting clouds, and at sundown it glows again through subtle, continuous, indivisible transformations in all the named and unnamed hues of fire.

On the slopes and flanks of the mountain and within its desiccated range the Sonoran plant life flourishes, a complex and various growth that for a desert region might be called luxuriant. Here is the saguaro cactus with its tall fluted col-

umns expanding or contracting in accordance with varia-
tions in water supply; the arms reach out and upward in
semihuman gestures; flickers and woodpeckers drill holes in
the tough trunk, where smaller birds and the elf owl will
later build their nests. After several hundred years the
saguaro sickens, rots and dies; and in all of nature there is
nothing more deathly than a rotting saguaro: The bare ribs
of the trunk form a cage around a hollow core; blackened,
corrupt flesh hangs from the sagging limbs.

Various types of jointed cactus grow in dense stands near
the saguaro; the most conspicuous is the cholla, *Opuntia bige-
lovii,* known locally as teddy bear cholla or sometimes as
jumping cholla. The branches of this plant are covered so
thickly with long spines that from a distance they wear a
furry look, shining against the light with a luminous glow.
The short joints depend like fruits from the branches; easily
detached, they cling impartially to leather, cloth, or skin. Not
easily removed.

Present too are the barrel cactus (sometimes growing six
feet tall); the hedgehog cactus, the buckhorn cactus, the pen-
cil cactus, the fishhook cactus, the beavertail cactus, the
Engelmann prickly pear, all well equipped with hairs and
bristles, thorns and needles, all equally at home in the
desert, democratically beautiful.

Oddest of plants out here is the one called ocotillo. Not a
cactus, it looks like some kind of undersea creature turned
on its back, eight to a dozen whiplike and thorny legs writh-
ing in the air. In blossom time each of these woody octopods
is wreathed in little green leaves, soon shed, and tipped with
a flamelike cluster of scarlet flowers.

Las Vegas: Fremont Street

HOWDY PARDNER . . . These friendly words were ad-
dressed to me by a steel-and-neon cowboy fifty feet tall, with
a six-foot-wide grin, and one moving arm. He towers above
the street. On the evening of November 22, 1963, I had ven-

tured for the first time into Las Vegas, Nevada, looking for the men's room.

Howdy to you too, sir, I replied.

And the cowboy repeated his greeting, by rote and rheostat, and repeated it again and again, with mechanical persistence, at rigid one-minute intervals, all night long.

HOWDY PARDNER . . .

The open city. Some of the big casinos on Fremont Street never close their doors. They have no doors. But what was the plain, homely face of Walter Cronkite doing on all the TV screens? Why was he weeping on all of them at once? I couldn't hear what he was saying because of

HOWDY PARDNER

and the California traffic and the clatter of dice, the rattle of chips, the jingle of silver dollars—

> Oh give me a big silver dollar
> To slap on the bar with a bang.
> A bill that is creased
> May do in the East,
> But we want *our* money to *clang!*

—the click and whir of the roulette, the flutter of cards, the chant of the keno callers, the shuffle of the crowd, the slap of leather, the tramp of the guards, the creaking pelvises of the change girls, the twinkling buttocks of the barmaids, the PA system paging

MR. CLYDE CLAUNCH, MR. CLYDE CLAUNCH TO THE TELE-PHONE PLEASE

and, of course,

HOWDY PARDNER

and the clash, roll, jangle, rumble, and rock of 10,000 concentrating mothers of America jerking in unison on the heavy members of 10,000 glittering slot machines.

Not a wide-open town at all. The police—public, private, plain, and secret—are everywhere, watching you with stony eyes, marking every move. It's a tight, clean, prim, bright, businesslike town, run not by hoods but by sober-sided middle-class gangsters—Mormons from Utah, Baptists from Oklahoma, Presbyterians from Pennsylvania, Roman Catholics from New Jersey, Jews from Texas. No nonsense.

HOWDY PARDNER . . .

It was business as usual that night too as on any other though one of the croupiers admitted to me that volume had fallen off slightly because of the distractions of the TV that day (ordinarily not allowed in the casinos; banned, like clocks), the weeping Mr. Cronkite, etc. A slight adjustment had been made in history and the juggernaut of empire turned a few points to the right. I myself was among the majority in Las Vegas not overly concerned. A president assassinated? Men as good as he were being murdered every day, I thought. Only much later did I come to understand how a minute change in course could make an extreme difference

HOWDY PARDNER . . .

in point of destination.

Or catch the connection between the spirit of Dallas and the bombed pagoda the burned-out village the napalmed child the machine-gunned water buffalo the poisoned ricefield the defoliated forest the immolated priest the bombs bursting like flowers in that tiny country which seemed to have more bridges barges and *structures* than any other nation on earth. Which somehow absorbed more bombs than were dropped in all of World War II. All that—and the tortured prisoner. On a pleasant evening in May in 1966 you could have seen on your television screen in the comfort and convenience of your living room (on Channel 13, WNET, educational TV) a guerrilla soldier being slowly choked to death with water-soaked rags while American officers stood by watching, and heard when it was over (the prisoner refused to talk) one of the officers mutter sheepishly near the microphone of Bernard Fall's tape recorder

HOWDY PARDNER . . .

No, he didn't say that. He said, "Well, that's the way it

goes." The voice as incorrigibly down-home as corn pone, pecan waffles, mince pie or hominy grits. The eyes of Texas are upon you.

HOWDY PARDNER . . .

The girls of Nevada are skillful and efficient. For $100 a trip halfway around the world and back. By jetstream. A good buy at twice the price, more therapeutic by far than any osteopathic massage, psychoanalysis, colonic irrigation, or Gestalt group encounter known to man—the only honest game in the state.

HOWDY PARDNER . . .

Goodbye to Las Vegas, but we'll be back. Unavoidable. Las Vegas is creeping out everywhere. Very early next morning by the dawn's early light we lit out north by west, passing en route a portion of the Las Vegas Bombing and Gunnery Range where the Pentagon plays furtively with its secret toys. Among the several lifeless desert hills in the area are two named by the poetry of pure coincidence Skull Mountain and Specter Mountain. Check your map if you don't believe it.

We were bound for Death Valley.

HOWDY PARDNER . . .

7

Death Valley

Summertime

From Daylight Pass at 4,317 feet we descend through
Boundary Canyon and Hell's Gate into the inferno at sea
level and below. Below, below . . . beneath a sea, not of
brine, but of heat, of shimmering simmering waves of light
and a wind as hot and fierce as a dragon's breath.

The glare is stunning. Yet also exciting, even exhilarating—a world of light. The air seems not clear like glass but
colored, a transparent, tinted medium, golden toward the
sun, smoke-blue in the shadows. The colors come, it ap-

pears, not simply from the background, but are actually present in the air itself—a vigintillion microscopic particles of dust reflecting the sky, the sand, the iron hills.

On a day in June at ten o'clock in the morning the thermometer reads 114 degrees. Later in the day it will become hotter. But with humidity close to zero such heat is not immediately unpleasant or even uncomfortable. Like the dazzling air, the heat is at first somehow intoxicating—one feels that grace and euphoria that come with just the right ration of Old Grandad, with the perfect allowance of music. Sunlight is magic. Later will come. . . . Yes, out of the car and standing hatless under the sun, you begin to feel the menace in this arid atmosphere, the malignancy within that silent hurricane of fire.

We consider the dunes, the sea of sand. Around the edges of the dunes grow clumps of arrowweed tall as corn shocks, scattered creosote shrubs bleached out and still, a few shaggy mesquite trees. These plants can hardly be said to have conquered the valley, but they have in some way made a truce—or found a point of equilibrium in a ferocious, inaudible struggle between life and entropy. A bitter war indeed: The creosote bush secretes a poison in its roots that kills any other plant, even its own offspring, attempting to secure a place too near; in this way the individual creosote preserves a perimeter of open space and a monopoly of local moisture sufficient for survival.

We drive on to the gas station and store at Stovepipe Wells, where a few humans huddle inside beneath the blast of a cold-air blower. Like other mammals of the valley, the human inhabitants can endure its summer only by burrowing deep or by constructing an artificial environment—not adaptation but insulation, insularity.

Sipping cold drinks, we watch through the window a number of desert sparrows crawl in and out of the grills on the front of the parked automobiles. The birds are eating tourists—bugs and butterflies encountered elsewhere and smashed, baked, annealed to the car radiators. Like the bears of Yellowstone, the Indians of Arizona, and roadside businessmen everywhere, these birds have learned to make a good thing off passing trade. Certainly they provide a useful service; it's a long hot climb out of here in any direction and a clean radiator is essential.

The Indians of Death Valley were cleverest of all. When summer came they left, went up into the mountains, and stayed there until it was reasonable to return—an idea too subtle in its simplicity for the white man of today to grasp. But we too are Indians—gypsies anyhow—and won't be back until September.

Furnace Creek, September 17. Again the alarming descent. It seemed much too hot in the barren hills a mile above this awful sinkhole, this graben (for Death Valley is not, properly understood, a valley at all), this collapsed and superheated trench of mud, salt, gravel, and sand. Much too hot—but we felt obliged to come back once more.

A hard place to love, Death Valley. An ugly place, bitter as alkali and rough, harsh, unyielding as iron. Here they separate the desert rats from the mice, the hard-rock prospectors from the mere rock hounds.

Cactus for example. There is none at all on the floor of the valley. Too dry or too brackish or maybe too hot. Only up on the alluvial fans and in the side canyons 1,000 feet above sea level do we find the first stunted and scrubby specimens of cholla and prickly pear and the pink-thorned cottontop—poor relation of the barrel cactus.

At first glance, speeding by car through this valley that is not a valley, one might think there was scarcely any plant life at all. Between oases you will be impressed chiefly by the vast salt beds and the immense alluvial fans of gravel that look as hostile to life as the fabled seas of the moon.

And yet there is life out there, life of a sparse but varied sort—salt grass and pickleweed on the flats, far-spaced clumps of creosote, saltbush, desert holly, brittlebush, and prickly poppy on the fans. Not much of anything, but a little of each. And in the area as a whole, including the surrounding mountains up to the 11,000-foot summit of Telescope Peak, the botanists count a total of 900 to 1,000 different species, ranging from microscopic forms of algae in the salt pools to limber pine and the ancient bristlecone pine on the peaks.

But the first impression remains a just one. Despite variety, most of the surface of Death Valley is dead. Dead, dead, deathly—a land of jagged salt pillars, crackling and tortured crusts of mud, sunburnt gravel bars the color of rust, rocks and boulders of metallic blue naked even of lichen. Death Valley is Gravel Gulch.

Telescope Peak, October 22. To escape the heat for a while, we spend the weekend up in the Panamints. (Summer still baking the world down below, far below, where swirls of mud, salt, and salt-laden streams lie motionless under a lake of heat, glowing in lovely and poisonous shades of auburn, saffron, crimson, sulfurous yellow, dust-tinged tones of white on white.)

Surely this is the most sterile of North American deserts. No matter how high we climb it seems impossible to leave behind the influence of aridity and anti-life. At 7,000 feet in this latitude we should be entering a forest of yellow pine, with grassy meadows and freshwater brooks. We are farther north than Santa Fe or Flagstaff. Instead there are only the endless barren hills, conventional in form, covered in little but shattered stone. A dull monotonous terrain, dun-colored, supporting a few types of shrubs and small, scattered junipers.

From 7,000 to 9,000 feet we pass through a belt of more junipers and a fair growth of pinyon pines. Along the trail to Telescope Peak—at 10,000 feet—appear thin stands of limber pine and the short, massive, all-enduring bristlecone pine, more ancient than the Book of Genesis. Timberline.

There is no forest here. And fifty or sixty airline miles to the west stands the reason why—the Sierra Nevada Range blocking off the sea winds and almost all the moisture. We stand in the rain shadow of that still higher wall.

I walk past three wild burros. Descendants of lost and abandoned prospectors' stock, they range everywhere in the Panamints, multiplying freely, endangering the survival of the native bighorn sheep by trespassing on the latter's forage, befouling their springs. But the feral burros have their charm too. They stand about 100 feet from the trail watching me go by. They are quite unafraid, and merely blink their heavy eyelashes like movie starlets when I halt to stare at them. However they are certainly not tame. Advance toward them and they trot off briskly.

The bray of the donkey is well known. But these little beasts can make another sound even more startling because so unexpected. Hiking up some arid canyon in the Panamints, through what appears to be totally lifeless terrain, you suddenly hear a noise like a huge dry cough behind your shoulder. You spring ten feet forward before daring to look around. And see nothing, nothing at all, until you hear a second cough and scan the hillsides and discover far above a little gray or black burro looking down at you, waiting for you to get the hell out of its territory.

I stand by the cairn on the summit of Telescope Peak, looking out on a cold, windy, and barren world. Rugged peaks fall off southward into the haze of the Mojave Desert; on the west is Panamint Valley, the Argus Range, more mountains, more valleys, and finally the Sierras, crowned with snow; to the north and northwest the Inyo and White mountains; below lies Death Valley—the chemical desert— and east of it the Black Mountains, the Funeral Mountains, the Amargosa Valley and farther mountains, wave after wave of wrinkled ridges standing up from the oceanic desert sea until vision gives out somewhere beyond the curving rim of the world's edge. A smudge hangs on the eastern horizon, suggesting the presence of Death Valley's counterpart and complement, the only city within 100 miles: Las Vegas: Glitter Gulch West.

Echo Canyon, November 30. A hard place to love. Impossible? No, there were a few—the prospectors, the single-blanket, jackass prospectors who wandered these funeral wastes for a century dreaming of what? Sudden wealth? Not likely. Not Shorty Borden, for example, who invested eight months of his life in building by hand a nine-mile road to his lead and silver diggings in Hanaupah Canyon. Then discovered that even with a road it would still cost him more to transport his ore to the nearest smelter than the ore itself was worth.

Echo Canyon. We are deep into the intricacies of the Funeral Mountains. Named not simply for their proximity to Death Valley, but also for shape and coloration: lifeless escarpments of smoldering red bordered in charcoal, the crags and ridges and defiles edged in black and purple. A primeval chaos of faulted, uplifted, warped, and folded dolomites, limestones, fanglomerates of mud, sand, and gravel. Vulcanism as well: vesiculated andesite, walls embellished with elegant mosaics of rose and yellow quartz. Fool's gold—pyrite—glittering in the black sand, micaceous shales glinting under back light, veins of pegmatite zigzagging and intersecting like an undeciphered script across the face of a cliff: the writing on the wall: "God Was Here." Shallow caves, holes in the rock, a natural arch, and the canyon floor littered with boulders, deep in coarse gravel.

Nowhere in Echo Canyon can I find the slightest visible trace of water. Nevertheless, it must be present under the surface, at least in intermittent or minute amounts, for here and there stand living things. They look dead but are actually dormant, waiting for the resurrection of the rain. I mean the saltbush, the desert fir, the bladderweed, a sprinkling of cottontop cactus, the isolated creosote bush. Waiting.

You may see a few lizards. In sandy places are the hoof-prints of bighorn sheep, where they've passed through on their way from the high parts of the range to the springs near Furnace Creek. Sit quite still in one spot for an hour and you might see a small gray bird fly close to look you over. This is the bird that lives in Echo Canyon.

The echoes are good. At certain locations, on a still day, one clear shout will create a series of overlapping echoes that goes on and on toward so fine a diminuendo that the human ear cannot perceive the final vibrations.

Tramp far enough up Echo Canyon and you come to a ghost town, the ruins of a mining camp—one of many in Death Valley. Deep shafts, a tipple, a rolling mill largely intact, several cabins—one with its inside walls papered with pages from the *Literary Digest.* Half buried in drifted sand is a rusted model-T Ford without roof or motor, a child's tricycle, a broken shovel.

Returning through twilight, I descend the narrow gorge between flood-polished walls of bluish andesite—the stem of the wineglass. I walk down the center of an amphitheater of somber cliffs riddled with grottoes, huge eyesockets in a stony skull, where bats hang upside down in the shadows waiting for night.

Through the opening of the canyon I can see the icy heights of Telescope Peak shining under the cloud-reflected light of one more sunset. Scarlet clouds in a green sky. A weird glow pervades the air through which I walk; it vibrates on the canyon walls, revealing to me all at once a vision of the earth's slow agony, the convulsive grinding violence of a hundred thousand years. Of a million years. I write metaphorically, out of necessity. And yet it seems impossible to believe that these mountains, old as anything on the surface of the planet, do not partake in some dim way of the sentience of living tissue. Genealogies: From these rocks struck once by lightning gushed springs that turned to blood, flesh, life. Impossible miracle. And I am struck once again by the unutterable beauty, terror, and strangeness of everything we think we know.

Furnace Creek, December 10. The oasis. We stand near the edge of a grove of date palms looking eastward at the soft melting mud hills above Texas Spring. The hills are lemon yellow with dark brown crusts on top, like the frosting on a cake. Beyond the hills rise the elaborate, dark, wine-red mountains. In the foreground, close by, irrigation water plunges into a pool, from which it is diverted into ditches that run between rows of date palms.

The springs of Furnace Creek supply not only the palms but also the water needs of the hotel, the motel (both with swimming pools), Park Service headquarters and visitor center, an Indian village, and two large campgrounds. I do not know the output of these springs as measured in gallons per minute. But I do know that during the Christmas and Easter holidays there is enough water available to serve the needs of 10,000 people. Where does it come from? From a natural reservoir in the base of the bleak, fatally arid Funeral Mountains. A reservoir that may be joined to the larger underground acquifers beneath the Amargosa and Pahrump valleys to the east.

This does not mean that the Furnace Creek portion of Death Valley could support a permanent population of 10,000 drinking, back-scrubbing, hard-flushing suburbanites. For the water used here comes from a supply that may have required 20,000 years to charge; it is not sustained by rainfall—not in a country where precipitation averages two inches per year.

That's the mistake they made in central Arizona—Tucson and Phoenix—and are now making in Las Vegas and Albuquerque. Out of greed and stupidity, but mostly greed, the gentry of those cities overexpanded their investment in development and kept going by mining the underground water supply. Now that that supply is dwindling, they set up an unholy clamor in Congress to have the rest of the nation save them from the consequences of their own folly. Phoenix might rise again from ashes—but not, I think, from the sea of sand that is its likely destiny.

There are about 200 springs, all told, within the boundaries of Death Valley National Monument, counting each and every tiny seep that produces any flow at all. None except those in the northeast corner of the park are comparable to the springs at Furnace Creek. In addition to the springs, there are the heavily saline, undrinkable waters of Salt Creek, Badwater, and the valley floor itself.

All this water is found in what meteorologists believe to be the hottest place on earth, year in and year out hotter than the Sahara, the Great Karroo, the Negev, the Atacama, the Rub'-al-Khali ("Empty Quarter") of Arabia, or the far-out-back-of-beyond in central Australia. The world's record is held by Libya, where a temperature of 136 degrees Fahrenheit was once recorded at a weather station called Azizia. Death Valley's high so far is a reading of 134 degrees at Furnace Creek. But Azizia has been unable to come near repeating its record, while temperatures at Furnace Creek consistently exceed the mean maximums for Azizia by ten percent. And Badwater, only twenty miles south of Furnace Creek, is on the average always four degrees hotter. It follows that on the historic day when the thermometer reached 134 at Furnace Creek, it was probably 138 at Badwater. But there was nobody around at Badwater that day (July 10, 1913).*

Official weather readings are made from instruments housed in a louvered wooden box set five feet above the ground. In Death Valley the temperature on the surface of the ground is ordinarily fifty percent higher than in the box five feet above. On a normal summer's day in Death Valley, with the thermometer reading 120 degrees Fahrenheit, the temperature at ground surface is 180.

Curiosities: There are fish in the briny pools of Salt Creek,

---

* I am indebted for these data to Ruth Kirk's guidebook, *Exploring Death Valley*, Stanford University Press, 1965.

far out on the hottest, bleakest, saltiest part of the valley floor—the inch-long cyprinodon or pupfish. There is a species of soft-bodied snail living in the Epsom salts, Glauber's salt, and rock salts of Badwater. There are fairy shrimp in the *tinajas* or natural cisterns of Butte Valley in the southwest corner of the park; estivating beneath the clay most of the year, they wriggle forth to swim, rejoice, and reproduce after that rarest and most wonderful of Death Valley events, a fall of rain.

More curiosities: Blue herons enter the valley in winter; also trumpeter swans; grebes, coots, and mallards can be seen in the blue ponds of Saratoga Springs; and for a few weeks in the fall of one year (1966) a real flamingo made its home among the reeds that line the shore of the sewage lagoon below Park Village. Where this flamingo came from no one could say; where it went the coyotes most likely could testify. Or perhaps the lion.

A lean and hungry mountain lion was observed several times that year during the Christmas season investigating the garbage cans in the campgrounds. An old lion, no doubt—aging, possibly ill, probably retired. In short, a tourist. But a lion even so.

But these are mere oddities. All the instruments agree that Death Valley remains the hottest place on earth, the driest in North America, the lowest in the Western Hemisphere. Of all deathly places the most deadly—and the most beautiful.

Badwater, January 19. Standing among the salt pinnacles of what is called the Devil's Golf Course, I heard a constant tinkling and crackling noise—the salt crust expanding in the morning sun. No sign of life out there. Experimentally I ventured to walk upon, over, among the pinnacles. Difficult, but not impossible. The formations are knee-high, white within but stained yellow by the dusty winds, studded on top with sharp teeth. Like walking on a jumble of broken and refrozen slabs of ice: At every other step part of the salt collapses under foot and you drop into a hole. The jagged edges cut like knives into the leather of my boots. After a few minutes of this I was glad to return to the security of the road. Even in January the sun felt uncomfortably hot, and I was sweating a little.

Where the salt flats come closest to the base of the eastern mountains, at 278 feet below sea level, lies the clear and sparkling pool known as Badwater. A shallow body of water, surrounded by beds of snow-white alkali. According to Death Valley legend the water is poisonous, containing traces of arsenic. I scooped up a handful and sampled it in my mouth, since the testing of desert waterholes has always been one of my chores. I found Badwater lukewarm, salty on the tongue, sickening. I spat it out and rinsed my mouth with fresh water from my canteen.

From here, the lowest point in all the Americas, I gaze across the pale lenses of the valley floor to the brown outwash fan of Hanaupah Canyon opposite, ten miles away, and from the canyon's mouth up and up and up to the crest of Telescope Peak with its cornices of frozen snow 11,049 feet above sea level. One would like to climb or descend that interval someday, the better to comprehend what it means. Whatever it means.

I have been part of the way already, hiking far into Hanaupah Canyon to Shorty Borden's abandoned camp, up to that loveliest of desert graces, a spring-fed stream. Lively, bubbling, with pools big enough and cold enough, it seemed then, for trout. But there are none. Along the stream grow tangles of wild grapevine and willow; the spring is choked with watercress. The stream runs for less than a mile before disappearing into the sand and gravel of the wash. Beyond the spring, up-canyon, all is dry as death again until you reach the place where the canyon forks. Explore either fork and you find water once more—on the right a little waterfall, on the left in a grottolike glen cascades sliding down through chutes in the dark blue andesite. Moss, ferns, and flowers cling to the damp walls—the only life in this arid wilderness. Almost no one ever goes there. It is necessary to walk for many miles.

Devil's Hole, February 10. A natural opening in the desert floor; a queer deep rocky sinkhole with a pond of dark green water at the bottom. That pond, however, is of the kind called bottomless; it leads down and down through greener darker depths into underwater caverns whose dimensions and limits are not known. It might be an entrance to the subterranean lakes that supposedly lie beneath the Funeral Mountains and the Amargosa Valley.

The Park Service has erected a high steel fence with locked gate around the hole. Not to keep out tourists, who only want to look, but to keep out the aqualung adventurers who wish to dive in and go all the way down. Within the past year several parties of scuba divers have climbed over and under the fence anyway and gone exploring down in that sunless sea. One party returned to the surface one man short. His body has not been found yet, though many have searched. If supposition is correct, the missing man may be found someday wedged in one of the outlets of Furnace Creek springs.

Death Valley has taken five lives this year—one by water, two by ice, and two by fire. A hiker slipped on the glazed snow of the trail to Telescope Peak and tumbled 1,000 feet down a steep pitch of ice and rock. His companion went for help; a member of a professional mountaineering team, climbing down to recover the victim, also fell and was also killed.

Last summer two young soldiers from the Army's nearby Camp Irwin went exploring in the desert off the southwest corner of Death Valley. Their jeep ran out of gas, they tried to walk home to the base. One was found beside the seldom-traveled desert road, dead from exhaustion and dehydration. The body of the other could not be found, though 2,000 soldiers hunted him for a week. No doubt he wandered off the trail into the hills seeking water. Absent without leave. He could possibly be still alive. Maybe in a forgotten cabin up in the Panamints eating lizards, waiting for some war to end.

Ah to be a buzzard now that spring is here.

The sand dunes, March 15. At night I hear tree toads singing in the tamarisk along the water channels of Furnace Creek Ranch. The days are often windy now, much warmer, and rain squalls sail north through the valley, obscuring both sky and sun. The ground squirrels scamper from hole to hole in the mud hills, the Gambel's quail swoop in flocks low over the ground, alight, and run in unison through the brush, calling to one another. Tawny coyotes stand bold as brass close to the road in broad daylight and watch the tourists drive by. And the mesquite thickets, black and lifeless-looking since last fall, have assumed a delicate tinge of spring green.

Death Valley's winter, much too lovely to last, is nearly over.

Between winds and storms I walk far out on the dunes. How hot and implacably hostile this sea of sand appeared last June when we saw it for the first time. Then it seemed to be floating in heat waves, which gathered among the dunes and glistened like pools of water, reflecting the sky.

I bear for the highest of the dunes, following the curving crests of the lesser dunes that lead toward it. On the way I pass a few scraggly mesquite trees, putting out new leaves, and a number of creosote shrubs. No other plants are deep-rooted enough to survive in the sand, and these too become smaller and fewer as I advance and the dunes rise higher. On the last half mile to the topmost point there is no plant life whatsoever, although in the sand I find the prints of ravens, coyotes, mice, lizards. The sand is firm, rippled as the seashore, and virginal of human tracks; nobody has come this far since the last windstorm a few days ago.

Late in the afternoon I reach the summit of the highest

dune, 200 feet above the valley floor. Northward the sand drops abruptly away to smaller dunes, mud flats, a scatter of creosote and mesquite—and what looks to be, not a mirage, but a pond of real water encircled by the dunes.

Glissading down the hill of sand, climbing another and down the far side of that, I come to the margin of the pool. The sandy shore is quick, alive, and I sink ankle deep in the mud as I bend to taste the water and find it fresh, cool, with hardly a trace of salt—fit to drink. The water must be left over from the recent rain.

I struggle out of the wet sand onto the dunes. Here I'll make camp for the evening. I scoop a hole in the sand, build a tiny fire of mesquite twigs and sear a piece of meat on the flaming coals. Mesquite makes excellent fuel—burns with a slow hot flame, touching the air with a nut-sweet fragrance, and condenses as it burns to a bed of embers that glow and glimmer like incandescent charcoal. Fire is magic, a purifying and sanctifying magic, and most especially a mesquite fire on a sand dune at evening under desert skies, on the shore of a pool that gleams like polished agate, like garnet, like a tiger's eye.

The sun goes down. A few stray clouds catch fire, burn gold, vermillion, and driftwood blue in the unfathomed sea of space. These surrounding mountains that look during the day like iron—like burnt, mangled, rusted iron—now turn radiant as a dream. Where is their truth? A hard clean edge divides the crescent dunes into black shadow on one side, a phosphorescent light on the other. And above the rim of the darkening west floats the evening star.

8

Come On In

The canyon country of southern Utah and northern Arizona—the Colorado Plateau—is something special. Something strange, marvelous, full of wonders. As far as I know there is no other region on earth much like it, or even remotely like it. Nowhere else have we had this lucky combination of vast sedimentary rock formations exposed to a desert climate, a great plateau carved by major rivers—the Green, the San Juan, the Colorado—into such a surreal land of form and color. Add a few volcanoes, the standing necks of which can still be seen, and cinder cones and lava flows, and at least four separate laccolithic mountain ranges nicely distributed about the region, and more hills, holes, humps and hollows, reefs, folds, salt domes, swells and grabens, buttes, benches and mesas, synclines, monoclines, and anticlines than you can ever hope to see and explore in one lifetime, and you begin to arrive at an approximate picture of the plateau's surface appearance.

An approximate beginning. A picture framed by sky and time in the world of natural appearances. Despite the best efforts of a small army of writers, painters, photographers, scientists, explorers, Indians, cowboys, and wilderness guides, the landscape of the Colorado Plateau lies still beyond the reach of reasonable words. Or unreasonable representation. This is a landscape that has to be seen to be believed, and even then, confronted directly by the senses, it strains credulity.

Comprehensible, yes. Perhaps nowhere is the basic structure of the earth's surface so clearly, because so nakedly, revealed. And yet—when all we know about it is said and measured and tabulated, there remains something in the soul of the place, the spirit of the whole, that cannot be fully assimilated by the human imagination.

My terminology is far from exact; certainly not scientific. Words like "soul" and "spirit" make vague substitutes for a hard effort toward understanding. But I can offer no better. The land here is like a great book or a great symphony; it invites approaches toward comprehension on many levels, from all directions.

The geologic approach is certainly primary and fundamental, underlying the attitude and outlook that best support all others, including the insights of poetry and the wisdom of religion. Just as the earth itself forms the indispensable ground for the only kind of life we know, providing the sole sustenance of our minds and bodies, so does empirical truth constitute the foundation of higher truths. (If there is such a thing as higher truth.) It seems to me that Keats was wrong when he asked, rhetorically, "Do not all charms fly . . . at the mere touch of cold philosophy?" The word "philosophy" standing, in his day, for what we now call "physical science." But Keats was wrong, I say, because there is more charm in one "mere" fact, confirmed by test and observation, linked to other facts through coherent theory into a rational system, than in a whole brainful of fancy and fantasy. I see more poetry in a chunk of quartzite than in a make-believe wood nymph, more beauty in the revelations of a verifiable intellectual construction than in whole misty empires of obsolete mythology.

The moral I labor toward is that a landscape as splendid as that of the Colorado Plateau can best be understood and given human significance by poets who have their feet planted in concrete—concrete data—and by scientists whose heads and hearts have not lost the capacity for wonder. Any good poet, in our age at least, must begin with the scientific view of the world; and any scientist worth listening to must be something of a poet, must possess the ability to communicate to the rest of us his sense of love and wonder at what his work discovers.

The canyon country does not always inspire love. To many it appears barren, hostile, repellent—a fearsome land of rock and heat, sand dunes and quicksand, cactus, thornbush, scorpion, rattlesnake, and agoraphobic distances. To those who see our land in that manner, the best reply is, yes, you are right, it is a dangerous and terrible place. Enter at your own risk. Carry water. Avoid the noonday sun. Try to ignore the vultures. Pray frequently.

For a few others the canyon country is worth only what they can dig out of it and haul away—to the mills, to the power plants, to the bank.

For more and more of those who now live here, however, the great plateau and its canyon wilderness is a treasure best enjoyed through the body and spirit, *in situ* as the archeologists say, not through commercial plunder. It is a regional, national and international treasure too valuable to be sacrificed for temporary gain, too rare to be withheld from our children. For us the wilderness and human emptiness of this land is not a source of fear but the greatest of its attractions. We would guard and defend and save it as a place for all who wish to rediscover the nearly lost pleasures of adventure, adventure not only in the physical sense, but also mental, spiritual, moral, aesthetic and intellectual adventure. A place for the free.

Here you may yet find the elemental freedom to breathe deep of unpoisoned air, to experiment with solitude and stillness, to gaze through a hundred miles of untrammeled atmosphere, across redrock canyons, beyond blue mesas, toward the snow-covered peaks of the most distant mountains—to make the discovery of the self in its proud sufficiency which is not isolation but an irreplaceable part of the mystery of the whole.

Come on in. The earth, like the sun, like the air, belongs to everyone—and to no one.

9

Manhattan Twilight, Hoboken Night

Hoboken, New Jersey, is not one of the five boroughs of New York City. But it should be, for it's closer and quicker to the center of Manhattan from Hoboken than from any point in Brooklyn, the Bronx, Queens, or Staten Island. Fifteen minutes by bus, via the Lincoln Tunnel, takes you from Washington Street in Hoboken to the Port Authority Bus Terminal on Forty-First Street; ten minutes by train via the Hudson Tubes takes you from the Erie-Lackawanna Terminal to Ninth Street and Sixth Avenue—the Village. A dash under the river, a roar of iron, and you're there: in Glitter

Gulch, U.S.A.—Times Square, the Big Midway, the hanging
gardens of electricity. Or down yonder in Green Witch Village. What more could you want? And if New York is not
Manhattan, it is nothing. A little worse than nothing. Meanwhile the insane, medieval burgs of New Jersey—Union
City, West New York, Jersey City—lie divorced from Hoboken by a wall older than the Great Wall of China. I mean the
Palisades, that sill of diabase left over from the Triassic
period.

I make this effort to incorporate Hoboken into New York
City (where it belongs) rather than allowing it to remain in
New Jersey (for which it is much too sweet, pure, romantic)
because it is from the Hoboken point of view, the Hoboken
mystique, the Hoboken metaphysic, that I must describe
what I remember and what I know of New York. Meaning
Manhattan. Of the rest I know nothing. The other four
boroughs are as remote to my imagination as the Malebolges
of the Eighth Circle of Hell. Perhaps only Dante could tell us
the truth about them. Perhaps only Dante—and Dos-
toevski—could tell us the truth about New York.

For two years I lived in Hoboken, far from my natural
habitat. The bitter bread of exile. Two years in the gray light
and the sulfur dioxide and the smell of burning coffee beans
from the Maxwell House plant at the end of Hudson Street.
In a dark, dank, decaying apartment house where the
cockroaches—shell-backed, glossy, insolent *Blatella ger-
manica*—festered and spawned under the linoleum on the
sagging floors, behind the rippled wallpaper on the sweating
walls, among the teacups in the cupboard. Everywhere.
While the rats raced in ferocious packs, like wolves, inside
the walls and up and down the cobblestone alleyways that
always glistened, night and day, in any kind of weather, with
a thin chill greasy patina of poisonous dew. The fly ash everywhere, falling softly and perpetually from the pregnant
sky. We watched the seasons come and go in a small rectan-
gle of walled-in space we called our yard: in spring and sum-

mer the black grass; in fall and winter the black snow. Overhead and in our hearts a black sun.

Down in the cellar and up in the attic of that fantastic house—four stories high, brownstone, a stoop, wide, polished bannisters, brass fittings on the street entrance, a half-sunken apartment for the superintendent, high ceilings, high windows, and a grand stairway on the main floor, all quite decently middle class and in the better part of town, near the parks, near the Stevens Institute of Technology—hung draperies of dust and cobweb that had not been seen in the light of day or touched by the hand of man since the time of the assassination of President William McKinley.

In the sunless attic the spiders had long since given up, for all their prey had turned to dust; but the rats roamed freely. Down in the basement, built like a dungeon with ceiling too low to permit a man of normal stature to stand erect, there were more rats, of course—they loved the heat of the furnace in winter—and dampish stains on the wall and floor where the great waterbugs, like cockroaches out of Kafka, crawled sluggishly from darkness into darkness. One might notice here, at times, the odor of sewer gas.

The infinite richness. The ecology, the natural history of it all. An excellent workshop for the philosopher, for who would venture out into that gray miasma of perpetual smoke and fog that filled the streets if he might remain walled up with books, sipping black coffee, smoking black Russian cigarettes, thinking long, black, inky thoughts? To be sure. But there were the streets. The call of the streets.

We lived one block from the waterfront. The same waterfront where Marlon Brando once played Marlon Brando, where rust-covered tramp steamers, black freighters, derelict Dutchmen, death ships, came to call under Liberian flags to unload their bananas, baled hemp, teakwood, sacks of coffee beans, cowhides, Argentine beef, to take on kegs of nails, jeep trucks, Cadillacs, and crated machine guns. Abandoned by the Holland-American Line in '65, at least for passenger service, the Hoboken docks—like Hoboken bars and Hoboken tenements—were sinking into an ever deepening state of decay. The longshoremen were lucky to get two days' work a week. Some of the great warehouses had been empty for years; the kids played Mafia in them.

The moment I stepped out the front door I was faced again with Manhattan. There it was, oh splendid ship of concrete and steel, aluminum, glass, and electricity, forging forever up the dark river. (The Hudson—like a river of oil, filthy and rich, gleaming with silver lights.) Manhattan at twilight: floating gardens of tender neon, the lavender towers where each window glittered at sundown with reflected incandescence, where each crosstown street became at evening a gash of golden fire, and the endless flow of the endless traffic on the West Side Highway resembled a luminous necklace strung round the island's shoulders.

Who would believe the city could be so beautiful? On winter evenings when the sun went down early and all the office lights stayed lit, the giant glass buildings across the river glowed like blocks of radium with a cool soft Venusian radiance, magnetic and fatal. And above them all stood the Vampire State Building with its twin beams stroking through the mist and the red spider eyes on the radio mast blinking slowly off and on, off and on, all through the New York night. While deep-sea liners bayed in the roadstead, coming up the Narrows, and tugboats shaped like old shoes and croaking like alligators glided by in the opposite direction, towing freight trains or barges filled with traprock. Once I saw a large dark ship, no visible running lights at all, pass between me and the clustered constellations of the city—a black form moving across a field of stars.

One night Manhattan itself became that dark ship. Under moonlight the city appeared to be deserted, abandoned, empty as a graveyard except for the dim beams of automobiles groping through the blacked-out canyons, fumbling for the way home. From where I stood in Hoboken, on a hill above the waterfront, I could hear not the faintest sound of life, not a heartbeat, from New York. The silence was impressive. But by the next night the power was back and the city shining like a many-colored vision of wealth and glory. From the little park in Weehawken where Aaron Burr shot Alexander Hamilton (good shot!) you could look right down the center line of Forty-Second Street. With glasses powerful enough, you could watch the sports and pastimes of the folk who dwell in the City of Dreadful Night.

If the Lower East Side is now the East Village, Hoboken was (still is, if urban renewal has not yet destroyed it all) the West Village. Down on River Street just past the gothic gables of the Christian Seamen's Home began our own little Bohemia, where the otherwise omnipresent odor of sewer gas, burning coffee beans and the Hudson River was sweetened by the smell of marijuana and smoking joss sticks. Under the vacant eyes of condemned tenements lived the Peace People, the Flower Children, in happy polygamous squalor. Woven god's-eyes dangled from the ceilings; on once blank and dusty storefront windows appeared the American flag, handpainted, with five, six, or seven stripes and anywhere from a dozen to twenty stars, asymmetrical as nebulae. The men wore bands on their heads, beards on their jaws, and their old ladies were as slender, sweet and comely as their tresses were long. My friend Henry the painter was painting nothing but gas stations that year. Esso gas stations. And Rini the sculptor was busy welding and reworking junked auto parts into surreal hobgoblins of iron.

"Look here, Rini," I said to her, "instead of dragging the goddamn junkyard into the art galleries, why don't you throw the goddamn art galleries into the junkyard?"

"That's exactly what we're doing," she replied.

They had a coffeehouse—the Baby Bull—and nocturnal police raids and finally even a murder of their very own. Anything Haight-Ashbury had we had too.

Hoboken may be the only city in America where some of

the police were actually caught red-handed in the act of tampering with the voting machines: There was a resolution on the ballot in the election that year which if approved would have authorized a substantial pay increase for the fuzz and the firemen.

Which suggests the role of *power* again: When I lived in Hoboken it was the most densely populated, square-mile city in the United States, inhabited largely by babies; you could not walk down the main drag, Washington Street, at any time during daylight hours without threading your way through traffic jams of loaded baby carriages, many of them containing twins, some triplets, each carriage powered by a pregnant mother with two or three toddlers dragging at her skirts. And who ruled this fecund mass?

The character of the population was mixed, a typical American polyglot boiling pot of Italians, Irish, Puerto Ricans, Poles, Jews, Germans, and Blacks. But there could be little doubt which *ethnos* dominated the structure of authority when you read in the local paper of the latest gathering of dignitaries at the Union Club: "Present were *Mayor Grogan, Councilman Hogan, Bishops Malarkey* and *Moone, Commissioners Hoyle* and *Coyle* and *Boyle.*"

Who were those others we sometimes glimpsed on rare occasions, those heavy short swarthy men with Homburg hats, velvet-collared overcoats, fat cigars, who rode far back in the rear corners of black limousines rolling swiftly, quietly (no sound but the hiss of rubber on asphalt) down the evening streets? Who were the two Mongolian wrestlers in front dressed like FBI operatives, one driving, one scanning the sidewalks with stonefish eyes?

Hoboken. Weehawken. Hohokus. Secaucus. Paramus. Manhattan. And the five boroughs of New York. True, we were separated by a river from the center of the city. But are not the others also cut off by water? The Harlem River. The East River. What is the Brooklyn Bridge for? What is the function of the Staten Island Ferry? New York is a city of waters and islands, like Venice, floating on sewer lagoons, under a sea of fog and smoke and drizzling acid mists. You have to be tough to live there—even the clams on the off-shore shelf are full of polluted pride. The chickadees, star-lings, sparrows and alley cats of Hoboken were a hardier meaner breed than you find elsewhere. The old trees in the little parks along Boulevard East and Hudson Street seemed lifeless as statuary most of the year; yet in April there came an astonishing outburst of delicate green along the length of those blackened limbs. As if leaves should grow upon gun barrels and—but why not?—bright, fuzzy flowers spring up from the mouths of cannon.

Perhaps I liked best the sunflowers along the railroad tracks, and the little purple asters that rose between the ties, out of the cinders. Or the cattails in the ditches and the rank nameless weeds that flourished by the iron wheels of rotting boxcars—*Erie-Lackawanna—The Great White Way—Route of Phoebe Snow*—forgotten on sidings. Or the feral hollyhocks tall as corn along the walls of the gate tender's shack at the railway crossing, transpiring through July. There was a bit-ter, forlorn yet stubborn beauty everywhere you looked in Hoboken. Even the smog of heavy summer evenings played a helpful part, enhancing the quality of light and shadow on old brick walls, lending to things only a block away the sem-blance of magic and mystery.

When I was there I thought New York was dying. Maybe it really is. I know I was dying to get out. But if it's dying then it's going to be a prolonged, strange, infinitely complex process, a death of terror and grandeur. Imagine a car-cinoma 300 miles long, a mile thick, embracing 50 million souls. Whatever else (I tell myself) you may think about New York now, looking back at it from this desert perspective, you've got to admit that Wolf Hole, Arizona, can never have so rich a death.

There are three ways to get from Hoboken to Manhattan. There were four. You can take the Number 6 bus, dive into the Lincoln Tunnel (holding your breath), roar through that tube of tile and light, where the tunnel cops pace forever up and down their cement walkways or stand in glass boxes built into the walls (we used to discuss the question, which is the world's worst job: subway motorman? city bus driver? slaughterhouse worker? switchboard operator? or tunnel cop?), to emerge suddenly into the blue air of the Port Authority Bus Terminal. Or you can take the Hudson Tubes under the river, ride the trains through the sweating tunnels, where little green lights blink dimly beside the rails, and come out in the Village or stay on the train and ride it uptown as far as Macy's, Gimbel's, Herald Square. The third way, if you have a car, is to drive it yourself through either the Lincoln Tunnel or the Holland Tunnel and drive it back through the other way when you realize finally that there is almost no place on all of God's Manhattan where you can park your machine.

The fourth way was to take the Lackawanna Ferry and although the slowest this was by far the best. (A fifth way will be to walk on the water when the Hudson finally coagulates.) Getting to the ferry slips at the railway terminal was part of the pleasure: For whether you went by Washington Street, Hudson Street or River Street, you passed not only such places as the hippie communes and the Christian Seamen's Home but also the most shabby dingy rundown smelly half-lighted dangerous and downright picturesque little Mom and Pop bars in North America.

It was said, on good authority, that Hoboken had more taverns per square block than any other city in the world except Anchorage, Alaska. I believe it. I never did get into all of them, though for two years I tried. Some I remember: the Old Empire, the Seven Seas, Allie and Jopie's, Anna Lee's, Portview, El Jim's, the Dutch Mill, the Elysian Fields Bar and Grill, the River Street, the Cherokee, the Old Holland House, McSharry's Irish House, the Continental, the Little Dipsy Doodle, the Grand, the Inn, the Idle Hours (how true), Pat's, Pete's, Lou's, Joe's, and Mom's. And the Silver

Trail, Hoboken's only genuine western bar, with live western music and authentic cowboy stomp dancing every Saturday night; and Nelson's Marine Bar and Grill, my favorite, where the bartender, Herman Nelson, sole owner and proprietor, is or was the man who *almost* became world welterweight champ in 1931; and the stand-up bar of the Clam Broth House, men only (then), free clam broth, Löwenbrau on tap, the crackle of clamshells underfoot.

Anyway, if you made it past all the bars and the three Chinese laundries—Sam Toy's, Harry Lew's, Gong Lee's—and past the hash peddlers, cops, hippies, Christian seamen, bohemes, bums, panhandlers, whores, winos, shoeshine boys, muggers, rapists, and shiv artists, you arrived at the Erie-Lackawanna building. End of the line. Mouth of the tubes. Home of the ferryboats. The E-L building (is it still there?) looked like a square fruitcake coated with green mold. It was enormous, its cavernous interior capacious enough for a dozen trains plus shops and offices and waiting rooms. Paying our fare at the turnstiles, we stormed up the ramp onto the "Next Boat."

All on board, gangplanks winched up with a rattle of chains, the ferry surged out of the slip and bore east-southeast across the Hudson toward the Barclay Street docks on the far side. Moving partly with the current and partly across it, the ferry left a curving wake as it churned from shore to shore. In winter we glided among drifting ice floes the color of urine; in summer through trails of garbage bobbing in the wake of ships, seagulls screaming as they wheeled and dove for supper. I liked to stand on the open forward deck facing the wind and the solemn monuments of lower Manhattan. For a few minutes at least we were all free, commuters, drifters and students alike, liberated from the confines of lubberly life and at home—so we thought—with sailors and seabirds, the allure of the open sea. It seemed to me I could read on the faces of even the most resigned commuters an emotion the same as mine: exultance.

It was strange, that approach to Manhattan over the open

water. No sound but the slap of waves, the wind, the gulls, the distant signals of other boats. The city itself swung slowly toward us silent as a dream. No sign of life but puffs of steam from skyscraper chimneys, the motion of the traffic. The mighty towers stood like tombstones in a graveyard, leaning against the sky and waiting for—for what? Someday we'll know.

And then as we came close we began to hear the murmur of the city's life, the growing and compelling roar, the sound of madness. Newspapers were folded, overcoats buttoned, hat brims tugged—those gray near-brimless little felt hats that all the men wore and which had the peculiar virtue of rendering the wearer invisible. Everyone crowded toward the front of the boat. You could see the tension stealing over each face as 200 full-grown men prepared themselves for the stampede to taxis, buses, the subway trains.

But those were the mornings. Mornings were always absurd and desperate in New York. In the evening, going to the city, the mood was different, only a few of us on the boat, going the wrong way—the right way—against the mainstream of human traffic. In the evening the great glittering ship of Manhattan seemed to promise the fulfillment of every desire, every wish; one sailed toward it through the purple twilight with a heart full of hope. Hope for what? Hard to say—hope for those things a young man desires so much he hesitates to name them: for love; for adventure; for revelation; for triumph. All of it waiting there in that golden city of electric glory. All of it almost within reach.

That was the view from the water, the fantasy of the river crossing. Close to, the scene came into a different focus; we found ourselves back in the profane world of people with problems, embittered cab drivers, Sam Schwartz and his roasted chestnuts, the quiet tragedy of human relationships. No amount of weed or booze or sex or heavy art could permanently alter any of that.

I was a walker. I usually walked from Barclay Street up to

the Village, preferring the grim and empty downtown streets to the infernal racket and doomed faces of the subway. Pausing at the White Horse for a drink to the memory of Dylan—the one from Cardigan Bay—the real Dylan, and thence to Dillon's where I *might* meet somebody I knew, and from there to the Cedars, international intersection of all Volkswagen Bohemia where I *always* met somebody I knew, where anybody meets somebody, we threw a few back while deciding whose opening, whose screening, whose party to crash on this wild, full-of-wonder, high-blossoming night.

After a quick trip to the john to read the writing on the wall—Socrates Loves Alcibiades; Joy Shipmates Joy!; Here I Sit Anonymous as Hieronymus Bosch; Caligula Come Back; Mene Mene Tekel—it was out on the jam-packed streets again, through the multitudes, and up a tunnel of stairways into somebody's loft—THIS FLOOR WILL SAFELY SUSTAIN A LOAD OF 70 LB PER SQUARE FOOT—and into The Party.

The Party was permanent, like the revolution, always in swing somewhere, with the same conglutinate crowd, the same faces, the same wilted potato chips, the same red wine, the same dense atmosphere of smoke and heat and intellection, the same blonde lovely girls down from Boston for the weekend, the same paintings of Esso gas stations on the walls, the same racoon-eyed lank-haired crepe-clad palefaced vampire lass hesitating in the doorway, to whom some catty chick would say, "Well do creep in." Somebody like Norman Mailer was always there, a drink in each hand, and Dwight MacDonald, and Joel Oppenheimer, and Joseph Heller, and the man who invented Happenings, I forget his name. Everyone was there but the host, who usually could not be found.

There were other parts of the town I got to know, a little. For a while I had a girl friend who lived on Fourteenth Street, near Union Square; I worked briefly as a technical writer for General Electric in an office building on Lower Broadway, editing training manuals for DEW Line soldiers on how to dispose of sewage in permafrost; we all had to wear white shirts—that was mandatory—and I was fired at the end of two weeks for spending too much time staring out the window. I was invited a few times to publishers' offices in the midtown region, to an agent's office in Rockefeller Center, to lunches at Sardi's. My wife had an M.D. with an office in the East Sixties. Once I went to Wilt Chamberlain's nightclub in Harlem. And I worked for a time as a welfare caseworker in the Atlantic Avenue district of Brooklyn—but that is another story, that was another world, that was lower Mississippi we were dealing with there; let us now praise famous men. But I lived in Hoboken.

The Party is over, for me. In the gray light of dawn with the Sunday *Times,* world's most preposterous newspaper—all those dead trees!—rolled under my arm, I navigated the deserted streets. Bleak and God-forsaken Sunday. Down into the subway entrance, down into the dim calamitous light of the tubes. Into an empty car. The placards on the walls implored me: GIVE: multiple sclerosis; muscular dystrophy; heart disease; lung cancer; mental illness; cystic-fibrosis; nephritis; hepatitis; cerebral palsy; VD; TB; acute leukemia. Buy Bonds: Keep Freedom in Your *Future!* Good God. The train jolted forward, began to move; the dripping steam pipes, the little blue lights, the sweating walls slide greasily by. Just a happy little journey through hell. The train paused at the Christopher Street station. Before it moved on again I had time to contemplate a pair of rubber gloves lying in a pool of oil beside the tracks.

We plunged beneath the river. I slept all day. At evening I walked once more along the waterfront and gazed across the river at the somber forms of Manhattan, the great towers largely dark, for on Sunday no one is at work over there but the janitors. I don't know how New York can survive.

I believe the city is doomed. The air is poisonous, not so much with filth and disease as with something deadlier—human hatred. Yes, there's hatred in Arizona, too, but here it is easily dissipated into the nothingness of space: Walk one-half mile away from the town, away from the road, and you find yourself absolutely alone, under the sun, under the moon, under the stars, within the sweet aching loneliness of the desert.

That loneliness is not enough. We must save the city. It is essence and substance of us all—we cannot lose it without diminishing our stature as a nation, without a fatal wound.

My words therefore are dedicated to that city we love, that visionary city of the prophecies, humane and generous, that city of liberty and beauty and joy which will come to be, someday, on American earth, on the shore of the sea.

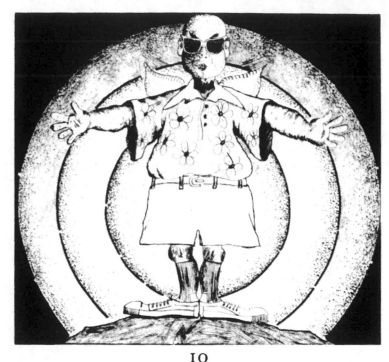

10

God's Plan for the State of Utah: A Revelation

We're riding along the rimrock above Pucker Pass Canyon, me and this red dun horse, minding our own business and generally at peace with the world, such as it is. His head was going one way and his legs was going that other way and he was dancing along the edge of the rim with that goldamn river 2,000 feet straight down below and ever now and then I give him a crack between the ears with this here piece of lead pipe I carry along for pleasure rides. That helped some but not much so we compromised by going in a direction neither of us wanted to go in the direction of. Me and my

horse, we spend a lot of our time like that, just enjoying ourselves.

Then we come across this stranger.

He was sitting on a warm rock in the middle of July looking out acrosst the canyons toward Poverty Flat and them La
Sal Mountains. There wasn't much to see in that direction
except the smoke from the Moab City Dump and them new
evaporation ponds the potash company built down by the
river but that's what he was looking at.

Now this stranger, he weren't much to look at hisself. Not
what you'd call a fine figure of a man. He was dough-bellied,
ewe-necked, and too short in the hind legs. I'm not even
talking about what he had for a face. Now they say a man
can't be blamed for the way he looks but if I was that fella
I'd want to have a long talk with my mother.

This stranger was a shade nervous, maybe because my red
dun makes everybody nervous, especially me. I better tell
you about my horse. Old Diablo he don't mean any harm
most of the time. It's that moon-eye he got on the left makes
him look undependable but it's the other eye you got to
watch out for. So long as you don't turn your back on him
for more than two seconds in a row you got absolutely nothing to worry about. All in all I'd say he's about as fine a horse
as you're likely to find here in Grand County, Utah. For the
price. I ain't denying he got some unusual habits. For instance, if you try to mount him by yourself you might need
help. I mean medical help. (Someday I hope to find the gen-
tleman sold me this gem. Want to thank him.)

Anyhow like I say there was this stranger and he was looking mighty red in the face from too much sun. He was ten
miles from the nearest road and he didn't even have any
water with him. He didn't look like no hiker and I couldn't
figure out how he got there. He was dressed up like one of
them California tourists—short pants, a shirt with palm trees
all over it, tennis shoes, great big sunglasses. Didn't even
have a hat on and he was bald as a hen's egg. That skinhead

of his was so sunburnt you could see a glow around it from the heat he was giving off. Hurt my eyes just to look at him.

Diablo didn't like the looks of this stranger none a-tall. For a minute I was real busy trying to keep that horse in reasonable connection to the ground where all that yucca and prickly pear grows so good. Maybe it was the hump the stranger had under the back of the shirt spooked him. That hump kind of quivered now and then, like it was alive. Course it was none of my business what he was hiding under his shirt. I ain't no game warden.

"Hello there," the stranger says as I rein in close on Diablo. He had a accent I couldn't exactly place. Harvard, maybe, or Oxford, one of them pointy-headed professor schools back East, where they study how to park a bicycle straight. Then he kind of barks at my horse. "Die-bally-cuss hick ate your beak," he says—or something like that. It was a language we ain't too familiar with in these parts. "How are you?" he says to me, while I'm trying to stay topside of that sunfishing bronc of mine.

"You sonofabitch," I says and give old Diablo a couple of good ones on the head with the lead pipe. He quieted down for a minute and stopped this four-legged two-step he was doing around the cactus. "Maybe that'll learn you, you goldamn shirt-eater." I catch my breath then and I say to the stranger, "Well, sir, we're just fine. Fine as a frog's hair."

"That's good," he says. "Do you have water in that vessel of yours? I'm afraid we forgot what the weather is like down here in the summer."

Vessel? I always thought a vessel was a kind of boat you sail on the ocean. Or maybe a leaky vessel like my old lady. Then I seen he was eyeballing my canteen.

"Fix you right up, pardner," I says. I take this plaited bull rope me and Diablo carry around and I slip off him quick while he's watching the stranger and tie him to a big pinyon pine nearby with a clove hitch, two half hitches, another clove hitch and a double lock knot. Actually you can tie my horse to most any tree if it's got a good solid root system.

Then I give my canteen to this stranger and he starts gulping down the water. "Don't cramp your gut now," I says. He keeps on drinking. Like I said he don't look like any hiker but I asked him anyhow, "You one of them there Sahara Clubbers?"

The stranger says, "I'm not familiar with that organization," and goes back to drinking my water.

I was kind of glad he said that. I'd hate to tell anybody what we done to the last Sahara Clubber we caught in Grand County after sundown. I looked him over some more. I been calling this character a "he" and a "him" but I ain't sure exactly what he was. Except for that bald head he didn't really look like a man and he didn't look like a woman neither. What he looked like was what they call a "androgyny" in that *Mizz* magazine. Oh yeah, I read *Mizz*. Me and my wife we're modern, we like to keep up. I read *Mizz* and she reads the *Shotgun News*. I guess we know where things is at. Or was at. (Mail gets in late to our town sometimes.) She ain't no beauty queen but she got a head on her shoulders, my old woman. Mind you I don't believe everything I read in my *Mizz*. Like they talk all the time about "human beings." Well I seen men and I seen women but I ain't never come acrosst one of them there "human beings." Least not in Grand County, Utah. But now looks like I'd got me a genuine androgyny.

"You out taking a hike anyway?" I ask him.

"That's not why I was sent down here," he says.

He might as well of dropped out of the sky for all I could see. "You ain't told me how you got here," I says. He didn't answer right away. I stood there watching my water circulate around *his* Adam's apple. I said, "This here's no kind of country for a fella to be a-chousin' around in on foot this time of year. A little fella like you could pucker up and blow away like a thistle ball inside twenty-four hours."

He lowered my canteen then. He looked kind of irritated. "What's your name?" he says.

"Name's Garn," I says. "J. Orrin Garn. Folks around here call me Big Jake. Some folks used to call me Jakie but you don't see much of them anymore. What's yourn?"

"What's my what?"

"What's your name?"

He thought it over. "Nehi," he says, raising the canteen.

I gave him my right paw. "Glad to meet you, Mr. Nehi. We used to drink your soda pop all the time. You might save a swaller or two of that water for me."

He finally gave back my canteen. I drank what was left quick before this stranger tried to grab it back. By God I'm thinking, any hammerhead dumb enough to wander around this desert in July without no water ought to have his brains inspected for leakage. If he got any. How could any one man be that stupid? Takes teamwork to be that dumb. Look at Watergate. This poor greenhorn probly wouldn't know how to pour piss out of a boot unless the instructions was printed on the heel. In basic English. Upside down.

The stranger appears to be getting a mite restless. "Mind your thoughts," he says—but don't explain. He shuffles around a minute, looking at that smudge in the sky and the potash ponds and he says, "Garn, I have a message to deliver to the State of Utah."

"We got a telephone down in Moab."

"This message has to be delivered personally to someone who represents Utah as a whole. The Executive Director insists on that."

"The who?"

"The Boss."

"I'll take it," I says. "There ain't nobody represents this state as a hole better than J. Orrin Garn."

Nehi looked doubtful but made up his mind. "All right," he says. "We're in a hurry. I guess you'll have to do."

Well now that remark didn't set quite right with me, no sir, but while I was figuring how to take it he starts to peel off his shirt. And about the time I decided I'd only remove his lower jaw and break his legs over my knee and maybe for the fun of it scale his sunglasses over the rim, why then he gets that shirt off and commences to fluffing out these little white wings he wore on his back. They looked like pigeon wings only bigger and they was a-growing right out of his skin. That took my mind off my project to improve his manners for a minute. I guessed I better humor him.

"You'll never get off the ground," I says. He looked like a bird like the kitchen stove looks like a airplane. He looked about as airy-dynamic as a bristleback hog. "You'll never get no pilot's license with them pigeon wings, Mr. Nehi."

The stranger, he didn't even smile. "Give me your hand, Garn," he says, sticking out his own. "We're taking off."

I knowed the sun must of fried his brains considerable but you got to be cautious with these little short-pants fellas that think they are airplanes. So I give him my hand and he takes a surprising powerful grip on it.

"Point your toes," he says.

Before I could work that out, there's this buzzing noise like some kind of giant bumble-assed bee and there we go, me and him, hand in hand flying over the rimrock 2,000 feet above the Coloraddy River.

I didn't like that much. Old Diablo he didn't like it neither. He give a snort and a screech and a backflip and broke that bull rope and made tracks for home. You wouldn't of thought it could be done but mainly I hoped he didn't tear up my new four-hundred-dollar Slim Fleming roper saddle taking shortcuts through barbed-wire fences.

Anyhow I had other things to occupy my mind. We was flying around 10,000 feet above the town of Moab where I live and you could see the whole damn stretch of Grand County from the Colorado line to the Green River.

Nehi pointed down to the potash evaporation ponds. Them ponds are so big and square you can see them from near anywhere. "Get rid of those," he says.

The wind was howling past my ears so hard I wasn't sure I heard him right. "Sir?"

He cuts the speed some and we drift lower. "The message," he says. "The Director says you've got to stop covering his canyonlands with that blue garbage."

"Sir?" I couldn't figure what the hell he was talking about but I guess it didn't matter because Nehi was picking up speed again and before I knew it we was whizzing north over the Book Cliffs and up toward Vernal where the new shale rock operation is. You could see the dust and smoke from fifty miles away.

"That also," the stranger says. "Close it down. You're tearing up good deer- and cattle-country. Not allowed."

"That's shale rock," I says. "They're gonna be squeezing oil out of them rocks."

"Can you eat oil?"

"I don't know. Ain't never tried, Mr. Nehi."

"Close it down." And then we're shooting west over the Wasatch Mountains above the Salt Lake City area. You couldn't see the city, exactly, but you could see all that brown-yeller smog down there stretching for about a hundred miles from Bountiful to Cedar City. Salt Lake was down in the middle of it somewheres. Nehi he says, "The Director wants that mess cleaned up, Garn. It doesn't look good. It offends His nostrils."

"Well, sir," I says, "I don't know about that. That all belongs to Kennecott Copper down there. This here's Kennecott country. They own it."

"Clean it up."

"Like they say, smoke means jobs." Had him there, I reckon.

He says, "Emphysema means jobs too. If you want to work in a nursing home. Clean it up."

"The copper companies are a-gonna build higher smokestacks," I says. "Spread it around better."

"We don't want that filth spread around. We want it kept out of the air. That's a direct order from the top."

"They say they might close down if this pollution control gets too strict."

"Where I come from," Nehi says, "blackmail is a mortal sin. Down here it's a felony. Prosecute."

"That ain't easy to do when the prosecutor works for the prosecutee."

"The Director gives you two years. No more. He has decided that the State of Utah shall be a clean-air refuge for sick tourists from Indiana."

"That's ree-diculous, Mr. Nehi. Utah's to make money in. Everybody knows that. Why, our state motto is 'Industry' and our state symbol is a gold beehive. We're busy little bees here, Mr. Nehi. A-packing in the honey."

"We're changing all that."

"That's the message?"

"Part of it. Now see those open pits in the mountains down there? We want those holes filled in, contoured, planted in bluestem and gramma grass, and stocked with mule deer, mountain lion, bighorn sheep, and prairie wolf."

"Filled in? Now looky here, stranger," I says, "them copper people spent fifty years digging them pits. There's one-half percent copper still down in there."

"Fill them in. And do it right."

"That'll cost millions."

"Spend it. The Director wants no more open pits in Utah except the ones He designed himself. He has *decreed* that Utah shall be a land of clean air, clear streams, abundant wildlife, natural beauty, and human delight."

"Well, sir, your director he's crazy as a jugful of crickets. Our state legislature and our governor, they ain't gonna stand for any foolishness like that."

"They'll have problems," Nehi says, buzzing up a little higher. The smell from below is kind of rank. I go along; he's got a good hammerlock on my right arm. "How many people down there, Garn?"

"About a million, I reckon, give or take a million or two."

"Too much," he says. "Too many. Thou shalt not lay up house against house. An abomination." He keeps muttering and grumbling. "Garn," he says, "the Director wants this brainless multiplying to come to a halt. It disgusts Him."

"We got to be fruitful, Mr. Nehi."

"Fruitful? Fruitful?" All of a sudden he starts roaring at me. "Then be fruitful like human beings!" he roars. "Not like fruit flies! Not like maggots! Not like rabbits!" He grumbles some more, then he says, "The Director wants the population of Utah kept at a human and humane level. That means no more increase. No more artificial cities in the desert. No more mining the water table. No more diversion of river waters. No more strip-mining of His sacred mesas."

"But *our* governor he says we need more people so we can attract more industry. He says we need more industry so we can attract more people to generate more jobs so industry can grow and help make Utah Number One."

"Number One what?"

"He didn't say."

"No more increase," Nehi says. "That's an order."

"But—"

"From On High."

He tightens his grip on my arm and shoots off toward the south. I'd estimate our airspeed at about five miles a minute but naturally I was a-dragging my feet some. We fly over the mountains again and down past Emery where they're building another power plant.

"That one too," he says.

"Yes, sir."

"No more smog!"

"Yes, sir."

"No more strip-mining!"

"Yes, sir."

We whistled over the Waterpocket Fold and across the Escalante canyons and around the Kaiparowits Plateau and there in front of us was Lake Powell and that Glen Canyon Dam. Over yonder was the town of Page. We slowed down some and circled around for a minute. I could see Nehi was studying that big plug of cement where the Colorado River used to be. He gives me a hard look.

"Garn," he says, "who did that?"

"Not me, Mr. Nehi, no sir." He keeps on staring at me. "Honest. Wasn't me. I don't know who done it."

He tightens the hammerlock another notch.

"I think it was them Government people," I says. He kept on giving me the hard eye. "Them goldamn Government men," I explained.

"The Colorado River is a sacred river," he says softly.

"Yes, sir," I says. "Weren't none sacreder."

Then he roared at me: "And we don't want anybody mucking around with it!"

"No, sir."

"Is that understood?"

"Yes, sir."

"Is that clear?"

"Yes, sir."

To myself though I was kind of thinking, these goldamn angels got no right come down here and try to intimidate us American citizens. They got no right.

He gives my arm an extra twist.

"Watch your thoughts," he says. He stares down at the dam and that long green reservoir behind it. "World's biggest silt trap," he grumbles. "World's biggest evaporation tank. And someday, before it all fills up with mud, it will be the world's biggest sewage lagoon. Let's get out of here."

He yanks me off into the sky again, bearing northeast.

"What you want us to do about that dam, Mr. Nehi?"

"*We* will take care of *that*," he says, cool as a Christian with aces wired.

His tone of voice made me shiver some, I don't mind telling you. Mighty glad *I* don't live down there in Page. Always was, come to think of it. Only town in the whole canyon country with thirteen churches and only four bars. Any town with more churches than bars has got a serious social problem. That town is *a-looking* for trouble. No wonder they call it The Shithead Capital of Coconino County. And now they got the angel Nehi on their backs. Got to remember to say a prayer for them Page folks if I ever get back to Moab. Whereabouts in Moab? Well, lemme say this much. I got a crooked elbow and I generally say my prayers with one foot on a brass rail. It steadies my mind. I know my church is agin it but I don't care. Ever' man's got a right to his own form of worship. My old daddy learned me that just before he disappeared in the great Moab flood. I mean the one that tore up the bridge and carried off the town whorehouse back in 1928. We ain't seen him since.

Well anyhow we're heading up north again at 600 miles an hour I reckon when these gray dots commence to rising toward us from the direction of the Green River Missile Base.

Nehi sees them. "What's that?" he says.

"I think maybe you'd better speed it up some," I says. "That there's the United States Flying Air Force and they don't play around."

"We crossed their air space?"

"We crossed it and we crisscrossed it about sixteen times."

So old Nehi he flaps those pigeon wings of his faster. I can feel the shock wave a-building up in front of my nose. There's sonic booms bouncing across Dugout Ranch and La Sal Junction and Beef Basin by now. But the Air Force is gaining on us and any second I expect to see tracers closing in. Just hope they ain't fired them heat-seeking rockets. Gets my asshole all puckered up just a-thinking about it.

"Better step on the gas," I says.

"Are you keeping your toes pointed?" Nehi says, looking kind of irritable again. "Maybe I ought to jettison some surplus cargo."

"What surplus cargo is that?" I says. But I'm already looking for a soft place to land. We're 5,000 feet above the Colorado River. I start to tighten my grip on *him*. But it's too late. Old Nehi he does a nose dive and a fast loop over and shakes me loose. I start a long glide down toward the rimrock all by my lonesome.

As I go sailing down he hollers after me, "Don't forget the message, Garn."

"Yeah sure," I holler back, "I'll memorize it on the way down. I'll engrave it on my big toe." I guess no goldamn short-pants angel is gonna have the last word with Big Jake if I can help it.

But I could see it was due to be a rough landing. The rocks and the cactus was whirling up to meet me in a lot bigger hurry than I was. It looked like the only choice was the rocks or the prickly pear or that yucca they call Spanish bayonet in between. I just shut my eyes and hoped for anything but the one in the middle—

KER-RUMP!

Guess I blacked out for a few minutes after the crash. When I come to I was spraddled out on the rocks not feeling too good. Not bad rocks but I seen better. Old Diablo is fifty feet away munching on some squawbush and looking mighty pleased with hisself. Reins dragging and the saddle halfway up his neck. That sonofabitch'd throwed me again and right close was the reason why: one little snot-eyed horny-headed coon-tailed buzzworm with his tongue sticking out at me. A goldamn rattlesnake.

Should of killed that snake. I don't hate all snakes but I got to admit I got no use for rattlers. Like my daddy always said, if them other snakes can get along without poison why can't a rattlesnake? That makes sense.

But I didn't. Don't know for sure why. Maybe it was this pair of peculiar white feathers in my hand reminded me of something I wasn't supposed to forget. Only what was it? Or maybe I'm just getting soft-hearted in my old age. They don't call me Big Jake for nothing. Do they?

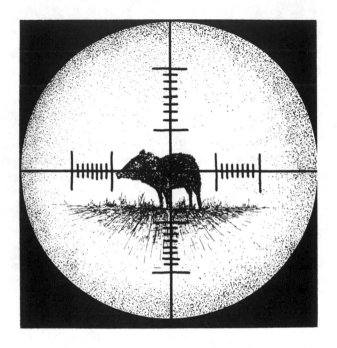

11

The Great Globe Arizona
Wild Pig and Varmint Hunt

I have lived half my life in a state called Arizona, which means "arid zone." It also means Mississippi of the West. A popular local slogan, often seen on bumper stickers, is Keep Arizona Medieval. Some members of the state legislature here once proposed to send a committee to New York to investigate the United Nations. Ours is the only state in the Union that sends Barry Goldwater to the U.S. Senate. Quaintness is a strong point. Despite the infernal summers, the kissing bugs and scorpions, the lung fungus, and the mushroom cities, Arizona is still a pretty good place to live. I

like it here. Part of it, part of the time. At any rate we still
have the flashiest sunsets in the Western world, when you
can see them through the belts of smelter smog.

One of Arizona's most important smog producers is a
mine and mill town called Globe. Globe, population about
10,000, lies deep in the rocky hills east of Phoenix, not far
from the Superstition Mountains. This is good desert country, of the lower Sonoran zone, rich in giant cactus, such as
the saguaro, and unusual wildlife, such as the javelina. It is
the javelina, together with certain other small mammals—the
coyote, the bobcat, and the fox—which is innocently respon-
sible for a controversy often swirling through the pages of
Arizona newspapers.

For fifteen years the Globe Chamber of Commerce has
been sponsoring an annual event called the Javelina Derby.
Each year prizes are awarded to the sportsmen who bring in
the first dead javelina and the heaviest dead javelina, with
separate categories of prizes for in-state and out-of-state
hunters, for bow hunters and gun hunters.

One of the questions raised by this affair is why anyone
would want to kill a javelina. The javelina, also known as
peccary, is a small piglike animal that never weighs over fifty
pounds. Almost half the bulk of this creature is taken up by
the head, so that it looks like a caricature of a pig, as a child
might draw one. The javelina subsists chiefly on the pads,
fruit, and roots of prickly pear and barrel cactus and in
higher desert terrain on the acorns of scrub oak. It does not
compete, therefore, with cattle or deer. Being mostly bone,
bristle, gristle, and hoof, the javelina is not generally considered desirable eating. The javelina comes with teeth and
tusks but is harmless to humans, unless you should happen
to corner one in a telephone booth. I have several times
strolled into herds of these delightful little animals; their
only reaction is to panic in all directions.

Why then should anyone wish to shoot a javelina? The
only answer seems to be, because it's there. Or was there.

The javelina, which used to roam the southwestern deserts in great number, has now been reduced by hunting and loss of habitat to a few small scattered bands in isolated or protected areas in southern Arizona. Nevertheless, it is still classified as a game animal by the Arizona Game and Fish Department.

This is more protection than the mountain lion, bobcat or fox gets in our state. All these predators must be considered rare in the Southwest and possibly in danger of extinction. All but the mountain lion are regarded as varmints, without protection. Although the mountain lion was recently given big-game status in Arizona, it may still be trapped or hunted at any time by any rancher who claims he is losing livestock to lions. On this basis alone twenty-four lions were trapped and killed in one county in Arizona in 1972. At that rate of loss, the lion will not last long as a species.

Perhaps because the javelina, like the carnivores, is becoming hard to find, the Globe Chamber of Commerce decided to combine the annual Javelina Derby with a predator hunt, in that way giving sport hunters something extra to compete for. The competition is based on a point system: five points for a bobcat, three for coyote, and two for fox. (Zero for hunter.) To receive points for a predator kill the hunter must bring in both ears of the animal, held together by skin. There is no limit on the number of these predators a sportsman may kill. Nor any limitation on hunting methods: It is considered sporting, for example, to use "varmint callers" to lure an animal within easy shooting range.

Why does the Globe Chamber of Commerce desire to kill coyotes, bobcats and foxes? The justification offered by Mrs. Donna Anderson, manager of that organization, is that these animals prey on domestic livestock to such an extent that they inflict serious financial losses on local cattlemen. One rancher in the area, Mr. Jimmy Griffin, claims to have lost $10,000 worth of cattle to predators (including mountain lions) in 1972. The Arizona Cattle Growers' Association claims total losses of over $500,000 statewide in 1972. The biggest villain in the picture, to the stockman's way of thinking, is the coyote, which is supposed to have killed 1,636 sheep and 1,539 calves. The lion is second. Even the bobcat, an animal not much larger than a domestic housecat, weighing from fifteen to thirty-five pounds, is accused of killing seven calves. How is this possible? A bobcat, some ranchers say, will attack a newborn calf when the mother cow is still too weak to defend her young. What's the evidence? Bobcat tracks in the vicinity of a dead calf.

The evidence against the other predators is similar. A dead calf is found, body mangled or half-devoured and the remains scattered about. On the ground nearby, inevitably, appear the tracks of the omnivorous coyote, sometimes the tracks of a cat or fox. Was the calf killed by a predator or did it die of disease, exhaustion, starvation, or weed poisoning? Even an expert pathologist would find it impossible to determine the answer with any certainty. In the Southwest, which has been severely overgrazed for a century, and in most areas is still being overgrazed, the most common cause of death to domestic livestock is malnutrition and the diseases attendant upon malnutrition. The dead or dying animal attracts whatever predatory animals, such as coyote or lion or bear, may be lurking in the vicinity.

This does not mean that predators are innocent of causing losses to the livestock industry. When you find a cow with its skull bashed in and bear tracks over the carcass there can be little doubt who did it. Nor can there be doubt that coyotes and mountain lions (and loose dogs) actually do destroy some number of livestock each year. But how many? No one knows.

The predator hunt at Globe has caused trouble in this state because many wildlife defenders are upset at having bobcat and fox among the victims. The fox, which in Arizona means the gray fox, is an animal even smaller than the bobcat, with an average weight of ten to eighteen pounds.

Like the coyote, the fox and bobcat feed mainly on hares, rabbits and rodents and could be considered beneficial to the livestock industry. How beneficial in dollars? No one knows.

Perhaps the economic aspect of the argument will never be settled to the satisfaction of all contenders. But conservationists in Arizona raise a further point: Wildlife, if it is the property of anyone, belongs to all. Sportsmen and ranchers, both of whom depend chiefly on use of the public lands for their activity, are making private use of a natural resource—wildlife—which should be public property, to be enjoyed by the public.

The Globe Chamber of Commerce may have stirred up more publicity by this combined Javelina Derby and Predator Hunt than it really wants—or needs. Even staunch defenders of sport hunting, like columnist Bill Quimby of the Tucson *Daily Citizen,* have attacked the Globe event on the grounds that hunting contests bring out the worst in sportsmen and give sport hunting a bad reputation. Such an affair attracts the attention of fanatics on both sides of the wildlife-and-predator controversy and adds further passions to an already adequate supply of misunderstanding. When I interviewed her in Globe, Mrs. Anderson showed me a sheaf of letters, one of them written in red ink (simulating blood?), all of them attacking her or the hunt or the Globe Chamber of Commerce. But she took comfort, she said, in the fact that at least nobody in Globe itself objected to the hunt. That was Monday.

On Wednesday, a group was formed in Globe calling itself Christian Citizens for Humane Treatment of Animals. They are now distributing free bumper stickers with the slogan, Javelinas Need Love Too.

12

Telluride Blues—
A Hatchet Job

The town of Telluride was actually discovered back in 1957, by me, during a picnic expedition into the San Miguel Mountains of southwestern Colorado. I recognized it at once as something much too good for the general public. For thirteen years I kept the place a secret from all but my closest picnicking cronies. No use: I should have invested everything I had in Telluride real estate.

In 1970 a foreigner from California named Joseph T. Zoline moved in with $5 million and began the californication of Telluride. Formerly an honest, decayed little mining town of about 300 souls, it is now a bustling whore of a ski resort with a population of 1,500 and many more to come. If all goes badly, as planned.

"We shall develop," announced Zoline, "a ski area bigger than Vail, as large as Ajax, Aspen Highlands, and Buttermilk combined, and twice as big as Mammoth Mountain in California." Two cheers for Zoline. The county Chamber of Commerce was delighted, but those who preferred Telluride as Telluride wept in their beers, prayed in the alleyways. It didn't help. Nothing worked.

Men weep, men pray and kneel, but *money talks*. Money. walks and talks and gets things done. Four years after his announcement (four years! it took twenty years to get the Wilderness Preservation Act through Congress, forty years to have one tiny remnant of the California redwoods given shabby and inadequate protection as a national park), Zoline has completed five operating double chairlifts, thirty-two miles of trails, and an eighty-seven-cell condominium.

Merely the beginning. Though the town offers only 1,200 beds for hire at present, Zoline's Telluride Company expects 170,000 skiers by 1978. To accommodate such multitudes, Zoline plans to build a village for 8,000 on the mountain meadows at the foot of the lifts; cabin sites or "ski ranches" are already being offered for sale (at $5,000 to $10,000 per acre); and Holiday Inn has begun to make inquiries. The twenty-year plan for Big-T envisions, on paper, a cable monorail system and a total of seventeen lifts with the combined capacity for transporting 17,000 skiers per day up a vertical distance of 4,000 feet; from there dropping them at the head of sixty miles of trail. Bigger than Vail! Better than Aspen!

What—*another* Aspen?

Yes, but different. Telluride's growth will be controlled and orderly, say the company executives, with "full environmental protection." The vague phrase rolls easily from the mouths of all developers these days. "Aspen grew without controls, under inadequate zoning laws," says Zoline. "We shall profit from that lesson here."

Will they? One may hope so; but the ambitious plans make the nature of that profit ambiguous. How can anything so big happen in a place so small as Telluride without changing the town beyond recognition? For those opposing the change the best hope is that Telluride will never make it as a big-time ski resort. There are problems.

Telluride is a hard place to get to. The nearest big town is Denver, 325 miles away on the other side of the Rocky Mountains, an eight-hour auto drive under the best conditions. The nearest primary air access terminal is at Grand Junction, 130 miles to the north. There is no rail line to Telluride, and the buses, at present, arrive only on weekends. If you elect to go by car, during the winter, you must drive the last thirty miles on a two-lane winding mountain road often surfaced with snow and ice, chains advisable. Below the road is the deep canyon of the San Miguel River. Above are the high-pitched mountain walls and thousands of tons of snow, hanging there.

Avalanches have been a problem in Telluride ever since the 1880s. Built in a narrow valley under 14,000-foot peaks, Telluride was hit by death-dealing avalanches in 1902, 1926, and 1927. Smaller ones occur every winter. With an average annual snowfall of 165 inches (Aspen averages 135), the next killer avalanche may come at any time. Even the summertime visitor to Telluride can see on the steep slopes above the town the swaths of destruction cut through the forest by snowslides both old and recent.

Of course, this heavy snow cover makes possible good skiing and a long season. Among the runs already open is one called The Plunge. The Plunge drops 3,200 vertical feet in a distance of 2.5 miles—perhaps the longest continuous steep run in North America. Even the experts need time to work their way down that one. The Big-T also offers helicopter transport to areas above and beyond the lifts, providing those skiers who can afford it a chance to play in the deep and virgin powder of the more remote mountain snowbowls.

But the skiing is good everywhere in the Rocky Mountains, and the scenery at Telluride, though magnificent, is merely routine Rocky Mountain magnificence—no grander, for example, than the landscape of Sun Valley, Taos, Vail, Aspen, Alta, Snowbird, Park City, or any of a hundred other crowded, frozen, expensive established ski resorts in the intermountain West. What some of us liked so much about Telluride was not the skiing but that quality of the town which Zoline and his developmental millions must necessarily take away: its rundown, raunchy, redneck, backwoods backwardness. That quality is one you cannot keep in a classy modern ski resort, no matter how much money is spent for preservation, no matter how many town ordinances are passed attempting to protect Telluride's antique Victorian architecture.

Some Telluriders, naturally, the crafty few who got in on the ski boom early, are becoming rich. Do I begrudge these native few their sudden unearned wealth? I sure do. That's normal spite and envy. (Christ, I could have bought the old Senate Bar and Whorehouse for $4,500 in 1962, if I'd had the $4,500. Last year the place was sold for $100,000. Vacant lots that used to sell for five or ten dollars in back taxes now are priced at $10,000. And so on.)

Others among the town's original population, those too slow to speculate, manipulate, scam, and scheme are going to have to suffer. A lot of the old folks who have lived in Telluride for many years, sometimes for most of their lives, are going to have to leave. Why? Most of them are pensioners; their fixed and humble incomes will not permit them to pay the runaway property taxes that have multiplied ten times over in the past three years. For instance, a lot formerly assessed at $100 is now appraised at $1,000; a leaning clapboard shack with gingerbread filigree had a valuation of $300 before—now it's $2,500.

You might think it a simple matter to change the rules so that the old folks are taxed for the inflated value of their homes only if they choose to sell out. It would be a simple matter; but that's not the way we do business in this country. Business in this country depends on high volume and fast turnover. That's what keeps the real estate industry operating—displaced human beings. "Our retired people with fixed incomes will have to leave," says Don O'Roarke, the county treasurer.

In came the hippies then, the trust funders, the freaks, the rootless ones, the middle-class proletariat with their beards and unisex ponytails, all of them, male and female, wearing the same bib overalls, Goodwill workshirts and waffle-stomper boots, all trying to look different in the same way. The air is thick with flying Frisbees, the sweet smell of *Cannabis sativa,* the heavy rock electric jungle sound, the industrial beat of hard-core imitation-Negro music. *Rock,* beneath the mountains, where once we heard only the sigh of spindrift from the snowfields and Eddie Arnold on the jukebox. But they have money, these freaks, and want to invest.

All of which poses a serious problem for the natives. A serious psychic bind. On the one hand, the natives want the newcomers' money; on the other hand, they hate their guts. Excruciating inner conflict. What to do? Well, why not take their money first, then call in the cowboys from the outback every Saturday night and have them beat the living shit out of these long-haired weirdos? Such has always been the traditional style of hospitality in the Golden West; still is in Wyoming.

But something has gone wrong with the Colorado cowboys. Although they continue to wear the funny hats and the tight snap-button shirts, they don't seem to like to fight so much anymore, even when they've got the opponent outnumbered by the customary ratio of ten to one. Even on Saturday nights. The bartender at the Sheridan Hotel and Opera House explained it all to me: "It's like this. It's that sex revolution. It finally come to San Miguel County about two years ago. Now even cowboys can get laid."

A break for the horses. And the sheep. With the cowboys pacified by sex, the solution to the hippie problem came to rest in the hands of Telluride's former one-man law-enforcement agency, Town Marshal Everett Morrow. Born in Oklahoma, seven years in Telluride, a welder by trade and police officer in his spare time, Morrow wore the classic western lawman's costume: boots, leather vest with tin star, concho-banded Stetson, the quick-draw artist's low-slung .45. Each shady looking newcomer got a personal welcome to Telluride from Marshal Morrow, including identification check with police-record follow-up. His tactics, sometimes rough on the younger generation, made Morrow a focal point of the cultural conflict between Telluride's conservative native establishment and the long-haired newcomers who have swarmed into the town during the past four years.

"The ski area will be the best thing ever happened to this town," says Marshal Morrow, "if we can get it without the goldamn hippies. It ain't the hair bothers me, it's the drugs."

The chief drug being dispensed in Telluride today, however, is the same as it was ninety years ago—alcohol. The town has twelve bars, three package stores, and a special 3.2 beer joint and poolroom for teenagers. With a current population of 1,500, that's one liquor establishment for every 100 citizens—man, woman, child, babe in arms. Contrariwise, there are only three churches and one part-time barbershop. That's the way things go in Telluride: downhill.

One afternoon a couple of years ago a man named Wayne Webb purchased a bottle of peppermint schnapps in the Belmont Liquor Store, Telluride. (Peppermint schnapps!) From there he went on to every liquor establishment in town, which includes the restaurants, and had a drink or bought a bottle. An hour later he was followed on the same circuit by Town Marshal Morrow, who presented the manager of each place a summons charging him or her with the sale of liquor to a minor. Wayne Webb, who has the looks and manner of a man of thirty, was twenty years old. The legal drinking age in Colorado is twenty-one. Webb, employed by the marshal, was a plant. Every liquor dispenser in Telluride had been entrapped into breaking the law.

That kind of law enforcement does not set well in a town of only 1,500 people. A stormy town meeting promptly followed the citations, during which the bar owners and their partisans (an overwhelming majority of those present, mostly the young long-haired new residents) demanded the resignation or ouster of Marshal Morrow. The town council, consisting largely of old-timers, declined to take action against Morrow but also dropped all charges against the liquor dispensers. This compromise was not sufficient to appease the anger of the crowd, for whom Morrow's entrapment bit was simply a final straw in a long history of alleged abuses. One of the most indignant of those present at the meeting was young Pierre Bartholemy, owner and operator of a restaurant he calls, *naturellement,* Chez Pierre. Around Telluride they call him Chez. He is a newcomer, both to Telluride and to the United States. In the course of his harangue, which was long and passionate, Bartholemy urged the town council to take away the marshal's TV set. "Zis Marshal," he said, "he watch too much zat how you call it? horse *opera?* too much goddamn *Gunsmoke!*"

Marshal Morrow replied by asking for an interpreter, saying, "Sorry but Ah cain't understand Chez's kinda English. . . ." Someone in the back of the standing-room-only crowd shouted "Fucking bigot!" and crept quickly out of the hall. Another person suggested that it was Chez who needed the interpreter since no new arrival to the American hinterlands could reasonably be expected to understand Oklahoman Morrow's "boll weevil English."

I braced myself for action. Nothing happened. Morrow merely smiled. A stand-down. A draw. The cowboy had the long-hairs outnumbered: There were only 300 of them. He lounged in the swivel chair behind the judge's stand at the head of the hall, listening in scornful silence as the indignation against him ranted on, peaked, leveled off, waned, and petered out. Meeting adjourned. The mob straggled into the night, defeated by the bland inertia of the town council, and dispersed to Telluride's twelve principal establishments of nocturnal worship. Democracy had suffered another crushing setback. Nothing new in that.

I wanted to interview the town marshal and managed to intercept him at his car. "I'm writing a story about Telluride for a magazine," I explained.

Pause.

Morrow considers. He shakes a precise measure of Bull Durham into his ungummed Wheatstraw and checks me over briefly with a pair of the regulation chill blue eyes. "Let's see your ID," he says.

I offer him my old pink *Life* card with the scowling passport photo, plainly stamped "Good Only for March–April 1971." (Issued for a trip to Sinai, called off on account of sloth.)

"So you're from the media," he says.

"That's right. I'm a medium."

He rolls his cigarette with one hand, holding my card in the other, hardly glancing at it. His little cigarette, licked and twisted shut at one end, looks exactly like a joint. That *was* Bull Durham, wasn't it? In the little cotton sack with the black label and the yellow drawstrings?

"I ain't been treated too good by the media," he says. "They take a man like me, they like to make him look like a fool. Like a goddanged hick." (He'd been written up in *Colorado Magazine*.)

"I'm different from the others," I said.

"Yeah?"

"I'll treat you different."

He lights the little cigarette, takes a deep drag down into the delicate lung tissues, holds it for a moment, then blows it out past my nose. It doesn't smell much like tobacco. Smells like a blend of dried cornsilk and half-cured horseshit. That's Bull Durham all right. (And if he tries to draw on me,

I thought meantime, I'll grab the tag on his Bull Durham pouch and yank him off balance. That way he'll shoot me in the groin instead of the belly. The groin's nothing but a lot of trouble anyway.)

Marshal Morrow studies me for a few more seconds, his cold steady eyes looking straight into mine, if I'd been standing two feet to the left and about forty miles back.

"I kinda doubt it," he finally says, handing back my obsolete press card.

"Doubt what?"

"What you said."

"You mean the answer is no?"

"Yeah."

That old Morrow, the bartender at the Sheridan explained to me shortly afterward, he's mean but he's fair: He treats *everybody* like shit.

I sulked for a while in a remote corner of the bar, trying to hear myself think against the continuous uproar at ninety decibels from the speakers mounted on the walls. The juvenile voices of what sounded like criminal degenerates united in teeny-bopper song: I believe it was a group called the Almond Brothers. Followed by the Ungrateful Dead. I missed Hank Williams.

Next day I investigated Joe T. Zoline's million-dollar condominium. From the highway it looks like a haphazard arrangement of apple boxes; close up it looks bigger but the same. The roofs are flat. They won't hold up well under 165 inches—about fourteen feet—of snow. The walls seem to be made of plywood. I noticed some of the exterior paneling beginning to peel and warp already, though construction was completed only a year ago. The interiors are cleverly designed: Each of the eighty-seven apartments, whether big or small, has high ceilings, a view of the mountains, and a little private sun deck. Each apartment (priced at $31,000 and up) contains a fireplace, but the fireplaces are miniaturized, more decorative than functional; all heating, as well as all cooking, is by electricity. All-electric homes in the nine-month winters of Telluride, at 8,800 feet above sea level, must be *mighty* expensive. In more ways than one: I thought of the canyon and mesa lands of Utah and northern Arizona—my country—being disembowled, their skies darkened by gigantic coal-burning power plants, in order to provide juice and heat for frivolous plywood ski hutches like this. Sad? No, not sad—just a bloody criminal outrage, that's all.

I stopped at the office for a few words with Mr. Zoline. Not available, the secretary told me; back in Los Angeles raising more millions. As I walked out of the place I paused for a final look back. The whole condominium rests on a boggy piece of bottomland beside San Miguel Creek. Drainage problems are considerable. May the whole thing sink, I prayed, down into the muck where it belongs.

That afternoon I took the Telluride Company's free bus tour and chairlift ride. Anything to add to the overhead and help hasten the company into its inevitable bankruptcy. The chairlift ride up over the mountain meadows was quite enjoyable. The view of Mount Sneffels and Mount Wilson, two of Colorado's most spectacular 14,000-foot peaks, is certainly a good one. Routine but good. Our tour guide, full of enthusiasm, told us that Mr. Zoline had started his new ski empire by purchasing, for only $150,000, a 900-acre sheep ranch. Sheep ranch? I might have known that a goddamn *sheep grower* was at the bottom of all this.

On the way back I asked the guide about the Telluride Company's official symbol, the significance of which escapes me. The official symbol of the Telluride Company is a fried egg with one quarter section cut away.

"That ain't no fried egg," the guide (a local boy) said, "that

there's the sun a-comin up behint a mountain with sunshine all around it. What they call a logograph."

"It looks like a fried egg."

"Yessir but it ain't it's a logograph. Ask anybody."

Evasive answer and typical: All you ever get from these company people is doubletalk.

Telluride. To hell you ride. All-year mountain playground. And why not? The people need their playgrounds. We all need a place to escape to, now and then, as the prison of the cities becomes ever more oppressive. But why did they have to pick on my Telluride? One more mountain forest, virgin valley, untainted town sacrificed on the greasy altar of industrial tourism and mechanized recreation. Soon to become, like New York, like L.A., like Denver, like Tucson, like Santa Fe, like Aspen (thus the development proceeds), one more place to escape *from*. Someday soon, if this keeps up, there will be no places left anywhere for anybody to find refuge in. Whereupon, all jammed together in one massive immovable plenum of flesh and machinery, then we may think, at last, in Fullerian-Skinnerian-McLuhanian telepathic unison: Ah! if only! if we had only thought. . . .

Thought what? By that time perhaps even the thought, even the memory of what (if only) could have been, that too will be lost. Perhaps lost forever.

Forever? Never say *forever*, pardner. Forever is a long time. But say—for a considerable spell of time. For one long long hell of a ride. Until those little voices on the mountain summits, one mile above, calling

> don't fret Telluride we're a-coming

have their way, and the huge white walls come down.

P.S.: Since this story was written a few changes have taken place in the Telluride scene. Marshal Morrow's contract was not renewed; he has retired from the law-enforcement busi-

ness. Mr. Zoline has sold a majority interest in the Telluride
Company to Mr. William H. Lewis, a New York investment
specialist. The town now has a full-time resident physician.
The Idarado Mining Company, a subsidiary of the Newmont
Mining Company of New York, which owns the 1,500 acres
of prime flat land east and west of Telluride, plans to develop this property for second homes and recreational facili-
ties when skier volume makes it "feasible." The permanent
population of Telluride, now about 1,500, could grow to
10,000 or even 20,000 within a decade. (If the ski development does not fail.) The generational conflict within Telluride has largely faded away; many of the old-time residents have sold their homes (at an exponential profit) and
moved to places like Sun City and Youngtown in Arizona.
The freaks, long-hairs and hippies who have taken their
places now own and operate most of the shops, restaurants
and other small businesses within the town. They have also
taken over the town council and the local Chamber of Commerce and are determined to prevent—somehow—the transformation of Telluride into another Aspen. Two things have
not changed: Chez Pierre still offers the best French dinners
on the western slope of the Rockies; and Telluride remains
this writer's favorite mountain town. I go there every summer and have failed four times now (out of sloth, ineptitude
and fear) to climb nearby Mount Wilson, 14,247 feet of rotten rock and icy rotten snow. I plan to fail to climb it again
next year, thereby setting a new world's record.

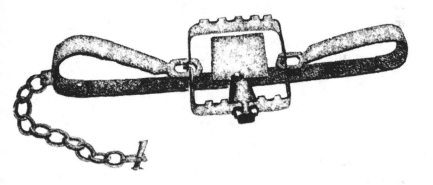

13

Let Us Now Praise
Mountain Lions

The mountain lion eats sheep. Any animal that eats sheep can't be all bad. It's also true, as lion lovers say, that the staple of his diet is deer, with an occasional side dish of porcupine, gopher, kangaroo rat, field mouse, and rabbit. Elk, when available. But mostly deer. Old deer, young deer, sick deer, wounded deer, inferior deer—the culls and leavings of the herd. In this process of natural selection, given a liberal allowance of time, it is the lion's claw, the lion's tooth and need, that has given the deer its beauty and speed and grace.

Dr. Maurice Hornocker, University of British Columbia, spent three years studying mountain lions in the Idaho Primitive Area. He found that a lion in normal health kills a deer every seven to ten days—just enough to feed itself and cubs. Sometimes, but seldom, it will attack a rancher's livestock, take a sheep or two. But why not? It should eat more. (EAT MORE SHEEP.) A man has a right to defend his private property. But when he runs his beasts on public lands, on *our* lands, as most wool growers do out here in the West, then he has to take his chances.

AESTHETIC THEORY

The mountain lion. *Felis concolor.* Except for the jaguar, it is the largest cat in the Western Hemisphere. One species, thirty races. Also known as cougar, from the French *cuguar* or *couguar,* based on a native American Indian name. Also known as panther, puma, painter, catamount, screamer, Indian devil, king cat. Range, Canada to Patagonia. Range of an individual, up to fifty miles; will sometimes travel twenty-five miles in one night.

What does the American lion look like? According to the Boston *Gazette* (1738):

> "The Catamount has a Tail like a Lyon, its Legges are like a Bear's, its Claws like an Eagle, its Eyes like a Tyger and its Countenance a mixture of everything Fierce and Savage. He is exceeding ravenous & devours all sorts of Creatures that come near." *

The mountain lion may weigh up to 220 pounds, grow eight feet long, have a front foot seven inches wide. Only the very lucky ever see this beautiful monster in the flesh in the wild. But you may, some purple evening, walking down the canyon, turn back suddenly on your track and find behind

---

* Quoted in *Wildlife News*, October 1968.

you this great footprint in the wet sand, slowly filling with water.

Our lion cannot, or at any rate does not, roar. But he—and she—are famed for the vehemence of their courtship and copulation. The screams at such a time have been compared to the cry of a woman in violent pain. Of this "most dismal distressing yell," Mr. Theodore Roosevelt said, "certainly no man could listen to a stranger and wilder sound." He once shot fourteen cougars in one year.

Why mountain lions? Because they are beautiful. For the same reason we need more bald eagles, golden eagles, coyotes, Gila monsters, alligators, redtail hawks, bobcats, badgers, wild pigs, grizzly bears, wild horses, red racers, diamondbacks, sacred datura, wild grapes, and untamed rivers. How to say once more what has been said so often? Who is listening?

BE A GOVERNMENT TRAPPER

Mr. Robert V. Shiver is the state supervisor for Arizona of the federal rodent and predator control agency. It *was* called the Predator Control Agency; now it's called the Division of Wildlife Services, Bureau of Sport Fisheries and Wildlife, U.S. Department of the Interior. The division's services to wildlife have consisted primarily of planting cyanide guns, poisoned meat, and steel traps in generous distribution over the landscape. The use of poison was banned in 1972 by presidential order; that order can be rescinded at any time, and has been under heavy attack by the livestock industry.

Mr. Shiver has the air of an aggrieved, much harassed man. He sees himself as the mediator in the middle, caught in the crossfire between conservationists (he calls them preservationists) and those on the other side—the stockmen, the state game department, certain hunters' organizations—who would like to see the population of what they call varmints, including lions, much reduced if not eliminated entirely from the face of Arizona. Attacked from both sides, defended by neither, he and his twenty-five full-time trappers continue to do their quiet work as best they can. Just doing our job, he says, when and where requested. Any time the people of Arizona want us to leave, he says, we'll leave.

How many lions left in Arizona, Mr. Shiver? He doesn't know. Nobody knows. How many left in the United States? Again, nobody knows for sure—estimates range from 1,500 to 6,500. How much damage done by lions? No reliable estimates available. Is the lion population increasing, decreasing, or static? Seems to be either static or decreasing, but nobody really knows. What are you people up to in the Music Mountains? Lion-control program. Why there? Requested by the state game and fish department. Why? Too many lions, not enough deer. How many lions do you plan to kill? It's an evaluation program. It's a what? It's experimental. What does that mean? We want to see what effect the program will have on the deer population.

THE QUIET CRUSADER

If wildlife get little comfort from government wildlife agencies, they still have some friends among the citizenry. Mr. Hal Perry, Phoenix, gave up a profitable construction business in order to devote most of his time to fighting the trappers and poisoners. Mr. Perry may or may not be a bleeding-heart wildlife lover; but he is certainly no Hindu. The mounted heads of bighorn sheep and pronghorn antelope hang on his study wall—and he likes guns, loads his own ammunition, opposes gun-control laws, eats meat. But most of all, he despises the professional wildlife exterminators. What kind of a man, he asks, can make the spreading of cyanide, ten-eighty, and other poisons his life work? In his opinion the mountain lion *is* in danger of extinction, not only in Arizona but in the American West, and the other predators are barely holding their own. The bounty, he feels, was a disgrace to the state.

THE HUNTERS

They sit around in drafty bars drinking sweet green Coors (a provincial brew) from soft aluminum poptop cans. Custer's Last Stand on the wall. Lawrence Welk and Engelbert Humperdinck squatting in the jukebox. A bumper sticker on a pickup truck reads, "Did the Coyotes Get Your Deer?"

Jimmy Owen—famous Arizona hunter in the 1920s—claims to have killed 600 mountain lions on the Kaibab Plateau in the period of twelve years. Soon after he completed his work, the multiplying deer began gnawing the bark from the aspens. Mass starvation. The porcupines are still girdling the pinyon pines, and neither the deer herd nor the forest has yet fully recovered. Greatest of all varmint hunters, according to Texan historian J. Frank Dobie, was a man named Ben Lilly, who hunted, trapped, and killed thousands, not because he hated lions—he admired them—but "from a sense of duty." Doing the Lord's work, as he said.

How To Get the Getter

Called "getters" locally, the cyanide guns are the predator hunter's favorite tool. These are cylindrical devices about six inches long, loaded with potassium cyanide powder and a spring or firing charge; they are half-buried, upright, in the ground. Baited cotton on the exposed end attracts the coyote, fox, bobcat, or maybe somebody's pet dog; when the animal pulls on the bait he gets a jet of cyanide in the mouth. Death is certain, but not necessarily quick—the victim may endure ten, twenty, even thirty minutes of what appears to be extreme pain before the end. According to wildlife agency regulations (not always followed), the cyanide gun wherever planted must be marked with "conspicuously placed" warning stakes and eight-inch by twelve-inch warning signs "posted and plainly visible on all roads leading to station area."

Look for these signs. When you find the station—usually a

group of four or five cyanide guns set close together—you can disarm the devices in any of several ways. Urinate on them—that will warn the wildlife away. Or pour kerosene on them—that will destroy the bait. Or shoot them up with a gun. Or drop a large flat rock on each one. But don't touch them with your hands; they are dangerous.

MUSIC MOUNTAIN

Nobody seems to know how the name was chosen. Wind on the cliffs? Lions in love? Spirits? Nobody seems to know.

The mountain lies east of Kingman and west of Williams in northern Arizona, just north of Highway 66. Music Mountain is not impressive to look at, does not in fact look like a mountain at all, but more like the exposed face of an upthrust block fault. Which is what it is. An escarpment facing west, about thirty miles long, 2,000 feet high, sloping gently on the eastern side into the plain. Rocky, rugged limestone cliffs, a grass-covered talus, a light growth of juniper and pinyon pine on top.

I talked with the gas-station man in the village of Truxton, on the highway. Old cars overloaded with children and baggage pulled in and out, going to and coming from California, as always. Who says the Joads are not still on the road?

The gas-station man seemed surprised to learn that the state and the wildlife services were planning a trapping campaign against the lions of Music Mountain. He said the trappers had been in there only four years earlier and killed about forty lions then. Did he think there were many lions on Music Mountain now? He thought there were probably a few. Did he go up in there himself sometimes? Yes. See any lion sign? Yes, some. Think there are as many lions around as there used to be? No, not as many as there used to be. "But," he added, "they are mighty shy creatures, you know."

GENERAL SITUATION

Arizona was the last state that still paid a bounty on mountain lions. But in Idaho, Montana, Texas, Wyoming and New Mexico the lion remains in the predator or varmint classification, which means that anyone at any time can legally kill a lion, male or female, young or old, nursing mother or suckling cub. In California, Oregon, Nevada, Washington, Utah and Colorado the lion is classed as a game animal, which means that it has some protection. (Cannot legally be trapped, can be hunted only during specified seasons and killed in limited numbers.) Only Florida—where the lion is rare—and New Hampshire—where it is probably nonexistent—give this scarce, elusive, magnificent animal the complete protection it needs.

FACE TO FACE

Chester Thomas, former ranger at Zion National Park in southern Utah, once walked to within ten feet of a mountain lion, which lay before him on the trail. Thomas stopped, a bit uncertain; the lion, though not hostile, appeared to have no intention of getting out of his way. Thomas shouted at the lion; it retreated, disappeared. He waited a few minutes before going on, then heard small noises above, looked up and saw the lion on a ledge about twenty feet away. This time Thomas attempted a different approach; he called softly to the big cat, tried to coax it toward him. The lion responded, took a few steps closer, hesitated, drew back, came forward again as Thomas continued to call. And then other humans came up the trail, talking loudly, and the lion turned and vanished.

Many people have reported being followed by mountain lions, for greater or lesser distances, but there are few authentic records of a lion actually attacking a human being.

Apparently they bear no malice toward us.

14

Return to Yosemite:
Tree Fuzz vs. Freaks

The first time I visited Yosemite National Park was in August 1944. The crowds were small, the waterfalls dry, and the hitchhiking tough. Since then everything I've heard and read about Yosemite has made it seem less and less worth returning to. But I went back for a big weekend recently to see for myself. Things are not as bad there as I'd expected; I was disappointed.

In the foothills of the Sierras, up through the old mining towns like Coulterville and Chinese Camp, the flowers were blooming—silverleaf lupine, California poppy, paintbrush and penstemon—and the traffic seemed light. When we saw a sign, Water Ahead, I looked forward to a drink of pure Sierra Nevada spring water, fresh from the rocks. We found the spring, but another sign beside it said, Water Contaminated—Unfit to Drink. Well, that was more like it. But getting into the park was easy. Instead of the traffic jam I expected, we found only two cars in front of us at Big Oak Flat and I was surprised when the ranger-cashier in the box office said that Yosemite Valley was already full. I wished him a Happy Easter and he rolled his eyes heavenward.

Somewhere near Cascade Creek we stopped at a turnout for the classic view of Yosemite Valley, as invented by Ansel Adams. There was El Capitan, Half Dome, Sentinel Dome, Bridalveil Falls, and a blue haze above the valley floor. Woodsmoke? Exhaust fumes? The friend with me remarked that she thought Bridalveil a nice name for a waterfall. Two long-haired boys went by, walking their bicycles up the grade. Looking hard, I found my first Budweiser can below the bridge, down in the clear snow water. I clambered down the slippery granite in my dude boots, not to retrieve the can—*Let Nature Alone*—but for a drink of real mountain water. Spray paint on the boulders read, Joe & Juanita Was Here 7-4-70, and, Running Bear 1851.

Down in the valley. More teenage gypsies with sleeping bags, backpacks, and ragged heads slouched along the road, thumbs out. Damn lazy city kids, I thought—let them walk. Good for them. And I spurred my Avis Rental Widetrack Catalina right on by. Hitchhiking is illegal in national parks anyway. Hitchhikers are poor, dirty, immoral. I was one, I should know. They rape your girlfriend, they steal your credit card, they leave a weird smell in the back seat, they contribute nothing to the economy.

The people at park headquarters were helpful and hospitable when I appeared to investigate their law-enforcement practices. "We have nothing to hide," said Staff Park Ranger Richard Marks. But he feels the media were unfair to the

Park Service in televising the battle of Stoneman Meadow but not the events that led up to it. I hadn't even heard of Stoneman Meadow or any battle there—that's what comes from hiding out in the woods all summer. He had to tell me about it.

Yosemite Valley has always been a popular place for hell raising. But in the fall of 1969 it began to attract long-hairs, the freaks and hippies from the San Francisco Bay Area. During the following spring and summer this "youthful element" began to take over an open space in Yosemite Valley known as Stoneman Meadow, with larger and larger crowds—up to 500—each weekend. These young people behaved in many and various ways, mostly illegal, mostly offensive to the sensibilities of the respectable park visitors who were forced to drive by Stoneman Meadow on their way to more wholesome places. There was singing and dancing, sometimes in the nude; there was marijuana and underage drinking; there was bad language, loud coarse music, couples making love in broad daylight, the burning of fenceposts for firewood, a general trampling of the grass. The air whistled with flying Frisbees.

The park rangers decided that the character and integrity of the park was threatened by this activity. On the evening of July 3rd they dispersed the crowd by force—on horseback, with clubs, according to some versions. The next day the crowd reassembled, the rangers attacked again. But this time the long-hairs were ready for them with stockpiles of rocks and bottles, hunting knives and Boy Scout hatchets. A battle took place which the outnumbered rangers and their bewildered trail horses lost. The triumphant freaks proclaimed Stoneman Meadow a People's Park and retired to their camps for more illegal smoking, underage drinking and illicit sex. If they thought they'd won the war, however, they were seriously mistaken: During the night Smokey the Bear became Smokey the Pig. (Pride, Integrity, Guts.)

Reinforced by state police, sheriff's deputies, and town

police from outside the park, the rangers raided the camp-ground at two in the morning, arresting hundreds and roughing up a few who resisted arrest. (Versions of what ac-tually happened during this nocturnal raid vary according to the source of information. The television crews were not there.) "Disorderly conduct" was the charge, later dropped in most cases; but the real purpose of the raid was to drive the undesirable elements out of Yosemite National Park and in this the Park Service was for the time being successful. Stoneman Meadow has not been taken over by any public gatherings since, the grass seems to have recovered, and even the deer—innocent and neutral civilians in the war—are drifting back. Surely that is the purpose of a meadow in a national park; quiet deer grazing on the grass. Is it not?

Ranger Tom Wylie, supervisor of the night shift, took me along on three of his patrols. In a car, of course—horses are used only for trail work now and . . . cavalry maneuvers. Mr. Wylie is a good, competent, decent man, with an im-mense amount of patience. Impossible to imagine him trying to club some kid over the head. Still, he was powerfully armed: .38 police special, Mace on his belt; a club, hand-cuffs, and extra ammo nearby, in the car. He is young, mar-ried, with one child born and a second on the way. A college graduate with a major in botany, he has so far spent his en-tire Park Service career—four years—in Yosemite Valley, enforcing the law. He says he likes police work, finds it "in-teresting," but does not wish to make it a lifetime job. He wants to be a ranger, not a cop.

We investigated the case of a stolen Porsche headlight, an arrest was made, the suspect hustled off to be booked and charged by other rangers. Then came a tour of the camp-grounds, all full. Litter and garbage everywhere. "Lack of funds," Ranger Wylie explained. Coming and going, we passed other patrol cars, some of them carrying two or three men; the shortwave radio in the car carried an incessant chatter—little troubles here and there, mostly traffic problems. Sometime in the future the Park Service hopes to ban all private automobiles from Yosemite Valley, substitute a clean quiet nonpolluting mass transit system. They'll need it.

On night patrol I witnessed an authentic bust. A teenage kid wanders through the campground, his head full of mush, eyes bleary; in one hand he holds an open can of beer, in the other a paper sack. The rangers stop him, he tries to run, gets about ten feet before they pull him down and snap the handcuffs on. Wylie shows me what's inside the paper bag; about a dozen lids of marijuana, each wrapped up in a neat little cellophane Baggie. The kid wails as they take him away, "I didn't do nothin' wrong. . . ." But he's wrong. Peddling dope is a felony in the state of California.

For two hours we cruise through the campgrounds, in and out of parking lots, around the drives. Wylie straightens out a campsite mixup, which involves a great deal of paperwork and radio exchanges. He speaks quietly to a hairy young man walking the street with a bottle of wine in his hand, sends him back to his campsite. The freak offers us peanuts from a poke; we eat some of his peanuts. Ten in the evening, beginning of campground "quiet time." The air is foggy with the smoke from 500 campfires, rich with the dreamy redolence of *Cannabis sativa.* Sounds of music and jubilation—Wylie has to caution the party against excessive noise. Others are trying to sleep, he reminds them, and indeed, all around us, we can see through the gloom and the trees the pale forms of pickup campers, camper trailers, and Winnebago motor homes, where Middle America is bedding down to another night of lawful conjugal bliss.

Why not segregate the campers, I ask, put all the young, long-haired, law-breaking element at one end of the valley, let them pluck their banjos and pass around the hand-rolled hepatitis all night long, if such is their weird wont? Won't do, I'm told, not enough space, too much of Yosemite Valley is under asphalt already. Well, that's sure true.

We pause at headquarters to check the prisoners in the

jail. Oh yes, Yosemite National Park has its own tidy little jail, which I inspected. I've seen worse; I've been in worse. For temporary custody only; no one is kept there more than a day or two. The park also has its own resident U.S. commissioner to administer the law. How escape it? On a typical summer weekend there may be anywhere from 20,000 to 30,000 people in and out of Yosemite Valley. It's a small city much of the year, but one in which the population is permanently transient, always changing. Which makes things even harder for the ranger-cops. They never have a chance to get to know the people they police except as types and stereotypes: as "hippies," "straights," "average families." The average family has 2.4 children; the freak family may have from 10 to 500. How to deal with them?

I went out a second night with Ranger Wylie and again nothing much happened. A routine patrol. We and some other rangers and some park police from Washington, D.C., on special assignment, gather at a place called Le Conte Memorial to listen to the sounds of festivity far back in the woods. Wylie and his rangers decide not to attempt to break it up: too many kids, not enough force, and besides the young people, contacted earlier, had promised to clean up their mess. We investigated some hitchhikers, let them go. They were trying to get out of the valley and out of the valley is where the Park Service wants them. Why? On the theory, based on statistical probability, that anyone too poor to own a car is likely to steal something if he gets a chance. Like a car.

I was shown the records and statistics. In 1952 the Yosemite district had 55 "cases" of illegal activity; in 1958 there were 182, mostly traffic violations; in 1970 the record shows 765 cases, with a total of 2,170 persons charged with various offenses, among them 92 for disorderly conduct, 13 as "runaways," 648 for larceny, 16 for auto thefts, 1 for rape, 2 for manslaughter, 2 for robbery, 24 for aggravated assault, 29 for burglary, 62 for narcotics, 34 for drunkenness, and 106 for "soliciting" (begging and hitchhiking). Of the 765 cases, 564 involved juveniles. That's life in the woods in Yosemite Valley. To handle this happy holiday scene, the Park Service employs seven permanent rangers in Yosemite Valley plus thirty to thirty-five summer seasonals, most of them without training in police work.

Perhaps the banning of private cars from Yosemite Valley will reduce the crime problem. Perhaps not. Probably not if the private cars are simply replaced by a mass transit system. For the basic trouble here is urbanism. Yosemite Valley has been urbanized. It's no more a wild or natural area than Manhattan's Central Park.

On my last night in Yosemite I walked alone through the meadows and listened to the bellowing frogs, maddened with moonlight. Out of a notch in the granite cliff I could see Yosemite Falls, that extravagant gush of milky foam dropping 1,400 feet through space, dissolving in mist, re-grouping in cascades below to fall 600 feet more to the valley floor. Through the inner smog of figures and problems I dimly imagined Yosemite as it must have been in 1851 when Chief Tenaya and his little band of renegades were driven out. (Renegades: Indians unwilling to camp in officially designated campsites.) No wonder they hid and fought and escaped and fought again and wept and died. Yosemite Valley was a wild, savage, splendid and precious place then.

The Park Service believes that Yosemite Valley is not the proper location for youth festivals, organized or disorganized. No doubt true. (The frogs, having an orgiastic celebration of their own, might not agree.) But I can think of other things that Yosemite Valley is not the proper place for. It is not the proper place for paved roads and motor traffic in any form. It is not the proper place for gas stations, supermarkets, bars, curio shops, barbershops, a hospital, a lodge, a hotel, a convention center, and a small city of permanent and transient residents. Above all Yosemite Valley is not a proper place for a jail, for administrators, for police wearing park ranger uniforms.

What should Yosemite Valley be? It should be what it once was: the kind of place where a person would know himself lucky to make one pilgrimage there in his lifetime. A holy place.

Keep it like it was.

15

The BLOB Comes to Arizona

"Obvious Arizona," as Nabokov called it in *Lolita*, has been part of my life for most of my life.

I was among the first of the displaced refugees, after the War, to give up on the swarming East. And so when Arizona began to grow, as they call it, it was as much my fault as anyone else's. Like the man and his wife who moved from Des Moines into Phoenix last night, each of us wants to be the last to arrive. Each wants to be the final immigrant. If we could we'd raise a glass wall about ten miles high somewhere along the one hundredth meridian.

Obvious Arizona, eh, Vladimir? Obvious Colorado, if you ask me. Colorado with its one big city and conventional alpinetype mountains is what *would* appeal to the European hotel-manager's imagination of Nabokov, the wide-eyed wonder of a pop music hack like John Denver, the myriad mannikins of this world. Let them have it. Colorado has gone to hell anyhow, sold out to industry by its loyal sons of the pioneers. Including a recent governor named Love!

But Arizona is something different. Or was. There is nothing in Arizona that much resembles Europe or the East except the slums along the railroad tracks in Flagstaff. Arizona has some pretty mountains too, like Colorado, but mostly and essentially Arizona is desert country. High desert in the north, low desert in the south, ninety percent of my state is an appalling burnt-out wasteland, a hideous Sahara with few oases, a grim bleak harsh overheated sun-blasted God-damned and God-forgotten inferno. Arizona is the native haunt of the scorpion, the solpugid, the sidewinder, the tarantula, the vampire bat, the conenose kissing bug, the vinegarroon, the centipede, and three species of poisonous lizard: namely, the Gila monster, the land speculator and the real estate broker. Arizona is where the Apaches live, who used to suspend their prisoners head-down above a slow fire, and will again when they get the opportunity. Arizona is where the vultures swarm like flies about the starving cattle on the cow-burnt range. In Arizona the dust storms carry lung fungus. In Arizona you'll often find yourself paying seventy cents for a gallon of unfiltered gasoline and a dollar-fifty for a short shot of watered bourbon. Arizona is the land-fraud capital of the world. Keep a firm grip on your shirt. Because of the parched air and the hard water, Arizonans come down with more kidney stones per pelvis than any place outside of Chad and southern Libya. In Arizona the trees have thorns and the bushes spines and the swimming pools are infested with loan sharks, automobile dealers and Mafiosi. The water table is falling and during a heavy wind you can see sand dunes form on Central Avenue in Phoenix. We have the most gorgeous sunsets in the Western World—when the copper smelters are shut down. I am describing the place I love. Arizona is my natural native home. Nobody in his right mind would want to live here.

But all the same they keep coming. The growth figures would shock even a banker. Tucson has grown from a population of 45,000 (counting dogs) in 1950 to an estimated 332,000 today. According to the U.S. Census, "Greater Metropolitan Phoenix" had a human population of 65,000 in 1940; 106,000 in 1950; 439,000 in 1960; 970,000 in 1970; and in 1976, swollen up worse than a poisoned pup, approximately 1,355,000. Horrifying statistics. The state as a whole has undergone corresponding metastasis, with its 1940 population of 449,000 multiplied to about 2,245,000 at present. As can be seen, nearly three-quarters of the state's population is now concentrated in the Tucson–Phoenix area, the two cities closely linked by the urbanizing artery of an interstate freeway. If present patterns of growth continue the two will become one in the near future. If the water holds out.

I keep mostly to the north side of the Grand Canyon, myself, having never forgotten an old horror movie called *The Blob*. The Blob, as some readers may recall, was a mad amoeba escaped from a laboratory. Pink, palpitating and running amok, egged on by the Chamber of Commerce and growing *growing* ever-GROWING, this thing threatened to devour the planet. I forget how they stopped it. Maybe they didn't.

Who are all these people anyhow? Where do they come from, all these damned foreigners overrunning our peaceful little country hellhole of a state? (Is it possible that life is even more trying in Wisconsin than here?)

Well, the trouble started with the Indians, or Native Americans as they now prefer to be called. They came here about ten thousand years ago, wiped out most of the large native mammalian wildlife (mastadons, horses, tapirs, giant bison, hairy mammoth and others) and have been subsisting on corn, beans and public welfare ever since. The most numerous tribes in Arizona are the Navajo, the Papago and the aforementioned Apache. Together with smaller tribes they now comprise some seven or eight percent of the state's population. Although they own and control nearly one-fifth of Arizona's real estate, they have not done well, on the whole, in our modern industrial economy. In other words, they are poor people. They live in shacks, drive secondhand Oldsmobiles and eat too much Wonder Bread. The reasons for this deplorable situation are many, varied and complicated, as any sociologist can explain to you, but basically it comes down to the fact, observed all over the world, that the descendants of hunters and warriors do not make good clerk–typists or computer tapers.

The cities of Tucson and Phoenix have their large Chicano and black minorities. As elsewhere, most of these people live on the wrong side of the freeway; many of them live underneath it. In this respect Arizona is quite up-to-date; we have as much ethnic strife and cultural conflict, proportionately, as even the most advanced states.

The remaining sixty percent or so of Arizona's population is of good sound Anglo-European stock, the smartest, toughest, meanest people you can find anywhere. (I'm one of them.) Most of us own no property but a mortgaged home, a mortgaged car, a pickup truck and a motorboat, but we work hard and die early, striving upward all the way. The dominant political minority here consists of the grandchildren of the so-called pioneers, who established themselves in Arizona a century ago when land was cheap and the living easy. Most of them are now dead, so to speak. "Hanged by mistake," in some cases. Not hanged by mistake in the remainder. As in all western states short of California, any property of actual profit-making value—such as the mines—belongs to out-of-state corporations with headquarters in Manhattan, Tokyo, Houston or Bonn.

The majority of the newcomers to our state are from the snow-plagued upper Midwest; many of them are retired farmers. Most of the younger "element" have been lured here by jobs in construction, in military installations (the most beautiful part of Arizona is a bombing and gunnery range), in the electronics business (Motorola is a big employer) and in dope-smuggling and dope-interception, our fastest-growing industry. Though we old-timers are a genial, easygoing and hospitable people without exception, there is a tendency among us to regard the newcomers with mixed emotions: We hate their guts but we want their money.

After thinking these facts over for a while, I decided I'd better have a talk with our governor, see what he thought about all this. I called his appointments secretary one morning from my suite in the Shady Rest Motel on East Van Buren; half an hour later I was ushered into the governor's spacious, tastefully appointed office in the new Capitol Annex. In this corner room with big windows, we enjoyed a fine view of the smog over northwest Phoenix as we talked. Or rather as he talked and I scribbled; in truth I hadn't had time to prepare any probing questions.

Governor Raul Castro—no kin to the genial Cuban administrator—seemed genuinely glad to see me, though we were complete strangers to each other. (And still are.) In fact I had the clear and distinct impression that the governor had been sitting there that morning, behind his huge empty desk, in his spacious, tastefully appointed office, with nothing much to do, feeling bored and maybe a little lonely, and wishing it would soon be lunchtime. Having idled away many a tedious hour behind government desks myself, I knew exactly how he felt. I sympathized and also approved: Like Lao-tse and Thoreau, Tolstoy and Kropotkin, I agree that that government is best which governs least; and the ideal government governs not at all, except to preside over its own demise. All government is bad, including good government. What can you do, anyway, with a runaway BLOB? It was the laboratory, not nature, that created the mutant monster in the first place.

It soon appeared that Governor Castro was against Growth—uncontrolled, undirected Growth, that is. Like all politicians he is in favor of *controlled* Growth, properly *directed*. But this, I wanted to object, was precisely the problem facing the scientists who unleashed The BLOB upon an unsuspecting world—how to control and direct its growth. All they got for their trouble was a broken test tube and a devastated laboratory.

Arizona, the governor explained, is the fastest growing state in the Union. The people come because of the climate—everybody, it appears, wishes to escape winter. Nobody wants to shovel snow anymore. (Although they still want to play on the stuff; people move to Arizona to live, then spend their winter holidays skiing in Colorado.) But there's nothing we can do about it; there is no Constitutional method by which we can prevent American citizens from coming here to live.

I mentioned the Petaluma case. Petaluma is a small city north of San Francisco, plagued by mushrooming growth problems. The citizens of Petaluma approved severe zoning ordinances, crippling the home-construction industry in that city. The leaders of the construction industry took the city to court, charging that Petaluma's new zoning laws interfered with the right of Americans to live where they choose. The growth group won the first court battle, lost the second on the city's appeal to a higher court; the U.S. Supreme Court declined to review the case, thus letting stand the appeal and reversal.

Governor Castro agreed that growth could be inhibited by planning and zoning and even agreed that it should be. But he also believed that growth is inevitable, especially in states such as Arizona that attract so many of the nation's retired population. He repeated the traditional belief that some growth is desirable in order to provide jobs for the unemployed. Thus, he supports a giant water-transferral scheme called the Central Arizona Project, which will cost U.S. taxpayers billions, because, among other reasons, the project if continued will create many new jobs by the end of 1977. "We do not seek new growth," he claimed, "but we need jobs for our present population."

Spoken like a true American politician. I tried to pin the governor down on the question of just how much growth is good and how much is too much? At what point, I wanted to know, should we in Arizona draw the line? The governor would not be pinned. Dismissing the question as hypothetical—and of course it is hypothetical, that's why I asked it—he went on with other matters.

The falling water table, for example. Arizona's continued growth depends upon a reliable water supply. At present most of the water comes from deep wells, or what geologists call "fossil water," that is, water that has accumulated underground during countless thousands of years. Since the water is now being consumed faster than natural processes can replace it, the level keeps dropping. Each year wells have to be drilled deeper in order to reach it. Someday this ground water supply will be exhausted. Then what happens?

That's why we need the Central Arizona Project, said Governor Castro. Unless we get our share of Colorado River water soon, cities like Tucson are going to die of thirst. How soon? Some hydrologists think the ground water may be exhausted in a decade; others think there's enough to last for centuries, if a curb is put on further population growth, if wasteful practices are stopped and if irrigation agriculture is phased out. Ninety percent of Arizona's water, say opponents of the C.A.P., is used for irrigation. The C.A.P., they say, is a gigantic boondoggle conceived back in the 1930s, whose only beneficiaries will be the owners of the cotton plantations—and of course the civil engineers, the construction companies, the construction unions and those politicians who have a passion for leaving to posterity monuments of masonry named after themselves. The pyramid builders. Furthermore, the Colorado River is already overused; not a trickle of it has reached the open sea for forty years. Whatever water the state of Arizona pumps out of the river and up over the mountains to the Phoenix–Tucson area will necessarily be taken away from the farmers of California's Imperial Valley. The cost, in dollars and electrical energy, will be greater than the benefits.

To these objections Governor Castro had a long and elaborate reply, the gist of which is that he was elected to serve the people of Arizona, that historical compacts must be honored, that Arizona's future well-being (growth) depends upon the C.A.P., that California can find other water sources—somewhere.

The monologue went on and on. The governor never even glanced at his watch. I kept expecting his secretary to announce new visitors but no one appeared. Although I realized that the governor needed somebody to talk to and that I was apparently the only person available, I finally insisted on terminating the interview. As I left, the governor was beginning a conversation with his secretary in the outer office. No one waited in the waiting room.

I strolled through downtown Phoenix, through the lunchtime heart of the spreading BLOB. I decided I should get at least one opinion from a man in the street, and promptly accosted the first pretty girl I encountered. She identified herself as Jo Ellen, gave her occupation as fashion coordinator for a chain of department stores. I asked her what a fashion coordinator is. She tried to explain. I asked her how she felt about Growth? She looked alarmed. "What growth?" she wanted to know. I explained. She pondered the issue for a moment and then announced that in her opinion Phoenix was big enough; much too big, in fact, for such a small town. What did she think the optimum population of Arizona should be? "40,000 savages," she replied at once, "and me." Perfect; I've never met a pretty girl I didn't like.

In the afternoon I drove east of the city to investigate one of the biggest and newest of the area's many real estate de-

velopments, a place its promoters have named Fountain
Hills. The hills abound, covered with a lush and lovely
growth—paradoxical as this may seem—of desert vegetation:
giant saguaro cactus, mesquite, ironwood, flowering palo-
verde, many other plants peculiar to the Sonoran desert.
Within the development itself, however, all natural plant life
has been scraped away by bulldozers, except for a few isolated, token saguaros left standing amid the acres of dust
and mud. The fountain is a 200-foot-high jet of water rising
from an artificial pond set in the middle of the inevitable
golf course. The evaporation loss from that pond and fountain alone would be enough to supply many households. But
this is idle carping. The people who live here find it all quite
beautiful.

I talked with a few of the ladies out watering their newly
planted lawns. Their husbands, mostly business and professional men, were off in the city earning the daily bread. The
homes looked big and expensive, in the $50,000-and-up
class. The women I consulted had few complaints; they were
glad to be out of Phoenix itself, or Los Angeles, or Min-
neapolis, wherever they'd come from. For them this satellite
suburb ten miles beyond the metropolitan limits was a step
upward toward the fulfillment of the American dream. At
least they had escaped, for a time, the noise, the crowding,
the crime, the denser smog of the city. It would have been
cruel to remind these cheerful and friendly people that
Fountain Hills is destined to become, if growth trends continue, a part of The Thing creeping toward them from
beyond the hills. There is no escape.

Southeast to Tucson on the Interstate. Except for the barren hills of the little Gila River Indian Reservation (and the
Gila River, dammed and diverted into the white man's irrigation system, is a river no more), the scene is one of nearly
continuous industrial development: cattle feedlots, packing
plants, cotton and sorghum fields, truck stops, tourist traps,
suburban towns, all the way to Tucson. At one point I

passed the turnoff to something called Arizona City; a huge billboard featuring the grinning face of a movie actor named Rory Calhoun invited me to check out the delights of yet another "planned community"—"Five Different Life Styles to Choose From," says Rory. I stepped harder on the gas. But there is no escape. Monstrous semi's from the trucking industry, Whites and Macks and Peterbilts weighing forty tons, each half a block long, thundered past me on the left, each with its "cowboy" at the wheel crouching over his hemmorrhoids, his sick kidneys, his CB radio. No escape.

No escape. The faster I drove the sooner I came to Tucson; from fifty miles away you can see the smoke from the copper smelters enveloping that city in its perpetual shroud of noxious gases. Tucson lies within a half-circle of smelters. For years the citizens of Tucson have been fighting the copper companies and the politicians (who all work for the copper companies), trying to get them to clean up their act, do something about the pollution. The principal corporate response so far has been to build higher smokestacks in order to spread the filth around better, over a larger area. The democratic way. "The solution to pollution is dilution," goes the slogan of the company PR men. The mining and refining of copper is a big, powerful industry in Arizona—and in Arizona, as everywhere else, industry dominates state politics.

Tucson also lies within a ring of ICBM missile silos, making the city a certain target when the next war begins. How did this come about? Quite naturally, through the helpful graces of the county supervisors, the county Chamber of Commerce. The construction of the missile silos meant jobs, growth, profit—all in the name of patriotism. Hard to beat that.

I had a little talk with Steve Auslander, an editorial writer for the *Arizona Star,* Tucson's morning newspaper. He told me that nobody really knows how much water remains in the city's underground water supply. Perhaps enough for only eight more years, at present rates of growth and consumption, according to some hydrologists. Enough for 500 years, according to others. "Growth," says Auslander cautiously, "is a serious problem in Tucson." He went on to venture as his opinion that the people already living here are the ones who have to subsidize future development. Of all community factions, he says, the poor benefit the least from economic growth. Why so? Because economic growth always creates jobs, not for the local unemployed, who are usually unschooled and unskilled, but for the well-trained and aggressive people attracted from elsewhere.

I spoke with Peter Wild, a teacher at the University of Arizona, poet, writer and active environmentalist, who has lived in Tucson since 1958. "The basic problem," he says, "is that we in Arizona are attempting to live beyond our means." His contention is that Arizonans are mining their capital—the water, the rangelands, the air, the metals and minerals—in order to finance current expansion at the expense of the future: enriching ourselves, in David Brower's phrase, by stealing from our children.

The citizens of Tucson are not unaware of the issues involved and in recent years have been expressing their awareness at the polls. The city council is now dominated by a slow-growth majority; an outspoken conservationist named Dave Yetman has been elected to the county's board of supervisors; and Morris Udall, the nearest thing to an environmentalist among Arizona politicians, draws most of his support from the Tucson area.

Yet this new resistance to mindless expansion and population growth may have come too late, as it usually does in other places, to southern Arizona. Massive economic forces have been set in motion which are difficult to slow down, let alone halt. Touring the city I could see the advance of tract developments into the Catalina foothills where I had once lived myself only a few years before; new roads, shopping centers, banks, golf courses and sewage treatment plants now occupy what formerly had been open range, the home of deer, bighorn sheep, javelina. To me, a saddening but not unforeseen transformation, which is why I left. Frank Lloyd Wright once said, "If you don't want to live in the city pick a spot ten miles beyond its outermost limits—and then go fifty miles further." Wright's advice was based on personal experience. His own Taliesin West, which had once seemed to him safely remote from the city of Phoenix, has been leapfrogged by such developments as Fountain Hills; and a high-voltage powerline now transects his front yard.

Perhaps Paolo Soleri, another Arizona resident and architect, will prove to be a better prophet. Believing that we are doomed to crowded living whether we like it or not, Soleri proposes making the best of a dreary situation by packing us all into mile-high human formicaries, allowing at least a minimal amount of open land surface around each structure. Down there on the hard-packed grounds (glittering with broken glass) we will each have our ration of time on what's left of the earth. Anyone who has lived in or walked through a big-city public housing project would understand this vision of the future that Soleri has in mind.

Fantasies. Nothing of the sort will ever come to Arizona. Impossible. Just about the time that Tucson and Phoenix conglomerate, the two amoebae becoming one United Blob, the Colorado River will be drained dry, the water table fall to bedrock bottom, the sand dunes block all traffic on Speedway Boulevard, and the fungoid dust storms fill the air. Then, if not before, we Arizonans may finally begin to make some sort of accommodation to the nature of this splendid and beautiful and not very friendly desert we are living in.

16

The Second Rape
of the West

*The first time around we took care of the easy stuff—Indians,
buffalo, hills filled with gold—but this time we're getting
serious.*

—General George C. Custer IV

Rumbling along in my 1962 Dodge D-100, the last good
truck Dodge ever made, I tossed my empty out the window
and popped the top from another can of Schlitz. Littering
the public highway? Of course I litter the public highway.
Every chance I get. After all, it's not the beer cans that are

ugly; it's the highway that is ugly. Beer cans are beautiful, and someday, when recycling becomes a serious enterprise, the government can put one million kids to work each summer picking up the cans I and others have thoughtfully stored along the roadways.

Indian country. American country. Coming down out of the piny forests near Flagstaff, Arizona, headed north, you are led into one of the most exhilarating landscapes in the Southwest. On your left, the San Francisco Peaks, 12,660 feet above sea level; on your right and ahead, a group of dormant volcanoes and cinder cones, scattered over grasslands. One of those cinder cones, Sunset Crater, erupted only 910 years ago. We pray to God, my friends and I, for a little precision vulcanism once again; nothing could do our Southwest more good.

From 7,200 feet at the pass, the highway descends into the rangelands, bearing straight toward the valley of the Little Colorado and the Painted Desert. To the north, you can see the forested bulk of the Kaibab Plateau, through which the big Colorado has carved the Grand Canyon. To the northeast stand the red walls of the Echo Cliffs, the blue and sacred dome of Navajo Mountain, visible from fifty miles away. Indian ponies lounge along the highway looking for something to eat—Kleenex, hotdog buns, tumbleweed, anything more or less biodegradable. Out among the slabs of sun-burned rock the Navajo kids are herding sheep; among the scattered junipers are the hogans of The People, as they call themselves. And why not? They've been here a long time. By each dome-shaped hogan is an old car, on its back, cannibalized to keep another running, and a pickup truck, on its wheels. All seems to be in order.

Not quite. Something alien and strange has invaded the Southwest, a gigantic and inhuman power from—in effect—another world. You first notice the invaders as you approach the village of Cameron and the turnoff to Grand Canyon. They look like Martian monsters in this pastoral scene: skeleton towers of steel 90 to 120 feet tall, posted across the landscape in military file from horizon to horizon. From the crossarms of the towers hang chains of insulators, bearing power-line cables buzzing with electricity, transmitting power from Glen Canyon Dam and the new coal-fired generators near the town of Page to the burgeoning cities of Las Vegas, Phoenix, and southern California. From the silence of the desert to the clamor of Glitter Gulch, the fool's treasure of one region is transported and transmuted into the nervous neon of another. Energy, they call it, energy for growth. And what is the growth for? Ask any cancer cell.

The power lines are merely the first, outward signs of this war between the worlds. Deep in the heart of Indian country, on a plateau called Black Mesa, is the chief current battleground, a huge strip mine where walking dragline excavators 300 feet high, weighing 2,500 tons each, remove and overturn what the Peabody Coal Company calls "overburden." Blasters shatter the coal seam underneath; power shovels scoop the coal into trucks bigger than a house, trucks that look like stegosauruses on wheels. They haul it to processing plants nearby, from which it is shipped by pipeline in slurry form to a power plant in Nevada or by conveyor belt and rail to the plant at Page.

Strip mining destroys the rangeland on which the Indians once grazed their sheep and horses, and it threatens the underground water supplies that feed their few springs and wells. Strip-mined land has yet to be reclaimed successfully anywhere in the arid West. But from the point of view of the mine operators and the power companies, strip mining is cheap and profitable. A mine producing 1 million tons of coal a year may require only twenty-five workers. The machines are expensive, but machines never complain, never go on strike, never make demands for safety standards, medical insurance, retirement pensions. What about the displaced Indians and the unemployed miners back in Appalachia? Let them go on welfare; let them eat food stamps. Society at large will pay those costs. And so the strip mining goes on at an ever-growing pace and now consumes about 4,650 acres of American farm, forest, and rangeland each week. Every week of the year. An area the size of Connecticut, some 5,000 square miles, has already been strip-mined for coal alone. Can this land be reclaimed? According to the 1973 report from the National Academy of Sciences: "In the Western coal areas, complete restoration is rarely, if ever, possible." Even simple revegetation, in the West, "will require centuries."

In the case of the Black Mesa mine, what do the Indians get out of it? The Navajo tribal treasury is paid an annual royalty of $3 million, or about $25 per Navajo. The Indians also get 300 jobs paying an average of $10,000 per year. The royalty and the jobs are good for about thirty-five years, the estimated life of mine and power plant operation. Then what? No one knows for sure, but the fate of Appalachia provides a pretty good hint. Poverty, a blighted land, forced migration to the welfare slums: That has been the fate of Appalachians since King Coal moved into their homeland.

Meanwhile the Indians and everyone else living 100 miles downwind of the present and projected power plants (Warner Valley, Escalante, Caineville—all in south central Utah) will receive as a bonus a concentrated steady treatment of fly ash, sulfur dioxide, and nitrogen oxide. Even if such air-pollution-control devices as electrostatic precipitators, wet scrubbers, and baghouse filters, operating constantly at maximum theoretical efficiency, capture 99.5 percent of these pollutants at the plant smokestacks, the plants will still pump into the public air (which is all we have for breathing purposes) wastes on the order of 50,000 tons of particulates, 750,000 tons of SO_2, and 600,000 tons of NO_x per annum. These are magnitudes greater than those that now profane the Los Angeles Basin.

For those rare few who may not already be familiar with these forms of aerial garbage, a few words of explanation:

Fly ash is fine black soot, the stuff that coats windowsills and car tops and other horizontal surfaces in most industrial cities of the Western world; sulfur dioxide is a gaseous poison harmful to all varieties of plant and animal life, including the human—it reacts with moisture in the atmosphere to form sulfuric acid and comes back to earth mixed with rain or snow, often causing damage to crops; nitrogen oxide is a noxious gas that combines with ozone and carbon in the air to form the eye-smarting, sun-obscuring brown haze known as smog. All these major pollutants, plus others, including trace elements of radon and mercury, are known to cause or aggravate such respiratory ailments as asthma and emphysema; all may be and probably are carcinogenic.

Only we dumb locals may suffer physically from the power plants; but all Americans who enjoy—actually or potentially—the Grand Canyon, Lake Powell, Monument Valley, Shiprock, Canyon de Chelly, Zion, Bryce Canyon, Capitol Reef, Arches, and Canyonlands national parks will be forced to accept the degradation of the national heritage. The strip mines will tear up only a few hundred square miles; the accompanying power lines, railways, truck roads, dams, waste-disposal sites, industrial sites, and trailer-house towns will cover only a few hundred more square miles; but the filth spewed out by the power plants will smog the air for hundreds of miles in all directions, reducing visibility from the customary 50 to 100 miles to an average of something like 15. That's what you have to look forward to, tourists, next time you come west to enjoy what is, after all, *your* property.

Try to keep cool, calm, and objective, I tell myself, driving the familiar road up from Flagstaff through my favorite towns of Cameron, Tuba City, Cow Springs, and Kayenta. Don't get overagitated, Abbey, and try to keep a steady bead on the ceramic insulators that carry the lines that conduct the 50,000 volts of blue juice above the tracks of the Black Mesa and Lake Powell Railroad. Anger is bad for the aim, hard on the stomach, and makes for a nervous trigger finger. Rage is self-defeating, say all the wisest philosophers (all of whom are dead).

So much for ulcerdom. We have barely begun to discuss the difficulties that will follow mining and coal-fired power plants in the American Southwest, if the ambitious plans of the federal government and the power combines are carried to completion. We have said little, for example, of the impact on water supplies in an arid land. Every river in the Southwest is already overcommitted to agricultural and local municpal use; it was, in fact, for this purpose that the Glen Canyon Dam was built, together with secondary dams in Utah, Colorado, and New Mexico. The proposed power plants will require enormous quantities of water, primarily for cooling purposes. Since no surplus water is available, the water will have to come from sources presently allocated to agriculture. That means, of course, smaller food supplies and higher food prices. This touches on the problem; but the dislocation of groundwater supplies by mining may have more serious long-term effects, drying up some wells and streams, polluting others, on which the Indians, the farmers, and the cattle growers of the Southwest now depend.

The Four Corners Power Plant near Shiprock, New Mexico, may be the worst single industrial polluter in the world. The smog from the Four Corners plant drifts on the prevailing winds as far as Durango, Colorado, and down the Rio Grande Valley of New Mexico to obscure the skies above the historic towns of Taos, Santa Fe, and Albuquerque. This smog was the sole human artifact visible from the moon. Despite years of protest, the utility company has done almost nothing to abate this public nuisance and menace to public health. Yet several of the same companies which built and operate the Four Corners monster are now involved in the building of the Navajo Generating Station at Page, on the shore of Lake Powell, one of the most scenic and popular recreational areas in the Southwest.

With the help and/or interest of the Bureau of Reclamation, another combine consisting of Arizona Public Service Company, Southern California Edison Company, and San Diego Gas and Electric Company proposed in 1964 a third power plant in the area of the Kaiparowits Plateau, a presently uninhabited wilderness of forest and canyons within visual range of Page and Lake Powell. Though defeated in 1976, we may be sure that the power combine will attempt to revive this project when they think the political climate more favorable. You can trust your public utility about as far as you can hand roll a bulldozer.

All these Southwest power projects, actual or potential, violate the law of the land. According to the provisions of the Clean Air Act of 1971, passed by Congress and signed by the president, not only must the air of industrial regions be cleaned up to meet federal standards, but also, and equally important—perhaps *more* important—the air of nonindustrial regions, such as the Southwest, the intermountain West, and the northern plains, must be kept as is: clean. The intent of the act was to prevent utilities and industrial concerns from evading the law by building new plants in rural areas where the air is still reasonably clean.

Yet this violation of the act is exactly what the power companies, the mining corporations, and the public utilities hope to get away with. Although most of the energy produced will be consumed in Tucson, Phoenix, Las Vegas, and southern California, the mining and burning of the coal will take place in northern Arizona and southern Utah, where a small and docile population is being cajoled into giving up its birthright of fresh air, clear skies, and open space in exchange for a few hundred temporary jobs.

The coal could be mined and shipped by rail and truck to southern California and the big cities and burned there, at the place of need. Such a policy, while still damaging to the canyonlands and the Indian country, would at least assure the nondegradation of one of America's last large reservoirs of pure air. Local citizens who want the jobs coal mining would create but are opposed to the air pollution resulting from power plants have suggested this alternative to present policy. Their pleas go unheeded, despite the fact that the law reinforces their argument. The reason is simple: The public utilities and the oil, coal, and power combines want mine-site burning of the coal so they can escape air-quality standards imposed on the cities.

From the energy industry's point of view, it is more profitable to transport electricity long distances, via power lines, than to transport the raw coal and pay for the sophisticated technology required to clean up their urban area power plants.

The economics of the matter are more complicated than this summary indicates, involving such things as the manner in which public utility rates are set and the relative ease with which certain costs can or cannot be passed on to the consumer (fuels and power transmission costs are relatively easy to pass along, while other costs, such as improvements in pollution technology and the recovery of large-scale investments and mineral leases, are more difficult). But the core of the case is monetary profit: With profit margins fixed by state regulation at a percentage of total investment, it is more profitable for the utilities and their stockholders to develop their business to the largest scale and volume possible, no matter what the cost to the environment and the health of the citizenry.

The Environmental Protection Agency (EPA) is mandated by Congress to prevent exactly such degradation of air quality as the power combines are bringing into the Southwest. The EPA, however, blandly ignores the law and refuses to perform its clearly defined duty on the curious ground that enforcement of the law, in this case, would "retard or prevent industrial development" in presently nonindustrial areas. This may well be true; and it might well be a wise national policy to restrict or ban industrial development in areas that have a higher value for other uses, such as agriculture and human recreation.

Whether or not true, and whether or not wise, industrial development is not the concern of the EPA. The EPA's job is to protect the environment, not to assist in promoting its further industrialization. Apparently, the EPA is obeying, in this instance, not its congressional mandate but orders from higher up—from the Federal Energy Administration, the Federal Power Commission, the Department of the Interior, and the White House—that conglomerate of federal agencies and administrative powers that acts, in Ralph Nader's words, as the "indentured servant" of corporate industrialism.

The EPA has been taken to court by citizens' conservation organizations in an effort to compel it to obey the law and live up to its obligations. The federal courts have ordered the EPA to enforce the policy of nondegradation of air quality. Appealed by the EPA to the highest court, the orders of the lower courts were sustained by the Supreme Court of the United States, which ruled that the EPA may not allow "significant deterioration" of air quality anywhere.

No matter: The EPA continues to avoid, evade, and defy the law through various ruses, the latest of which is the drawing up of a complicated national map of air-quality "zones" and turning the problems of selection and enforcement over to state governments. In Utah, Arizona, Wyoming, New Mexico, and Nevada, we know well what that means: The rules will be dictated by the extractive industries—the coal, oil, and power combines.

Not only do our state politicians fail to resist these alien forces, they bid against one another to invite them in. Our good old boys would sell their mothers' graves if they could make a quick buck out of the deal; crooked as a dog's hindleg, tricky as a car dealer, greedy as a hog at the trough, these men will sell out the West to big industry as fast as they can, without the faintest stirrings of conscience. Governors,

U.S. senators, congressmen, and our chamber of commerce presidents don't give a hoot in hell for future losses; they figure, rightly, that they personally will all be dead by the time the extent of the disaster becomes clear.

So much for the canyonlands of Utah and Arizona: nothing but a barren wasteland, anyway, as any local Jaycee will tell you, nothing but sand and dust and heat and emptiness, red rock baking under the sun and hungry vultures soaring on the air. Quite so, men, quite so: nothing but canyon and desert, mountain and mesa, all too good for the likes of us.

I drove north and east into historic South Pass, through which the pioneers had made their way on foot, on horse, and in wagon trains to Oregon and California, guided by legendary mountain men like Jedediah Smith. At the summit of the pass I crossed the continental divide, leaving my trail of empty Schlitz cans by the roadside (to be recovered later). Bunches of pronghorn antelope watched my progress; I'd seen at least thirty small herds of those elegant beasts since entering Wyoming, all within sight of the paved highway.

In the high, cold mountain town of Lander (population 7,500), I stopped for a few hours to visit the people who write, edit, and produce the only newspaper in the entire Rocky Mountain West concerned primarily with environmental issues. The *High Country News*, founded six years ago and published by native Landerian Tom Bell, is a biweekly of small circulation but widespread coverage, dealing with the whole range of developments that threaten the people of the West: strip mining, power plants, air pollution, water diversion, urbanization, overgrazing, clear-cutting, land speculation, and other issues.

In the cubbyhole office of the *News*, I found Joan Nice, Bruce Hamilton, and Marjane Ambler. These young people, none of them looking over thirty, make up the entire editorial staff of the newspaper. They pay themselves a monthly salary of $300 each—enough for rent and beans and shoes. Though many of the feature articles published in the paper come from contributors, the staff writes the bulk of it, sixteen pages every two weeks. They are good people—a new breed of westerner.

Armed with names and addresses by the *HCN* staff, I went on north to Billings, Montana. In my room at the General Custer Hotel, I watched a TV commercial sponsored by the Montana Power Company promoting the attractions of strip mining, power-plant construction, and extra-high-voltage (EHV) transmission lines.

Next morning, I paid a call on Roger Rice, senior geologist for the Western Energy Company, a subsidiary of Montana Power. With him was Mike Grende, reclamation manager for the same outfit. Patiently and courteously, they explained to me why Montana Power wanted more strip mines, more power plants, and two new EHV lines across the length of Montana—some 410 miles at 500 kilovolts.

Why? To meet anticipated growth in industry and population. For example, Montana's Big Sky resort town, founded by the late Chet Huntley, is an all-electric community and, by itself, if all goes according to plan, will require more electricity than any city now existing in the state. The transmission lines, by tying in the power complex in eastern Montana with the northwest power grid of Oregon and Washington, would enable Montana Power to transfer energy to the urban centers of Seattle, Puget Sound, and Portland, where the need is greatest. Why there? Aluminum manufacture, they said; population growth; the aerospace industry; the new methods of irrigation; a twelve percent annual increase in power demands in the Northwest as a whole.

Why not ship the coal by rail, truck, or slurry line to Seattle, I asked, and let the power companies burn it there, pollute *their* skies? Because, they told me, it is more economical to transmit the power by high-voltage cable than to ship it in the form of coal. So Montana is to be sacrificed, I said, to the energy needs of the Northwest—and of the Midwest, where much of the electrical energy will also be transferred. Rice replied that we've got to think of the greatest good for the greatest number. The few (Montana's presently small and until now lucky population) cannot be allowed to obstruct the needs of the many (the teeming millions of Washington, Oregon, California, Michigan, Minnesota, Iowa, Illinois, Ohio, etc.). Besides, said Rice, the energy industry will give the Montana economy a much-needed shot in the arm.

I didn't argue; you don't argue with engineers—you have to derail them. Why the TV advertising campaign? I asked; if this deal is good for the people of Montana, why do you have to spend so much (tax-deductible) advertising money in selling it to them? We're spending only $100,000, said Rice, and the program has been well received by the public. But why is it necessary? Because there are some well-meaning and concerned people in this state, he said tactfully, who are not familiar with all the facts and have been misleading the public. Who are they? A small group of ranchers in eastern Montana (site of the strip mining) called the Northern Plains Resource Council. Later the same day, I would learn that the staff members of this ad hoc resource council are paid, like my friends down in Lander, $300 per month each. Three hundred dollars per month seems to be the maximum income of conservation activists. This suggested my final, unfair, irrelevant, *argumentum ad hominum* question: Exactly how much, I asked Mr. Rice and Mr. Grende, did Western Energy pay them for the use of *their* talents?

None of your business, they explained.

In the afternoon, I took a flight over the Powder River Basin, the area in southeast Montana and northeast Wyoming where most of the strip mining, power generation, coal gasification, and coal liquefaction are taking place or are scheduled to take place—if permitted. My guide was a young man from the Northern Plains Resource Council. Due east from the city of Billings, we flew over the Sarpy Creek strip mine, operated by Westmoreland Resources (a partnership consisting of Westmoreland Coal Company, Penn Virginia Corporation, Kewanee Industries, Inc., and Morrison-Knudsen Company, Inc., one of the world's largest construction companies) and saw the black gash already cut in the grassy hills. Down in the open pit stood a GEM—giant earth mover—with its sixty-cubic-yard bucket, big enough to lift two Greyhound buses into the air. Surrounding the strip mine were wheatfields, subirrigated hayfields along the watercourse and endless rolling plains covered with the sere, brown, short, tough native grasses that are the best cattle feed in the world. Where the land is too arid for conventional farming, it will still support a beef-growing industry; this is, after all, part of the region where the American bison once roamed in herds of thousands.

We turned southeast, across the Crow and Northern Cheyenne Indian reservations (also facing strip mining and industrialization), toward the towns of Decker, Acme, Sheridan, and Buffalo, the last three in Wyoming. More strip mines, more GEMs, new roads and railways, new trailer slums. If the Federal Government and the energy combines have their way, some ten to fifteen coal-burning power plants will be erected in this region between Billings, Montana, and Gillette, Wyoming. Never mind the opposition of the people who make their living here now. I recalled something senior geologist Rice had remarked during our interview: "Public attitudes will change," he said, "after they've had a few power blackouts."

We flew north, across the state line again and over Birney and Colstrip, passing the strip mines of Peabody Coal and the conglomerate of Montana Power, Puget Sound Power and Light, Washington Water Power, Portland General Electric, and Pacific Power and Light, which is developing the Colstrip mines. Off to the southwest, beyond the smog and dust of all this fresh activity, the snow-covered Bighorn Range loomed against the sky, still visible fifty miles away. If the proposed power plants are actually built, those mountains will no longer be seen from so great a distance.

We passed over the Bull Mountains, north of Billings, one more prosperous ranching area under the cloud of King Coal, then returned to the Billings airport. What had I seen in this brief aerial survey? Mountains, forested foothills, tawny grasslands stretching for hundreds of miles, silver rivers, winding streams lined with willow and cottonwood trees, green hayfields, ranches, homes, small towns—the traditional American version of the good life. And the strip mines.

What is most difficult to grasp is the scale, the magnitude of the planned assault. Including the lignite deposits of the western Dakotas, the coal-development proposals take in some 250,000 square miles. Beneath that surface lie an estimated 1.5 trillion tons of coal, about forty percent of total United States reserves (most of the nation's coal, the remaining sixty percent, is in the East—Appalachia—and the Midwest). Though lower in BTU (heat) content than eastern coal, these Northern Plains deposits are also lower in sulfur content, which makes them attractive to an energy industry under pressure to lessen air pollution in urban centers. To develop this energy resource, the U.S. Bureau of Reclamation and a participating group of thirty-five public utilities propose not only vast strip mining in Wyoming, Montana, North Dakota, and South Dakota, but also the construction of twelve mine-mouth power plants to convert the coal to electricity, together with additional plants for coal gasification and liquefaction—synthetic fuels. The power would be sent east and west through thousands of miles of 765-kilovolt transmission lines. A single projected 10,000-megawatt power plant would be five times bigger than New Mexico's Four Corners plant. The water needed for these planned developments would total 2,600,000 acre-feet per year, an amount exceeding by eighty percent the present municipal and industrial needs of New York City's 8 million residents. Where will so much water come from? From the Yellowstone River, on which the agricultural economy of the region now depends. Through an elaborate system of dams, storage reservoirs, pump stations, and aqueducts—to be built, of course, by the Bureau of Reclamation—this water project would divert from the Yellowstone one-third of its flow in good (wet) years and one-half in bad (dry) years.

Coal requirements for the 1980 goal of 50,000 megawatts would be 210 million tons per year, stripping ten to thirty square miles of range and farmland annually, or a total of 350 to 1,050 square miles during the projected thirty-five-year life of the power plants. At the 200,000-megawatt level, the strip mines would consume from 50,000 to 175,000 square miles of surface during the same thirty-five-year period. The transmission lines would take up over 8,000 miles of right of way, or (with mile-wide utility corridors) a total of 4,800 square miles. The ozone zone. Power losses from the lines would approximate 3,000 megawatts, equal to the present average peak demand requirements of Manhattan.*

If carried out, this plan will create a population influx of up to 1 million people in the Northern Plains, a number almost as great as the current population of Wyoming and Montana combined (1,094,000). A dozen new industrial towns would revolutionize the style, not to say the quality, of life in the region. The new power plants would generate pollution greater than that of Los Angeles or New York, with an estimated annual production (assuming pollution-control efficiency at 99.5 percent) of 100,000 tons of particulate matter (fly ash) per year, 2,100,000 tons of sulfur dioxide (including sulfuric acid), and 1,879,000 tons of nitrogen oxides, plus traces of selenium, arsenic, and mercury.

Who's to blame?

* Facts and figures taken (mostly) from Alvin Josephy's article, "Agony of the Northern Plains," *Audubon,* July 1973, Vol. 75, No. 4.

I asked that question of Boyd Charter, a crusty old rancher from the Bull Mountains north of Billings. Charter is one of the supporters of the Northern Plains Resource Council. He was also, he told me, once a fellow rider with the present junior senator from Wyoming, Clifford Hansen, and Hansen, he said, "is one of the worst."

May I quote you on that? I asked.

"You can write it in capital letters," said Charter. "When it comes to who's to blame for tearing up the Northern Plains and the West in general, my old buddy Cliff is THE BIGGEST SON OF A BITCH IN WASHINGTON."

Why pick on Hansen? I asked. Is he any worse than Stan Hathaway (briefly President Ford's secretary of the interior after a Senate fight for confirmation)? Or look at Senators Garn and Moss of Utah, Senators Goldwater and Fannin of Arizona, Governor Rampton of Utah, Congressmen Steiger and Rhodes of Arizona, and about half a dozen others in our Western Dirty Dozen. Don't they qualify, from the conservationist point of view, as sons of bitches, too? Charter and I had a bit of discussion about this, each of us maintaining, out of regional loyalty, that his own politicians were the worst.

Take Moss, Garn, and Rampton, I said. All three backed the Kaiparowits project to the hilt. All three are doing their best for the power industry, the mining industry, and the oil shale industry, not to mention such incidentals as commercial tourism and building freeways through the canyon country wilderness. Utah, I pointed out, is the only state in the mountain West without a single acre in the Wilderness Preservation System, and Rampton and Moss, together with Garn's predecessor Wallace Bennett, must be given full credit for that accomplishment. They even oppose wilderness in the national parks. Our man Garn, I said with pride, though he's been in office for only two years, has already made his name by openly advocating that public lands be transferred to private ownership, that is, to industry.

He knew about that, Charter admitted, but you still can't beat old Cliff Hansen. Old Cliff, he votes for the Highway Trust Fund every time. Against the Land-Use Planning Bill. For the Alaskan Pipeline. Against the Strip Mining Control Bill, which would protect the surface rights of ranchers and farmers from the coal companies. Against requiring environmental impact statements in coal and natural gas leasing. Against the Clean Air Act. Against the Wild and Scenic Rivers Act. For converting and extending a small airstrip in Grand Teton National Park to handle jet traffic. Against the Freedom of Information Act. According to a score sheet compiled by the League of Conservation Voters, Hansen voted wrong ninety-two percent of the time on environmental issues. According to the same kind of score sheet tallied by the U.S. Chamber of Commerce, Hansen voted right ninety-five percent of the time. That shows you who he works for.

Not bad, I agreed, not bad. But take my own congressman, Sam Steiger of Arizona: He has voted the same way on every issue as your friend Hansen and, besides that, still wants to build a dam in the Grand Canyon, led the fight in the House against the Land-Use Planning Bill, against mass-transit bills, and against wilderness preservation. He's the one who helped the Bureau of Land Management try to get control of the Kofa Wildlife Reserve, which was a move for mining and against bighorn sheep. Our Sam, he's something special.

Okay, said Charter, but our Cliff is the oilman's oilman. When everybody else wanted to eliminate the depletion allowance for the oil industry, our Cliff wanted to raise it. He wanted to raise it for the coal industry, too. Hansen is doing everything he can to encourage the energy industry in the West. A magazine called *World Oil,* which speaks for the industry, named Hansen "Oil's Champion." That's our senator.

The debate could have gone on forever. Charter and I finally reached agreement by agreeing that almost all of *them* in political office, Republicans *and* Democrats, from Phoenix, Arizona, up north to Billings, Montana, are in general working for the mining and energy industries and against farming, ranching, and the conservationist cause.

Boyd Charter is among the many landowners in the region who have been harassed, threatened, and cajoled by representatives from the coal and power industries trying to buy them out or, failing that, to condemn their land, for strip mining. "We're being raped and we're being lied to," he says. "Show me one acre that's been reclaimed after strip mining. There isn't any. The businessmen who form the Economic Development Association of Eastern Montana want to strip-mine the high plains and then use the pits for a national garbage dump.

"My patriotism is wearing thin," says Charter. "They wanted to sell Montana coal to Japan. Some Japanese aluminum company had the deal all set up—they'd even bought loading docks in Oregon. We heard about it and got it stopped. But what's all this other coal development for? Well, for one thing, to help make more aluminum beer cans in the state of Washington. They'd tear up the best cattle range in the world to make beer cans. These native grasses we have here can't be restored. Sure, they can plant something like crested wheat on what they call reclaimed land; but cattle don't like crested wheat. Or sweet clover; sweet clover is a *weed* out here. You can't raise beef cattle on it. Why do you think the Texas cattlemen brought their herds up here a century ago? Because of the native grass—the little bluestem, the blue bunch grass, the western wheat grass, the needle-and-thread grass, the Indian rice grass—that's why. This high plains grass is the next best thing to grain—and grain is too precious to feed to cattle anymore. We're going to be eating range-fed beef from now on. That's all you're gonna get. When you come right down to it, it's a choice between food and more electricity. Which would you rather have? How much protein in a kilowatt?"

I asked Charter if he could maintain his cattle business if

gasoline were severely rationed or priced much higher or if electricity became more expensive. "We can get along without gasoline entirely," he said. "We can convert in a few days to the same kind of operation we had forty years ago." And he added that he and some neighboring ranchers were already switching from Rural Electrification Administration (REA) power back to the old reliable windmills for pumping water from range wells. That, he said, was his first step toward Project Independence.

Time for a visit to another strip mine and power plant. I drove east from Billings to the little town of Colstrip, soon to become a hive of industry if the planners fulfill their plans. On the way I paused for an hour of meditation at a monument on a ridge above the Little Bighorn River, in the heart of the Crow Indian Reservation. Here Custer made his last stand. On the memorial stone is a bronze plaque that reads, in part: "To the officers and soldiers killed . . . in the Territory of Montana, while clearing the district of the Yellowstone of hostile Indians." All is quiet and peaceful, at the moment. The sun beams down on the green fields along the river, on the lion-colored hills above, on the gleaming Bighorn Mountains far to the south.

If you think the Indians would resent this memorial to Custer set up in their own backyard, you have forgotten that the Crows fought *with* the U.S. Cavalry, not against it. It was the Sioux and the Cheyenne tribes, traditional sporting enemies of the Crow, who shot down Custer and 261 of his men, together with a few of his Crow scouts.

Divide and conquer: It worked for the Romans, it worked for Cortes in Mexico, it worked in the U.S.A. against the Indians. The same technique is now employed by the Bureau of Reclamation and the power combine against the farmers and ranchers (including the surviving Indians) of the contemporary American West. If Continental Oil, Montana Power, or Peabody Coal can buy out one rancher, then that rancher's neighbors come under greater pressure to sell out. You can't raise hay and cattle next to a strip mine, downwind from a power plant belching SO_2 into the air, amid the factories and furnaces of the petrochemical industry. Today, as a century ago, it is the Crow tribe that is willing to accommodate itself to the advance of power—although bargaining for a stiff price—while its old enemies and neighbors on the adjacent Cheyenne reservation are resisting the strip miners and the air polluters to the end, just as they did the pony soldiers, the bluecoats, the gold seekers, and the sodbusters. The Crows have a big reservation and a relatively high per capita income (for Indians); all the Cheyennes have is their sense of honor.

Through the Cheyenne capital, called Lame Deer, and north. Approaching the strip mine, I saw, as usual, the iron rigs of giant draglines looming over the landscape, digging into the earth beneath a pall of dust. On the skyline were the long gray ridges of spoil banks, the overturned soil. Beyond the mined area the original landscape remains, hills of ponderosa pine rising from the rolling plains of grass.

I interviewed Martin White in the Colstrip office. White, who looks almost as young as the $300-per-month staff members of the Northern Plains Resource Council but wears a more harassed expression on his face, is project manager for the Western Energy Company at Colstrip. He told me a little about the mine: 6.8 million tons of coal per year, current production, with 833 million tons in reserve, still under the ground. Two units of the power plant already are under construction, two more proposed; if the proposed units are built, the power will be sent to the Northwest through the projected 410-mile, 500-kilovolt transmission line. White scoffs at the notion that ozone from the line will damage vegetation in the line's vicinity; denies charges it will take hundreds of square miles of land out of agricultural production. As for the town of Colstrip itself, it will be, he says, a "planned community," with bicycle paths, playgrounds and parks, a new library, quality homes, and spacious, land-scaped mobile-home courts. Colstrip, he says, will be a net asset to the people of eastern Montana, providing hundreds of new jobs and supporting public facilities through its contributions to the tax base. State and federal pollution-control standards will be met, and even though the quality of air and quality of life may suffer a bit in the region, the *national interest demands that Montana do its share.* He showed me the tables and charts; the graphs, plans, and statistics. A good, competent man, White; he earns his salary. I asked him what Western Energy pays him; he said it was none of my business. I asked for a tour of the strip mine; that was granted.

My guide was a young woman from the front office, newly arrived from California. As we drove over the wastelands and down into the black hole, I asked her how she liked living in Colstrip. Not much, she admitted; she and her husband, a construction engineer, would be moving on when the power plant was finished; both looked forward to that day. We watched hauler trucks, each with a capacity of 120 tons, rumble into the pit and line up under the bucket of a power shovel. I looked closely at the front of the steel bucket: Some wise-guy welder back in Euclid, Ohio, where the machine was manufactured, had spot-welded on the front of the bucket the motto of the strip-mining profession: *Fuck.*

We drove on to another part of the mine where a giant dragline excavator sat inactive, awaiting repairs. I climbed into the empty cab of the machine and fiddled with the controls. Handy piece of machinery, I thought; think what one could do with this thing on the main street of Billings or Denver or Salt Lake or Phoenix or Laramie, where all those glittering new skyscraper banks stand cheek by glassy cheek. Everywhere you go out West, in every town and city, the biggest, newest, most expensive and pretentious buildings are the banks: sure sign of social decay. ("Ill fares the land. . . .") The working people live in plasterboard boxes, in fiberboard apartments, in mobile homes of tin, aluminum, and plastic; but the banks rise up in gleaming stone and glass and steel, dominating the surrounding mass of huddled hovels precisely as the medieval lord's castle brooded above his vassal village.

As we drove back to the office, my guide showed me the official Western Energy Company reclamation plot, almost 500 acres of formerly strip-mined grassland where the spoil banks had been recontoured, fertilized, and reseeded three years before. A number of knee-high ponderosa hold out there, still alive, and a thin, dried-up growth of sweet clover, struggling for survival in the midst of the thickest thicket of Russian thistle I've ever seen.

The tumbleweeds are doing nicely, I commented, picking the stickers out of my shins, and my guide smiled and shrugged. She didn't give a damn one way or the other. What happened to that tree? I asked, pointing to a tall snag in the middle of the plot that might have been, years ago, a yellow pine. The company stuck that dead tree there, she explained, to make a perch for hawks: Hawks keep down the rodent population.

That evening I visited Duke McRae, a rancher who lives a few miles south of Colstrip. His ranch, established by his grandfather in 1886, lies directly in the path of coal and industrial development. It has been home, livelihood, and a way of life for three generations of the McRae family, including two of Duke McRae's brothers and *their* families. Now the coal companies are pressuring them to sell out. The Department of the Interior is threatening to lease the coal beneath the surface of the land (although the McRaes own the land, they do not own the mineral rights, which belong to the federal government) and their children are already suffering the effects of overcrowded schools, rapid pupil and teacher turnover, the social impact of living near a boom-town community plagued with the usual boom-town problems.

The power companies already have two power plants under construction, McRae said. They've applied for a permit to build two more with four more on the drawing boards—all to be built right there in Colstrip. Plus a coal-gasification plant, which will take most of the water out of the ground, dry up the wells and streams. You can't raise cows or kids, said McRae, in the kind of place the power company wants to make here. It's going to be a planned community, I reminded him. Sure, he said. It's planned, all right—like they plan an invasion.

I mentioned the reclamation plot I had seen—the tumbleweed farm. Oh, yeah, he said, and did they show you the dead tree for the hawks? Yes, I said. McRae laughed. That dead pine has been there for fifty years, he said: The power company was afraid people might get a bad impression, seeing a dead tree in the middle of their reclamation plot, so somebody made up that dumb story about a roost for hawks. The power company lies about everything, he said: It's so used to lying it can't tell the truth even when the truth might do it a little good.

Time for me to go home, where I belonged. On my way south, driving toward Birney, I paused at the Peabody Coal strip-mine turnoff to take a leak, open another can of beer, and study my map. Two cars emerged from the mine area and stopped: Their occupants looked me over. Suspiciously. Maybe it was my wrinkled truck with the red paper rose on the hood; maybe it was the smell of my thermal underwear. No matter, they looked suspicious to me, too. Four middle-aged men in business suits and hard hats in the front car, four more in the second car—and two of those wore the green business suits with brass-and-silver regalia of colonels in the U.S. Army. What were two colonels doing with company officials in a Peabody (Kennecott Copper) strip mine? There is something in the juxtaposition of big business, big military, and big technology that always rouses my most paranoid nightmares, visions of the technological superstate, the Pentagon's latent fascism, IBM's laboratory torture chambers, the absolute computerized fusion-powered global tyranny of the twenty-first century. But before I could open my mouth and ask any questions or even button my fly, they were gone, flashing off down the highway.

I stopped to see one more rancher, a widow named Ellen Cotton. She is a beautiful woman, about fifty, I suppose, with silver-gray hair, wind-burned face and the clear eyes (undimmed by too much print) of one who has spent most of her life in the out-of-doors. She raises cattle and race horses on her Four Mile Ranch near the hamlet of Decker, Montana, just north of the Wyoming line.

Mrs. Cotton lives in a land of almost painful beauty—clear streams, grassy meadows, red-and-yellow outcrops of sandstone, the hills and ridges topped with ponderosa pine. The dirt road to her place follows the contours of the land, winding from ridge to ridge under a sky still blue as the Virgin's cloak; from high points on the road you can see the snowy Bighorn Range seventy miles to the southwest. The officials of the Interior Department call this place the Decker-Birney Resource Study Area, proposing to lease it out to the coal-and-energy combine.

How could such a thing happen to so beautiful a land? Mrs. Cotton and her sons have lived here for twenty years, having come from Sheridan, Wyoming. Consolidation Coal (Continental Oil) has already sent its agents around to buy her out. She refuses to sell; and if they come creeping around again, she says, she's going to run them off with guns. A neighbor was offered $13 million for his land and turned it down. Mrs. Cotton says he did right; the land here is worth more than any possible sum of money, the grass more valuable than all the coal beneath it. Like old Boyd Charter up near Billings, she says that this is the best rangeland and the highest quality grass in the country. And even if it were not, she loves the land as it is, wants to live out her life here, will not sell out, will not be driven out, refuses to move.

"We cannot keep moving on," says Mrs. Cotton. "No matter what the price, where could we find another place to go? This is our home. It's time we stop exploiting the land and tearing it up. We always used to think it didn't matter, that when you mined out one area, or farmed it out, or overgrazed it, you could move to new country beyond the hills, keep moving West. But there are no new places to go anymore. The land is full. We have to stay where we are, take care of what we have. There isn't going to be anything else."

Mrs. Cotton has been to Appalachia, she told me, and saw what happened there. She and her neighbors do not intend to let it happen in their corner of the Big Sky country. She showed me a sign she had made for display along the highway. The sign is a whole cowhide, on which the following words have been inscribed with a branding iron:

National Sacrifice Area

The U.S. govt. recommends strip mining
the divide north of here. We landowners are opposed. Ellen Cotton. Mrs.
Dan Wilson. Jim & Ruth Benedict. Canyon Creek Cattle Co. Ruth Jordan.
Charles E. Jordan. Bob & Eula Ebeling.

Let future generations judge.

Behold how rich and powerful I am. . . . Would you destroy this glorious incarnation of your own heroic self?

—Thomas Wolfe
You Can't Go Home Again

All very well, the reader thinks, for a few thousand farmers and ranchers to want to save their homes and livelihoods, to preserve a charming but no doubt outmoded way of life. And it would be nice if we could keep the pure air, the wide-open spaces, the canyons and rivers and mountains free from pollution from a rash of new power plants. But America needs the energy. Our political and industrial leaders assure us that the very survival of America as a great world power may be at stake. We cannot let our future be dictated by a cartel of Arab potentates. We have more coal than the Arabs have oil. Let's dig it. The assumption is that we must continue down the road of never-ending economic expansion, toward an ever-grosser gross national product, driven by that mania for Growth with a capital G that entails, among other things, a doubling of the nation's energy production every ten years. "Expand or expire" is the essence of this attitude, exemplified in the words of President Ford in a statement to an Expo '74 audience: "Man is not built to vegetate or stagnate—we like to progress—zero-growth environmental policies fly in the face of human nature."

But a child can perceive that on our finite planet there must be, sooner or later, a limit to quantitative growth. Any high-school math student can prove that if our production of electricity continued to grow at an exponential rate of 100 percent every ten years the result would be, in less than a century, a United States of America in which every square foot of land surface was preempted by mines and power plants, leaving no room at all for homes, cities, farms, living space, or even graveyards. Growth for the sake of growth *is* the ideology of the cancer cell.

Far ahead of their so-called leaders, as usual, the American people as a whole have already begun putting into practice the obvious need for zero population growth. If the trend continues, the population of the U.S. should level off at about 250 million by the year 2000. Even that is far too many bodies for a free society, but better than the overcrowding typical of European nations. Beyond that point the goal would be an eventual reduction of the population (through normal attrition, of course) to something like 100 million, a rational figure if we desire our grandchildren to live in a green and spacious America.

An immediate and required step forward is stabilization of the energy growth rate. This will be forced upon us sooner than expected in any case. As some economists (though still a minority in that dismally obtuse profession) and most ecologists have pointed out, it takes energy to produce energy. The law of diminishing returns is now in operation. When oil could be pumped from a sixty-nine-foot well in Titusville, Pennsylvania, in 1859, it was a cheap commodity. When it has to be piped 800 miles across Alaska, or extracted from the continental shelf, or shipped in supertankers all the way from the Persian Gulf, oil becomes an expensive luxury.

If we are driven to manufacture synthetic fuels from coal or to squeeze oil from shale rock—a silly proposition on the face of it—we shall find ourselves expending as much energy as we gain; the net profit becomes marginal. This is the reason the power companies and oil corporations are demanding subsidies from the government. Nor will nuclear energy solve the problem. The available evidence indicates that the construction of nuclear power plants and the mining and processing of reactor fuel will require in themselves more electrical energy than these proposed plants could produce for the next forty to fifty years.

Nuclear fusion offers the last best hope of the technophiles. But nuclear fusion remains at least a generation away, perhaps farther, perhaps forever out of reach. Even if it can be developed someday, fusion will doubtless prove to involve hazards now unforeseen. Any form of cheap and unlimited power, if placed in the hands of humanity as we know it today, would probably lead, not to a free and abundant life for all, but to the rapid transformation of our planet into a gigantic dormitory and food factory. Earth would become a ball of passive flesh, alive perhaps but scarcely human, wobbling slowly around the sun.

The way to zero energy growth has been outlined for us by the report of the recent Energy Policy Project sponsored by the Ford Foundation. Two years in the making, *A Time To Choose: America's Energy Future* is the work of a professional staff of economists, ecologists, physicists, engineers, and research specialists, with a panel of supporting consultants including such distinguished names as Barry Commoner, René Dubos, Harrison Brown, Kenneth E. Boulding, Daniel Bell, Alan Poole, Ben J. Wattenberg, and Robert H. Socolow and an advisory board consisting of leaders from the world of science, conservation, law, and industry. *A Time To Choose* presents various scenarios for the future, including the option of zero energy growth, which can be accomplished, according to this study, without lowering the American standard of living; indeed, providing for continuing economic growth by assigning first priority to the fields of medicine, education, the arts, and sciences, and to basic human needs such as decent housing, adequate nutrition, livable cities, a clean, attractive, healthy environment.

Predictably, the strongest objections to the report came from project representatives of energy-intensive industries— William P. Tavoulareas, president of Mobil Oil; D. C. Burnham, chairman of Westinghouse Electric; the late J. Harris Ward, director of Commonwealth Edison; and John D. Harper, chairman of Alcoa. These men get nervous when the focus of debate is shifted away from their territory (what energy supplies should be developed) and into that of the conservationists (how we can prosper with less waste). Reducing the production of junk is the key to the matter. We do not have to strip-mine the farms, rangelands, and wild lands of the American West; we do not have to pollute the skies and poison the waters and dam the last of our rivers if we are willing to give up what conventional economists call "goods" but most of us recognize as being *junk*. Draw up your own list. Think of the many things we make and buy, but do not need. My preliminary list begins with Detroit,

Michigan: Who needs Detroit's bloated, ramshackle, inefficient, and overpriced rolling stock? Who is not weary of supporting that army of crooked car dealers and incompetent, gouging mechanics that has been preying on us all for the past fifty-five years?

It is no accident that Detroit should be the first major industrial victim of inflation and recession. When times are hard, we all know one thing we can get along without—a new iron mastodon from Chrysler, GM, or Ford. It is time to begin the phasing-out of the auto industry, which long ago outgrew its usefulness and no longer even amuses. Put those men to work making things we need: passenger trains; small, lightweight, efficient buses; bicycles that will last a lifetime; simple refrigerators that work for more than two years; can openers that actually open cans.

Junk, trash, rubbish—our lives are debauched, our natural resources squandered, our native land ravaged in this mad production of metal, plastic, glass and paper garbage. Who needs throw-away beer cans? Bottle my beer (and let's go back to making real beer, by the way; no more of this watery green commercial angel piss) in solid, substantial, amber-colored jugs that fit a man's hand, that rest solidly on a table and can be washed out and used over again, for Christ's sake, like they do it in Bavaria and Austria, where beer began. Who needs color television? It's bad enough in black and white and wavy stripes. Who needs trail bikes, snowmobiles, electric razors? Winnebagos, power lawn mowers, Styrofoam packaging, bulk-rate mail? Ballpoint pens, glass office buildings with windows that can't be opened, tract homes made of green lumber and plasterboard? Condominiums with cardboard walls, polyurethane geodesic igloos, plumbing that doesn't work, blenders, dishwashers, dryers, plastic picnic plates, electric guitars and Moog synthesizers? Vinylite upholstery, synthetic textiles made from ersatz fibers, sour green oranges and acid-injected tomatoes and hormone-polluted beef shipped from 3,000 miles away, frozen grape juice, incomprehensible income-tax forms, short-life light bulbs, high-powered cabin cruisers on every pond and stream, spray deodorants, nondairy products, plywood ski hutches in the mountain valleys of Colorado and Utah, four-wheel-drive "recreation" vehicles, snow-making machines, Astrodomes, the Dallas–Fort Worth Airport, aluminum pie plates, Teflon frypans, artificial fruit "drinks," electric typewriters, all-electric homes, electric chairs, gas chambers, neon billboards, Las Vegas, Los Angeles, Los Alamos? The list goes on and on ad infinitum, and anyone who wants to can easily make up a list ten times longer than mine.

While real needs go unsatisfied: good beer, good fresh healthy food for all; homes and apartments for all that are well made, well designed, comfortable, durable and handsome; quick easy urban transit systems; good continental passenger train service; air that's fit to breathe, water that's fit to drink, food that's fit to eat; and now and then, when we want it, some space and solitude and silence. Is that too much to ask of a sane and rational political economy? God only knows it's too much to ask of the one we've got now. Like my old man always says, capitalism sounds good in theory but it just doesn't work; look around you and see what it has done to our country. And what it is going to do to our country—if we let it.

Not that socialism is any better. Socialism is worse. Then what is the answer? Some mixture of the two? Something in between? Or something entirely different?

That's what I thought about, something different, grumbling south to Arizona in my final Dodge, past the golden hills of Wyoming, through Spotted Horse, Gillette and Reno Junction, past Thunder Basin National Grassland, past the Laramie Mountains and the Medicine Bow Mountains, through the Red Desert down to Rangely, Colorado, and Moab, Utah—that grand symphony of names on the American land!—and on to Bluff, Mexican Hat, Monument Valley,

Kayenta, Kaibito, Bitter Springs, Echo Cliffs, House Rock Valley, up the Kaibab monocline and across the plateau and down the other side toward Moccasin, Kanab, Shivwits, Mount Bangs, Pakoon Spring, Wolf Hole: home. Thinking, where they won't find you, yet, for a while. (It's ten six-packs from Custer's Battlefield to Abbey's last stand.) Pausing only three times during the whole 800-mile journey: once near Recluse, Wyoming, to doctor up a pair of bulldozers belonging to the U.S. Bureau of Reclamation; once near Cisco, Utah, to cut down a billboard erected by the Utah Chamber of Commerce; and once near Black Mesa Junction, Arizona, to shoot some insulators off the power line of the Black Mesa and Lake Powell Railroad. And my conclusion, when I finally reached the Hole, was that what we need in our perishing republic is something different.

Something entirely different.

17

Down the River
with Major Powell

May 1971: Green River, Utah

Last minute confusions. Can't find my baggage tickets—
I've come by bus—and we have to sweet-talk the depot manager into yielding up my banana boat and kayak paddle and
dehydrated chop suey dinners and topo maps and other
items needed for a float on the Green River. Yes, and my
copy of the book, the classic, my favorite western book, *The
Exploration of the Colorado River* by Major John Wesley Powell.

He was first, of course, after the Indians, maybe, and a
few mountain men, to do the whole thing—all the way from

the head of the Green River in Wyoming down 1,000 miles of mystery to what is now (alas) the placid evaporation tank called Lake Mead near Las Vegas. With one arm—he lost the other in the Civil War—and nine comrades, in May 1869, with wooden boats, like Columbus, he ventured into the heart of the little known. Columbus's men were afraid of sailing off the edge of a flat world; Powell's could not be sure they would not descend upon a Niagara walled in by unclimbable cliffs. But off they went.

Down at the beach we inflate our little rubber boats and prepare to launch. Harvey Mudd from El Paso, Malcolm Brown from Taos, and myself. We discover we have more food and gear than we can quite comfortably crowd into the boats. But we're reluctant to leave anything behind, it's going to be at least a ten-day voyage. So Harvey goes to town and buys an inner tube from a truck tire; this becomes our baggage dinghy.

In the middle of the afternoon, finally ready, we slide into our voluptuous, pneumatic craft and paddle out onto the surge of the brown river. And into a headwind. The water is choppy, with whitecaps and foam, but the strong current carries us downriver despite the wind. Paddling enough to keep warm and keep our bows into the waves, we make good time. The river banks slide by, the cottonwoods and willows and tamarisk, the railroad bridge and a dead cow mired in the mud, the final outlying shanty on the outskirts of the town—all things moving slowly by in silent motion as we glide into the desert wilderness. It's the tenth of May; we're the first to go down the river this spring. The wind pauses, resting; we let our boats turn round on the water and in leisure and stillness survey the landscape that has barely changed since Powell saw it back in 1869:

> There are buttes, outliers of cliffs to the left. Below they are composed of shales and marls of light blue and slate colors; above the rocks are buff and gray, and then brown.

The buttes are buttressed below, where the azure rocks are seen, and terraced above through the gray and brown beds. A long line of cliffs or rock escarpments separates the tablelands . . . from the lower plain. The eye can trace these azure beds and cliffs on either side of the river, in a long line extending across its course, until they fade away in the perspective.

They fade away all right. Powell is describing the Book Cliffs, south face of the Tavaputs Plateau, which extend for 100 miles from northeast Utah into Colorado. The shales he mentions contain the famous shale oil—a multibillion-dollar treasure in fossil fuels belonging to the American people.

An hour before sundown we see on the east shore an alkaline conglomeration, like a big glistening ulcer in the golden sandstone, which descends by terraces into the river. Paddling over to investigate we find ourselves on the lip of Crystal Geyser. Just beyond it we pull ashore, build a bonfire, strip off our watersoaked clothes and dance around the flames until we're warm and dry again. I break out a bottle of rum; we celebrate our first evening away from home and loved ones.

After dinner we inspect the geyser. Peering down into its evil spout we can see and hear, twenty feet below, the sullen rumbles, the bubbling liquids of a convulsion under preparation. But for a time nothing happens. Sitting around the fire, after dark, we've nearly forgotten the thing. We're talking, watching the bats flicker about and the constellations unfold, when suddenly and without any warning we hear a noise like a jet fighter coming over the edge of the mesa. A whistling explosion, a roar.

We jump to our feet and there's the geyser going off— tremendous ejaculations of water rising higher and higher, straight into the air, glowing in the starlight with a silvery, almost phosphorescent sheen. In a series of impulses the fountain climbs still farther as we watch; in a minute it reaches a maximum height we can barely guess—100 feet?

200?; we have no standard by which to measure. And then it begins to subside, not steadily but with sporadic rallies, down to a gushing well overflowing its brim and rolling over the terraces into the river. There is no steam. Feeling the water, we find it cold, with a strong, salty taste. How can cold water boil over? None of us can explain this. Nor can Major Powell. Apparently the geyser did not exist when he came down the river. He writes only of "interesting rocks, deposited by mineral springs . . . which are no longer flowing."

Six hours later the geyser blows up again, shocking us all awake at four o'clock in the morning.

A beautiful morning, which I promptly ruin by getting into my boat the wrong way and capsizing. Good thing I've lashed all baggage to the boat, and in rubberized bags. But lost a half quart of rum.

Onward, downstream, we drift and paddle through the empty Green River desert. Miles of sandy wastes on either side, beyond which we can see mesas, buttes, plateaus, and far away, perhaps sixty miles by line of sight, the blue and laccolithic peaks of the Henry Mountains. No one lives out here, no one at all anymore; the Indians have gone, the few old homesteads we pass have long been abandoned, and the three or four ranchers who run cows in the side canyons and bottomlands of the river live in town and commute to work, once in a while, when they feel like it, by four-wheel-drive truck or by airplane or powerboat.

In the afternoon the weather turns bad: headwinds and cloudy skies. We have to paddle hard and long to keep up with the river, which seems to be slowing down anyway. Wet and cold, we stop ashore long enough to cook a meal, dry out and warm up, then push on. Toward evening we spy a long island in the middle of the river; I suggest we camp there in order to get away from the cattle that infest the bottoms along this part of the river, but on landing we find that the island too has been frequented by the cows—their sign is everywhere. Too late to go on, however; we clear an area in the sand and Malcolm, a terrible pyromaniac, builds a giant fire on which he piles still more limbs, logs, entire dead and uprooted cottonwood trees, while the wind moans through the willows and the river gurgles past over bars of quicksand tricky as jelly.

In the morning we pass the mouth of the San Rafael River, today merely a trickling stream choked with jungles of tamarisk. On the east bank we see the ruins of old waterworks of various kinds, water wheels, pipes, funnels, various devices by which homesteaders fifty years ago had tried to lift water from the river to irrigate the alluvial bottoms. A vain effort; all has now reverted to the deer, the jackrabbits, and the cattle-growing industry. Mute testimony to the latter, more dead cows, dead calves, half-buried in the mudbanks and coated with layers of silt.

But finally the country begins to change, the river leaves the open desert and carves its way into the rising plateaus of the canyon country. All cattle sign and human sign vanish as we enter the portals of what Powell named Labyrinth Canyon:

> Now we enter another canyon. Gradually the walls rise higher and higher as we proceed. . . . Back from the brink the hollows of the plateau are filled with sands . . . of a rich cream color, shading into maroon, everywhere destitute of vegetation, and drifted into long wave-like ridges.

A wind is blowing above the canyon, and as we float along I see something I've never seen before: streams of red sand pouring steadily over the edge of the rim and falling down, down, from ledge to ledge, like waterless waterfalls. Constant as an hourglass the sandfalls pour and are still pouring as they pass from our sight behind the bend.

Further side canyons appear, deep and narrow, and one with a clear stream flowing down its sandy floor. We disembark to fill our canteens and water jugs, for the dead cattle have made us distrust the river water. Exploring this side canyon, we find it to be actually the mouth of three side canyons all broaching upon the river through the same opening. I recognize the place as Trin-Alcove Bend, first described and named by Major Powell over a century before. And so far as we can see unchanged, except for the thickets of tamarisk, a type of shrub unknown to Powell. Like that other typical desert plant the tumbleweed, tamarisk is not native to the American West. It comes from North Africa, and as is often the way with exotics, has spread like a plague in its new environment, clogging the desert watercourses and driving out the willow, the cottonwood, the hackberry, the box alder. Nevertheless, it is lovely, this African intruder, with its lacy leafery, its subtle fragrance, and its delicate lavender blossoms.

Through ever deeper canyons, into another wet and windy afternoon. At one time the wind becomes so strong against us that we cannot make headway; we are forced to wade along the muddy shore towing our boats. It is with great relief that we finally set up camp for the night at the base of a sandstone wall, where Malcolm builds so fierce a fire the rock begins spalling in slabs from the face of the cliff. We agree to name this, in his honor, Spalling Rock Campsite.

Deeper into the labyrinth. As we glide silently down the river we come close to deer standing on the shore, to great blue herons and American egrets perched on the rocks, to occasional beaver swimming from one burrow to the next. There are killdeer on the sandbars and flocks of cliff swallows in the air; often we can see the swallows' mud nests plastered to the undersides of grottoes in the canyon wall. Ravens and magpies flap across the river; buzzards and redtailed hawks soar far above. And always there is the music of a variety of birds we can only glimpse flitting through the thickets on the flood plains: vireos, yellow warblers, rock wrens, canyon wrens, catbirds, mockingbirds, and others we cannot identify. Off in the distance, always in the distance, comes the wistful call of a mourning dove—that universal song.

Around noon we stop and go up a canyon named Hey Joe Canyon, looking for good drinking water. Here we find, not only water but a semi-recluse named Howell Nicholson, guarding a uranium mining camp soon to be reopened. Owner of 179 uranium claims, as he told us, Mr. Nicholson is calmly looking forward to becoming a millionaire, puzzled but not troubled by the problem of how he will spend his money, when it comes. Friendly and hospitable, he invites us into his shack for coffee and would keep us all day and all night if we were willing to stay.

But the fascination of the river and our silent effortless voyage is irresistible. We launch forth again and come in another hour to Bowknot Bend, where the entrenched meanders of the river come close to doubling back upon themselves. Climbing a 400-foot talus partition at the narrowest part of the bend, we can look down and see the Green flowing in two directions at once within a space of 600 yards, east and west, and curving again toward the south. Around us are the towering walls of the Wingate formation, sheer and monolithic sandstone, and above and beyond that the Kayenta and then the buff-colored domes and elephant backs of the Navajo. The new moon is waxing overhead, pale fragment of a moon in the same hot blue sky as the sun.

Back to the river and right on schedule comes the wind and another battle—for boatmen the wind always seems to be blowing upstream, no matter which way the river flows. After a struggle we camp on a strip of bottomland across from Spring Canyon. This is in a sooty grove of burntover cottonwoods; not a pleasant place. But we are too tired, wet, cold, and hungry to go on; and furthermore Malcolm has broken one end of his kayak paddle and my boat has sprung a leak.

In the morning there is frost on the ground. But this marks the turn in the weather—from now on each day will be hotter, calmer, more beautiful. My boat patched, Malcolm's paddle repaired, we forge ahead through perfect stillness under a flawless sky. The voyage becomes dreamlike, a reverie, as we drift on and on under golden canyon walls. The century that divides in time our trip from Major Powell's has dwindled to nothing, a mere abstract point in the temporal:

> There is an exquisite charm in our ride today down this beautiful canyon. It gradually grows deeper with every mile of travel; the walls are symmetrically curved and grandly arched, of a beautiful color, and reflected in the quiet waters in many places so as almost to deceive the eye and suggest to the beholder the thought that he is looking into profound depths. We are all in fine spirits.

Exactly: And just as he did, we amuse ourselves in bouncing echos off the magnificent walls; or meditate; or Malcolm plays the harmonica while Harvey trails a hook and line in the water, feeling for catfish, and I scribble these notes under the shade of my hat.

The canyon widens for a spell, the walls roll away toward the upland benches and mesas. We land at the mouth of Horseshoe Canyon. Malcolm climbs a sandy hill for a look at the outside world, while I go upstream with the jugs and canteens in search of spring water.

Back on the river, through a calm and beauteous afternoon, we pass the half-sunken wreckage of an old ferryboat, washed here from somewhere far up the river, perhaps from where the highway now bridges the Green at the town of Green River. We cruise into the midst of a flock of coots, small, dark brown water birds with bright orange eyes; they dive like mechanical toys as we come near, then surface quickly only a few feet away.

The canyon walls close in again and rise still higher, at least 1,000 feet above the river. Late in the afternoon we stop at Woodruff's Bottom, make camp on a fine sandy beach where big rocks jut into the current and bullfrogs croak in a muddy lagoon.

Taking the names from our topographic map, we pass a whole series of bottomlands today, including one called Queen Anne Bottom. Most of these have been named after or by early Mormon settlers, but who Queen Anne was we're not likely to find out down here on the river. On some of these places we see unbranded horses, a few burros and many deer, but no cattle. Many of these places are inaccessible by land.

At one bend in the river we find an old log cabin, abandoned but in good shape, and on a knoll above it an ancient ruin of unmortared stone, an Anasazi lookout tower that might be six or seven centuries old. We climb up to it and get a splendid view of the winding river, the buttes and mesas, and the high plateaus on the east and west. Certain landmarks I recognize—Grandview Point, Junction Butte, Bagpipe Butte, Land's End, the Orange Cliffs, Sixshooter Peak—but observed from below, at this unfamiliar angle, most of what I see is unknown to me.

The river cuts through the Cedar Mesa formation from here on, forming what is called the White Rim, overhanging walls full of glens and amphitheaters, polished with "desert varnish," painted with stains of organic material washed down from above.

In the afternoon we reach the rincon known as Anderson Bottom. There is a developed spring here, which makes it a popular stopping place for boating parties. We camp for the night and linger on for another day and night, exploring the deep and narrow grottolike canyons that wind off back into the tableland.

Somewhere in this region we leave Labyrinth Canyon and enter what Powell named Stillwater Canyon. The transition is difficult to mark; the river is running quite slowly, but it also ran slowly in Labyrinth Canyon, at a rate of only two or three miles per hour. In the whole distance from the town of Green River we have not met a single rapid; all the rapids, it appears, are concentrated below the confluence with the Colorado River in Cataract Cayon.

Today we see more ruins, tiny storage rooms in alcoves in the canyon wall, their approaches long since eroded away. We pass a great anvil-shaped sculpture in sandstone called the Turk's Head, a thing of formidable beauty 100 feet high and twice as long; my friend Malcolm, sculptor and painter, builder and creator, longs to try his hand at something similar—someday.

Near Horse Canyon, new rock formations rise on either side as our river works yet deeper into the crust of the earth. The sandstone walls are set back far above, out of sight; beside the water are rough, broken cliffs of red-coated limestone, eroded into a multitude of grotesque shapes of sinister aspect. The cliffs descend to the water on both sides. There is no place to land until we go up into the deep, dark, prisonlike recess of Horse Canyon. No water here, nothing but sand, mud, and gravel, and half a mile up the canyon an overhanging dry waterfall 100 feet high—we are enclosed, and if a flash flood should come, trapped. A night of bad dreams.

All goes well, however, and in the morning, gratefully, we leave the dark canyon and journey on.

Today is a day of discoveries, for we are entering the complex and fantastic region where the Green River meets the Colorado River, a little-known country that has been thoroughly mapped—from the air—but only partly explored from the ground. Many of the side canyons that enter the rivers here are shown on our 1963 Geological Survey topographic maps as without names. We are entitled, therefore, to name them ourselves, and everything else we discover, and we do.

Mud Hole Canyon, for example. This is our discovery and

our name, and because of the lovely things it contains I prefer not to specify its location. Say only that around noon, seeing this obscure and totally unpromising-looking canyon appear on one side, the sort of place no ordinary riverman would bother stopping to investigate, I suggest that we head in there and have a look. So we paddle across the current and through an eddy into an aisle of muddy water barely wide enough for our boats. We stroke up this passage in water six inches deep, around a bend between walls of clay and slime, and beach on a shore of pure gray bentonated muck, the kind of material that hardens like cement as it dries on your boots. No trace here of any stream coming down the canyon. We tie our boats to the tamarisk, in case the river should continue to rise, and slop through the mud, fight through the brush and into the rocky, open floor of the canyon.

Still no miracles to greet our eyes, only a view far up the canyon of a talus slope that appears to offer a way to the top, out of the depths in which we've been living for days now. We are terribly thirsty, sick of the silty river. We find a seep on the side of the canyon wall, the water trickling through moss and fern at the rate of about one drop every thirty seconds, each drop coming from a different point. We make futile efforts to catch the drops in the narrow opening of a canteen, finally give up and proceed farther up the canyon. Beyond the next bend we come to a slick rock chute, with a plunge pool in the sand, and sliding down the chute a rill of clear water.

Delighted, we climb the chute and find more running water, more and bigger pools filling the basins in the polished limestone beds. Cottonwood trees come in view as we go on, standing near ledges over which the stream tumbles in crystal waterfalls. Everywhere deer sign, nowhere the faintest trace of man. We have stumbled into a miniature Eden.

We climb the talus and from near the summit see, on the opposite wall, a great natural arch carved by weathering in a fin of the sandstone that overlays the limestone formations below. This arch, unnoted on our maps, lies beyond and above a branch of the lateral canyon we are now exploring, at a distance of a mile or more from where we stand, inaccessible, and so we can only guess its size. Judging from the junipers growing near its base, we estimate the opening of the arch to be fifty feet high and eighty or ninety feet wide. The span on top is slender and flat, like the handle on a water jug, and the buttresses thick and solid. The rock is rosy red on the sides, buff white on top. We name it Eden's Window.

We keep climbing until we reach the rim of our canyon and then a little higher onto the highest of the nearby sandstone domes. There we stand and look out upon a wonderland of color and form, a surrealistic never-never land of stone. This is the edge of the Maze, or what the Indians called *Toom'pin wunear' Tuweap'* ("Land of the Standing Rocks").

> The landscape everywhere, away from the river, is of rock—cliffs of rock, tables of rock—ten thousand strangely carved forms; rocks everywhere and no vegetation, no soil, no sand. . . .
>
> When thinking of these rocks one must not conceive of piles of boulders or heaps of fragments but of a whole land of naked rock, with giant forms carved on it; cathedral-shaped buttes, towering hundreds or thousands of feet, cliffs that cannot be scaled, and canyon walls that shrink the river into insignificance, with vast, hollow domes and tall pinnacles and shafts set on the verge overhead; and all highly colored—buff, gray, red, brown, and chocolate—never lichened, never moss-covered, but bare, and often polished. . . .
> On the summit of the opposite wall of the canyon are rock forms that we do not understand.

In page after page Powell strove to describe a kind of landscape neither he nor any of his men had ever seen before. He came closer than anyone else to evoking through words the character of the canyonlands. Yet the strangeness of it can barely be suggested through language. In fact, the land can hardly be understood through the eyes. The imagination cannot comprehend what is so remote from all previous experience—"rock forms that we do not understand."

Storms abuilding in the west, beyond Candlestick Spire, Lizard Rock, Bagpipe Butte, and Land's End. We take one last long look around—for who knows when or if ever we'll come this way again—from dazzling rock to the distant snow fields of the Sierra La Sal, then hurry down into the canyon, back to the boats, back on the motherly bosom of our river, the golden Green.

From here on all becomes faintly anticlimactic, at least for myself. We reach the confluence of the Green and Colorado rivers and cruise four miles beyond to Spanish Bottom at the head of Cataract Canyon. We camp on dunes of sand, beneath the shade of a giant willow tree. From downriver come the toneless vibrations of the rapids, and we see, looking that way, the brown waves leaping upward, curling with foam.

One wishes to go on. On this great river one could glide forever—and here we discover the definition of bliss, salvation, Heaven, all the old Mediterranean dreams: a journey from wonder to wonder, drifting through eternity into ever-deeper, always changing grandeur, through beauty continually surpassing itself: the ultimate Homeric voyage.

But for us, for the time being, the dream must end. We wait here on the dunes for the powerboat that will hustle us back to what they call Reality. Well, and with some justice, let's grant them that: We're damn near out of grub, mates, and the catfish are not biting. Put that in your pipe and smoke it—take a deep drag and hold it—you'll see what you thought was unseeable. Here comes the fool moon through the cloudy symbols. Godlike faces gape at the stars. Farewell for now, beloved river, and goodbye to you, too, old

comrade, one-armed vision seeker with your wooden boat
your moldy bacon and your silted flour, your gallant crew,
and your never-dying romance with the world:

> We are three-quarters of a mile in the depths of the earth,
> and the great river shrinks into insignificance as it dashes
> its angry waves against the walls and cliffs that rise to the
> world above; the waves are but puny ripples, and we but
> pygmies, running up and down the sands or lost among
> the boulders.
> We have an unknown distance yet to run, an unknown
> river to explore.

18

Walking

Whenever possible I avoid the practice myself. If God had meant us to walk, he would have kept us down on all fours, with well-padded paws. He would have constructed our planet on the model of the simple cube, so that the notion of circularity and consequently the wheel might never have arisen. He surely would not have made mountains.

There is something unnatural about walking. Especially walking uphill, which always seems to me not only unnatural but so *unnecessary*. That iron tug of gravitation should be all the reminder we need that in walking uphill we are violating a basic law of nature. Yet we persist in doing it. No one can explain why. George H. Leigh-Mallory's asinine rationale for climbing a mountain—"because it's there"—could easily be refuted with a few well-placed hydrogen bombs. But our common sense continues to lag far behind the available technology.

My own first Group Outing was with the United States Infantry. The experience made a bad impression on my psyche—a blister on my soul that has never healed completely. Of course, we were outfitted with the very best hiking equipment the army could provide: heavy-gauge steel helmet; gas mask; knee-length wool overcoat; fully loaded ammunition belt around the waist, resting on the kidneys; full field pack including a shovel ("entrenching tool"), a rugged canvas tarpaulin ("shelter half") and a pair of wool blankets for bivouac; steel canteen filled with briny water (our group leader insisted on dumping salt tablets into each member's canteen at the beginning of the hike); and such obvious essentials as combat boots, bayonet, and the M-1 rifle. Since resigning from the infantry, some time ago, I have not participated in any group outings.

However, some of us do walk best under duress. Or only under duress. Certainly my own most memorable hikes can be classified as Shortcuts that Backfired. For example, showing my wife the easy way to drive down from Deadhorse Point to Moab, via Pucker Pass, I took a wrong turn in the twilight, got lost in a maze of jeep trails, ran out of gas. We walked about twenty miles that night, through the rain, she in tennis shoes and me in cowboy boots. Better than waiting for the heat of the day. Or take the time I tried to force a Hertz rented car up Elephant Hill on the Needles Jeep Trail—another long, impromptu walk. Or one night on the eastern outskirts of Albuquerque, New Mexico, when a bunch of student drunks decided to climb the Sandia Mountains by moonlight. About twelve started; two of us made it, arriving at the crest sixteen hours later, famished, disillusioned, lacerated, and exhausted. But it sure cured the hangover.

There are some good things to say about walking. Not many, but some. Walking takes longer, for example, than any other known form of locomotion except crawling. Thus it stretches time and prolongs life. Life is already too short to waste on speed. I have a friend who's always in a hurry; he never gets anywhere. Walking makes the world much bigger and therefore more interesting. You have time to observe the details. The utopian technologists foresee a future for us in which distance is annihilated and anyone can transport himself anywhere, instantly. Big deal, Buckminster. To be everywhere at once is to be nowhere forever, if you ask me. That's God's job, not ours; that's what we pay Him for. Her for.

The longest journey begins with a single step, not with a turn of the ignition key. That's the best thing about walking, the journey itself. It doesn't much matter whether you get where you're going or not. You'll get there anyway. Every good hike brings you eventually back home. Right where you started.

Which reminds me of circles. Which reminds me of wheels. Which reminds me my old truck needs another front-end job. Any good mechanics out there, wandering through the smog?

19

The Crooked Wood

For four seasons I worked as a fire lookout on the North Rim of the Grand Canyon. To get to my job I walked for a mile and a half each morning up a trail through a dense grove of quaking aspens. I called this grove "the crooked wood" because the trees there, nearly all of them, have been curiously deformed. The trunks are bent in shapes that seem more whimsical than natural: dog legs, S-curves, elbows, knees. The deformity is always found in the lower part of the trunk, four or five feet above the ground. Above that level the trunks assume the vertical attitude normal to aspens, supporting the usual symmetric umbrella of graceful, delicately suspended, dancing leaves which gives this tree its specific name, *tremuloides.*

Why the deformation? The explanation is simple. On the North Rim, at an elevation of 8,000 to 9,000 feet above sea level, winter snows are heavy. In well-shaded places, such as the ridge where my crooked grove is found, massive drifts of snow survive through May and into June, overlapping part of the growing season. Under the creeping weight and pressure of these snowdrifts the young aspens—seedling and sapling—grow as best they can, in whatever direction they must, through spring after spring, seeking the sunlight that is their elixir, until they reach a height where their growth is not affected by the snow.

The life of trees. We know so little about this strange planet we live on, this haunted world where all answers lead only to more mystery. The character of trees, for example, their feelings, emotions, personalities—Shelley was not the first to speak of "the sensitive plant." The mandrake, they believed, screams when uprooted. Contemporary researchers suggest that plants respond to music (preferring Mozart to the Rolling Stones, I'm not surprised to hear) and to human emotions. I'm inclined to believe it. And I'm the type inclined to doubt. But four seasons of solitary walking under those aspen trees, through the green translucence of summer and the golden radiance of autumn, alone in the stillness of the forest, can do queer things to a man's common sense.

We think we perceive character or "personality" in the shape, face, eyes of our fellow humans; why not find something similar in the appearance of plants—especially trees? How avoid it? Obvious analogies come at once to mind: the solemnity of the dark, heavy, brooding spruce; the honest, hopeful nobility of the yellow pine; the anxiety of white fir; the remote grandeur of the bristlecone pine; the brightness, the gaiety, the charm, the feminine sensitivity, the aspiring joyousness of *Populus tremuloides.* (Our name; what the aspen calls itself we may never know.)

I can hear the laughter down in the pit and up in the peanut gallery as I write these vulnerable words. (I'm a hard-nosed empiricist myself, one who believes only in what he can hear, see, smell, grab, bite into, so I understand.) But—I repeat—if you could spend as I did the sweeter part of four good years in that forest, scanning a sea of treetops for a twist of smoke, walking beneath that canopy of leaves in the chill clear mornings and again in the evenings—evenings sometimes full of golden peace and sometimes charged with storm and lightning—you too might begin to wonder, not only about yourself but also about those *beings*, alive, sentient, transpiring, which surround you. Especially the aspens, the quaking aspens, always so vibrant with light and motion, forever restless, always whispering, in tune like ballerinas to the music of the air. Walking there day after day, among those slim trim trees, so innocent (it seems) in their white and green or white and gold, you become aware after a while not only of the trees but of the trees' awareness of you. What they felt I had no notion of; I never got to know them well as individuals. But their conscious presence was unmistakable. I was not alone.

My father has been a logger, sawyer, and woodsman for most of his life. I myself have put in a fair share of time with ax, crosscut saw, chain saw, sledge, and wedge at the reduction of trees into fuel, post, and lumber. I understand and sympathize with the reasonable needs of a reasonable number of people on a finite continent. All men and women require shelter. All life depends upon other life. But what is happening today, in North America, is not rational use but irrational massacre. Man the Pest, multiplied to the swarming stage, is attacking the remaining forests like a plague of locusts on a field of grain. Knowing now what we have learned, unless the need were urgent, I could no more sink the blade of an ax into the tissues of a living tree than I could drive it into the flesh of a fellow human.

20

Mountain Music

The Lure of the Mountains

What am I doing here? I don't know anything about mountains. I am not a geographer, understand nothing of geology, and have never gone near the foothills of Annapurna. I am certainly no mountaineer: My notion of a mountain climb is a hike up the trail to Mount Whitney or one of Colorado's easier 14,000-footers. My only qualification for writing about them lies in a certain reluctant affection I have for these wrinkles, bulges, eruptions, and fractures on the earth's surface that we call mountains.

For me it began in the Allegheny Mountains of western Pennsylvania, on the little submarginal farm where I was born and raised. Though called "mountains" on the map, those ancient and rolling hills are but the northern fringe of the real Appalachians, which are in turn only remnants of a much greater range that once existed there. Nevertheless, the Alleghenies are high enough to excite the imagination of a boy. My latent acrophilia was brought out soon enough by excursions upward across the cow pasture under the lightning-blasted shagbark hickories—trees thus endowed with magical powers, according to Shawnee Indian lore—up through the cornfields where we labored (not too hard) in the stifling heat of September, up through the second-growth woods of maple, white oak, beech, poplar, walnut, up the path to the spring where we kept a pint Mason jar up-ended on a root. From there, the path led to the summit of the hill, where tracts of wood shared living space with the wide-open fields of hay.

Where does the line "High on a windy hill" come from? I cannot remember. But it evokes at once the spirit and the atmosphere of those skyward excursions. Clouds soaring by, the soft and melting clouds of Pennsylvania on the gentle Watteau blue of the Pennsylvanian sky. Down below—far below I would have said then—I could see the red barns, the white farmhouses, the green and yellow fields, the meanders of Crooked Creek, the winding ways of the country roads passing among the hills from farm to farm, those narrow lanes surfaced with red slag from the mines; we called them "red-dog" roads.

From the hills of home to the heights of the Himalayas is a long journey. All downward, maybe. A journey which, in any case, I have yet to complete. But the next step, right or not, was westward to the Rockies. Seventeen years old and ignorant as any other yokel, I took off one summer to see the country.

On a bright day in middle June, walking out past the

junkyards, feedlots, and gas stations of a small town in Wyoming, I saw for the first time in my life the shining peaks of the Rocky Mountains. The snow-covered range gleamed in the morning sun, sixty or seventy miles away, floating like a rampart of clouds across the western horizon. To me, who had never before seen hills higher than 2,000 feet above valley level, it seemed a fantastic sight. The magnetic mountains.

After that came others, a lifetime of mountains viewed in the summers of youth. I saw the Wind River Range, the Sawtooth Mountains, the Absarokas, and the Bitterroots. In California I spent a month wandering through the High Sierras from Yosemite to Mount Whitney and down the other side to Lone Pine in the Owens Valley.

Hitchhiking across the Mojave Desert one August, I had my first taste of desert mountains: the Calicos, the Chocolates, the Panamints, the Chuckawallas, and the Needle Peaks of Arizona at the Colorado River. Out of the infernal valley, I came to high country again and saw Music Mountain, Bill Williams Mountain, the San Francisco Peaks near Flagstaff, and then the mountains of New Mexico—Mount Taylor, El Ladrón, the Sandias, the Manzanos, and the Sangre de Cristos.

A taste of mountains; I could not say I had come to *know* them in any significant way. All I had learned was something about myself. I had discovered that I am the kind of person who cannot live comfortably, tolerably, on all-flat terrain. For the sake of inner equilibrium there has to be at least one mountain range on at least one of the four quarters of my horizon—and not more than a day's walk away.

Shipped to Italy by the United States Army, the first thing I did on my first weekend pass was trudge up the cinder slopes of Mount Vesuvius for a look into its evil, stinking crater. I had missed the latest eruption by one year, but there was enough thermal activity still going on down in the volcano's burbling pit to give me an idea of the internal na-

ture of this planet we play on. One could do worse than be
an inspector of volcanoes. Months later, in the middle of
winter, I made a railway tour of the Alps. The spectacle of
the Matterhorn from Zermatt, the Jungfrau from In-
terlaken, roused ancestral memories: My father's father
lived in a village in Canton Berne. One might well become,
like Herr Settembrini in *The Magic Mountain,* a philosopher
of high places.

THE MADNESS OF THE MOUNTAINS

All very well to look at the things, I tell myself, and very
nice to have a view of snow-covered peaks out the picture
window, but why in God's name does anyone want to climb
them? A good question, as fitting now as when asked of
Leigh-Mallory back in the early twenties. Why? is always a
good question; the one question that distinguishes the
human from all the other brutes. Mallory's answer, "Because
it's there," is not entirely satisfactory, except of course to
other climbers, who climb first and seek answers afterward.
To the question, Why? Mallory answers in effect, Why not?
and disappears forever into the wind and snow at 28,000
feet. His answer is at once too broad and too narrow, all-
embracing yet not adequate. The nonclimber demands a ful-
ler reply.

In my opinion Mallory and his fellow climber Andrew Irvine did actually make it to the summit of Everest on that
desperate day in early June 1924. When last seen they had
surmounted all serious obstacles except the weather and the
lateness of the day; they were less than 1,000 feet from the
top. This was Mallory's third serious attempt, and he probably felt, as Thoreau had said, now or never. Never mind that
they were five hours behind schedule; no matter that they'd
have to descend in darkness. This was the best opportunity
they would ever have for the mountaineer's ultimate victory.
Why not? thought Mallory, plodding on and upward. And
What the hell, said Irvine. And they went on, and made it too;

they stood for a few moments on the top of the world, the highest place on earth, and planted the expedition flag there as sign of their conquest. (The same tattered flag and stick that Sir Edmund Hillary casually kicked over the edge, before Tensing could see it, in the spring of 1953.) But as we know they never found their way back down to the safety of Camp Six or the North Col and so we do not have Mallory's final answer to the question. We have only two more martyrs for the hagiography of mountain climbing and as relic the single ice ax, made by Willish of Tasch, that Wager and Harris found on the northeast ridge of Everest in 1933—nine years after the vanishing of Mallory.

Why? Was death his answer? It is not merely death by falling that threatens the climber. Such accidents can generally be avoided through care, skill, patience, the proper equipment. More difficult, often impossible to escape, are the pain and misery and sickness of mountaineering, especially as the English say, "at altitude." Above 20,000 feet, in that realm of everlasting ice and snow, where I for one have no intention of ever setting foot (probably), the human body encounters varieties of stress unknown to lowlanders. Nausea, loss of appetite, cruel headaches, heart strain, pulmonary edema, and pulmonary embolism can afflict even the young and healthy. Plus the usual risks found in the arctic weather of high altitudes: frostbite, hypothermia, pneumonia. At least fourteen men are known to have died in the various assaults, so far, upon Everest. Eight Russian climbers recently died of exhaustion and exposure at 22,000 feet in the Pamirs. The first successful climb of Annapurna by Maurice Herzog and his party almost resulted in fatalities, and several of his climbers lost fingers and toes because of frostbite. In Hillary's 1961 Himalayan expedition all his men suffered severely from altitude sickness after two months spent above 19,000 feet; one member of the party had to have both feet amputated as a consequence of frostbite.

Those are the hazards, but we have not yet mentioned

simple exhaustion, the ordeal of dragging one foot after the other, against all reason and gravity, up over rock and snow toward the sky, with pack on back, the agony of unnatural effort that begins at the very foot of the mountain. Here I can speak from personal experience. I find that first step upward so difficult that each time I begin the ascent of a mountain I swear to myself, Never again. I say, and mean it, This is the last time. The body objects, the heart and lungs complain, and gravity, with arms of lead, drags at our limbs, pulls down our vanity. And yet the pain of it all is soon forgotten (like childbirth, they say), and a week or a month or a half-year later we're at it again, trudging with iron shoes and pig-iron on the back up yet another mountain trail, toward one more ugly, meaningless, and brutal rockpile in the sky. If we did it for pay, we'd call it slave labor. What punishment could be so cruel and unusual as that which is self-inflicted?

And yet, and yet. . . . It is not enough to say we climb a given mountain because no one else has done it. Even if true, that is not sufficient. Nor will it do to say, simply, "Somebody has to do it." They won't believe you. Most mountains have now been climbed anyhow, some of them many times. (The trail up Mount Whitney looks, on Labor Day weekends, like a pilgrimage to Purgatory, each hiker bearing his cross, harnessed to an ass's pack, bent beneath the weight of guilt and conscience, silent and sullen, toiling upward, upward, ever upward on the stony path, toward the cold bleak repellent summit, through wind, sleet, the thin unnourishing air, threatened from time to time by fangs of lightning from the gloomy clouds.)

Then why? We have not yet answered this elementary question, and perhaps no one ever will answer it to the satisfaction of nonclimbers. But one must attempt the answer.

To dare! to dare! ever to dare! said Danton, speaking of revolution and giving us the metaphor we need. Reproduction and mere survival never have been good enough for humankind. We torture one another, we torture ourselves, we torture the universe with our questioning, our endless strife, the tedious struggle against death. Even a simple hike up Whitney, even the mild walk and scramble to the apex of Sierra Blanca in Colorado (last week's holiday), involves that element of risk and effort which compensates for the usual banality of our lives. *We love the taste of freedom. We enjoy the smell of danger.* We take pleasure in the consummation of mental, spiritual, and physical effort; it is the achievement of the summit that brings the three together, stamps them with the harmony and unity of a point. Of a meaning.

Trite solution to our problem, but there is no better: Men and women climb mountains—whether in the Rockies or in the Himalayas—for the same reason that they blast off in rockets to the moon, launch poems and prayers at the stars, send symphonies of thought, music, mathematics, and fiction into the highest and deepest reaches of the human soul. Because . . . it's something to do. Because, there's nothing better to do. Because of all our terrors none is more terrible than boredom, the nothingness of a static existence, the infantile paralysis of Saturday night in Page, Arizona. Anything, anything—death in a drunk tank!—rather than that.

THE TRIUMPH OF THE MOUNTAINS

Well, what the hell, all this rhapsodic bullshit explains nothing. Better just to drive the damn car as far up the hill as it would go, climb out and make camp and breathe in some altitude for a while. Some of that Colorado high. So—we turned off the pavement halfway between Ophir ("land of gold" in the Old Testament) and Rico (self-explanatory) near the summit of Lizard Head Pass, about 10,000 feet above sea level. We forded a brook, the water clear, deep as the hubcaps, drove up an old rutty road that leads north toward the peaks. The usual August afternoon rain had begun; the road was slippery and we only made two miles from the highway before it became impossible to go

on. I parked the car under some spruce and fir at the edge
of an overgrazed meadow grown up in thistle, dockweed,
and skunk cabbage. Not a beautiful meadow, I guess, but
there was plenty of firewood available, a stream rushing
nearby, and a good view of some excellent mountains.

The rain fell softly. We waited. When it slacked off, I got
out and chopped dry wood from the underside of a log,
built a fire. The air did not seem chilly, but my breath va-
porized as I exhaled. There was no wind. The blue smoke
from our chunks of burning white fir rose straight as a pillar
into the trees. The clouds broke up and the evening sun
shone through. Sheep Mountain, above Trout Lake, lit up
suddenly. Above timberline gleamed steep slopes of scree,
the gray and broken granite; above that lay the red rock, the
bands of iron and manganese oxides that give the San
Miguel Mountains a color most mountains lack, a touch of
the exotic and sinister; in the couloirs reposed beds of old
snow, dusted brown and red by the summer winds; a few icy
cornices clung to ridges. Crags, pinnacles, and battlements
of rotten-looking rock formed a jagged skyline.

The rain stopped completely a few minutes before sundown. My wife cooked supper, and I carried water up from
the stream and gathered more wood. The sky cleared toward the west and north. Now we could see Mount Wilson
emerging from the clouds and its neighbors Cross Mountain
and Wilson Peak. Lizard Head itself became visible, a chim-
neylike structure with vertical walls 500 feet high above its
immediate base.

My objective this time was Wilson Peak, 14,017 feet above
sea level. The previous summer I had tried to climb Mount
Wilson, a couple of hundred feet higher and much more
rugged. A friend and I walked up the southwest ridge, in
bad weather as usual. We got to the 13,000-foot level before
giving up in the midst of a blizzard. The visibility was down
to thirty feet, we did not know anything about the route
ahead, we were getting cold and hungry and decided we

didn't really want to go on up that mountain on that day anyhow.

Two years earlier I had made a half-hearted attempt on Mount Sneffels, another 14,000-footer in the Uncompahgre Mountains, and failed that one too, again turning back some 1,000 feet below the summit. Too much sleet bouncing off my head, too much lightning bombarding the rocks. One thing I like about mountain climbing is that there are always plenty of excuses for turning back before disaster strikes. As it inevitably will anyhow, one of these days—but I don't know of any better way to meet that little mystery. Unless it's down in the canyons or far out on the Gran Desierto. Anything rather than the ultimate horror: death in a hospital bed, surrounded by the engines of medical technology and technicians making notes.

It seems a nuisance that the subject of death should continually obtrude itself, when I would rather talk about silverleaf lupine and blue columbine. But somehow it keeps coming up, along with the bracing mountain air, the white roar of the waterfalls, the stillness of timberline, the clarity of the peaks. Nothing morbid in this. Quite the contrary; it is the sense of danger and mortality that adds to the excitement and the joy of being still here, friends, still hanging around.

The new moon followed the sun, down beyond the mountain. We sat for a while longer by the fire, Renée and I, sipping at a bottle of cognac, making contingency plans. Cold air mass gathering at our backs. We went to bed early, since I was planning to get up early for a head start on the weather. August is not the best of months for hiking in the Colorado Alps. Zipped together in our downy cocoon we watched the stars and clouds, listened to the tumbling stream, fell off the mountain into dreams.

The morning looked good, but I wasted too much time getting started. I put on fresh socks and threw some jerky and an orange and a parka into my day pack and started up the trail. My wife accompanied me for a couple of miles, then veered off to photograph flowers and mushrooms. This was going to be a solo hike. She does not suffer from the compulsion to keep walking upward until there is no farther upward to walk to.

As always I found the first part painful, begrudging the drag of gravity that seems like blind harassment on nature's part. But again as always the steady plod pays off, something truly like second wind comes into play. You forget the burden of uphill walking and begin to notice and think about more interesting things.

A pair of big brown mule deer, for example, on the far side of a marshy meadow. I noted them a moment before they spotted me and instinctively I froze. I waited. They shuffled around nervously, unhappy about my presence, but finally returned to their browsing. I sank slowly to my knees and flat on my belly and crawled toward a log that shielded me from their line of sight. I carried my walking stick like a rifle before me. I haven't done any deer hunting for ten years but it seems just as well to keep in practice. When I reached the log I slid my "rifle" carefully on top of it and raised my eyes for a good easy 100-yard broadside shot at the nearest doe. But all I saw was a black tail and pale rump vanishing into the woods beyond. Yes, we will need practice.

Upward through the forest under the dark and shaggy spruce, the tall tapered spires of the fir. Glens of quaking aspen here and there. Open meadows bright with yarrow, fireweed, goldenrod, and sunshine, despite clouds beginning to form above.

Aside from the deer the wildlife was keeping mostly hidden. I saw gray squirrels and chipmunks, the tracks and scat of coyote along the trail, a lot of jays, woodpeckers, and Clark's nutcrackers in the trees. At timberline I flushed a covey of white-tailed ptarmigan from among the rocks; pikas began to whistle at me, those plump rusty-furred rodents that spend their entire lives in the alpine zone.

The high forest has its charms, but I think I love most the timberline regions. The taiga, the tundra, and the tarn. Here the trees are few and scattered, growing close to earth. The world opens out and one begins to understand what we're doing up here. There's Lizard Head butte, which bears no resemblance to any lizard I ever saw, towering on my right. Above is the pass between Lizard Head and Cross Mountain, both of them over 13,000 feet above sea level, and beyond the pass loom Mount Wilson and Wilson Peak, fearsome-looking 14,000-footers joined to one another by a knife-edge ridge.

The trail leads ever upward, switchbacking through fields of flowers shimmering in the wind, shining with color— purple lupine, Indian paintbrush, scarlet penstemon, sky-rocket gilia, bluebell, larkspur, columbine, monkshood, sun-flowers, fleabane, chickory, purple aster—all massed together in an astonishing statement of first principles. That ancient creed which insists on the primacy of fecundity, an open invitation to what His Holiness called "the banquet of life." Whose holiness? Well, the flowers' holiness. Lewis Mumford has pointed out that flowers began to appear on earth at about the time the mammals were taking over from the dying dynasts of the giant reptiles. The association of flowers and warm-blooded love is more than a romantic convention; it is based upon one of the great advances in the evolution of life.

Flowers, the wind, the sound of waterfalls, the air like a clear thin music passing across the walls of rock, sun blazing down from a violet sky—though tired, sweating, hungry, I felt again the exhilaration of high places. Beyond the crest of the pass I sat down on the sunny side of a rock, out of the wind, and ate my lunch.

Mount Wilson hangs over me on the west, an appalling skyscraper of red and gray rock and suspended snowfields. Wilson Peak, its lesser mate, looks more reasonable, despite a sprinkling of fresh snow. That snow must have fallen during yesterday's storm. It lies deep in the cracks and crevices that zigzag up the mountain's flanks.

From the summit of the pass it is necessary to descend into the U-shaped glacial cirque of Bilk Creek. I walked down the trail, reluctant to lose hard-earned elevation, but the only alternative would have been an up-and-down scramble across the loose rock on the slopes of Cross Mountain and Mount Wilson.

Down in the bottom of the drainage basin I crossed the creek and resumed the upward trudge, following the cobbled remains of an old mining road. I was well above timberline. To the northeast I could see Sneffels and other peaks that rise above Telluride and Ouray. Clouds were gathering all around, high-piled billows of dazzling white. Below I saw two hikers with backpacks descending the trail along Bilk Creek, in retreat. There is a general rule: Get off the peaks by one o'clock. The sun was now noon-high. Even so, plenty of open sky remained; with a little luck in the weather I might still make it to the top before the storm began.

Plodding upward over the rock. Pausing every twenty or thirty paces for a blow. I was in lousy shape, as usual, hauling my beer belly and my flat feet and my irritable undisciplined brain up this absurd bulge of granite. How much nicer and more sensible, I thought, to be back in camp, sitting on a log, drinking Coors out of a can, watching my wife (bless her) cooking up some kind of a stew in the old Dutch oven. These treacherous thoughts did not slow my pace. I kept going, trying to avoid the streams of water running among the stones of the trail. Snowbanks were melting up above, torrents gushing from caves in the ice.

In the basin above the cirque I passed shallow lakes, emerald green when viewed from the trail, turquoise blue when seen from above. Cascades tumbled through gorges in the rock, disappearing beneath the casual wreckage of the mountains to emerge as flashing brooks at the head of the lakes. Almost everything in sight was stone or water or vapor, as in the beginning, except for the miniature pastures of grass and turf—like putting greens—where the pikas make their living. The mountain glittered under the sun with that harsh perfection characteristic of God's early work. Almost too perfect; I should have brought a few beer cans to throw around, give the place a natural look.

Near the sun, near the snow, in the highest fields. We're up in the world of broken stone, sliding rock, frozen snow. Life, however, continues even here. Little black spiders with gray abdomens scuttle over the stone; rosy-headed finches, busy at something, flit low across the scree.

A shadow passes, its chill touching my skin, and snowflakes, genuine August snowflakes, delicate, whimsical and ephemeral, come floating on the air. A big lid covers half the sky. The snow is followed by a drizzle of rain. I step into an old cabin at the 12,000-foot level, the remains of some gold miner's shack that the Telluride Mountaineering School has rebuilt. I wait there for a while, nibbling on jerky, but the light rain continues. I put on my parka and go on. The clouds are moving so fast across the sky it seems possible the weather may clear again.

The trail leads up to the saddle between the two great peaks. I plod up a snowfield, kicking steps as I go, then up more loose rock, following the vestige of a path, and reach the col. I look down the other side at red and gray rockslides, patches of snow, alpine lakes, old test holes, and miners' diggings. The sky looks unfavorable, with mountains of black clouds storming my way, trailing curtains of sleet, rain, snow, rumbling with thunder. The peaks are socked in, out of sight though no more than 1,000 feet above. Shall I go on? I feel exhausted but I always feel that way at 13,000 feet; I know my rubbery legs well enough to know that from here on up it's a matter of mind more than muscle, a simple choice between victory or defeat again, triumph or ignominy. Should I go on?

I can't see a thing up there but purling vapors. The wind wails through the pass, my ears are aching from the cold, pellets of frozen snow patter on my hood, gathering in clusters on the ground. The rock will soon be wet and slippery. And I don't like the sound of that thunder, though still miles away. A lightning storm can develop on these peaks within five minutes. Go on?

Remember Mallory! I tell myself, summoning up courage. Okay, I reply, I remember. He disappeared into eternity, becoming a hero. I want to be a hero too—but not just yet. Coward? Right! With the courage of conviction I turn and descend the rocks, glissade down the snowfield, retreat to Bilk Creek and up to Lizard Head and down the other side to camp, five miles away, while the sky boils and the lightning crackles and I realize that I might have done it anyway. That I almost did. No matter.

The mountain is still there, waiting for me. All of them out there, all those mountains around the world, waiting for us.

That's the good part. We'll be back.

2 I

Shadows from the Big Woods

The idea of wilderness needs no defense. It only needs more defenders.

In childhood the wilds seemed infinite. Along Crooked Creek in the Allegheny Mountains of western Pennsylvania there was a tract of forest we called the Big Woods. The hemlock, beech, poplar, red oak, white oak, maple, and shagbark hickory grew on slopes so steep they had never been logged. Vines of wild grape trailed from the limbs of ancient druidical oaks—dark glens of mystery and shamanism. My brothers and I, simple-minded farmboys, knew nothing of such mythologies, but we were aware, all the same, of the magic residing among and within those trees. We knew that the Indians had once been here, Seneca and Shawnee, following the same deer paths that wound through fern, moss, yarrow, and mayapple among the massive trunks in the green-gold light of autumn, from spring to stream and marsh. Those passionate warriors had disappeared a century before we were even born, but their spirits lingered, their shades still informed the spirit of the place. We knew they were there. The vanished Indians were reincarnated, for a few transcendent summers, in our bones, within our pale Caucasian skins, in our idolatrous mimicry. We knew all about moccasins and feathers, arrows and bows, the thrill of sneaking naked through the underbrush, taking care to tread on not a single dry twig. Our lore came from boys' books, but it was the forest that made it real.

My brother Howard could talk to trees. Johnny knew how to start a fire without matches, skin a squirrel, and spot the eye of a sitting rabbit. I was an expert on listening to mourning doves, though not on interpretation, and could feel pleasure in the clapperclaw of crows. The wolf was long gone from those woods, and also the puma, but there were still plenty of deer, as well as bobcat and raccoon and gray fox; sometimes a black bear, or the rumor of one, passed through the hills. That was good country then, the country of boyhood, and the woods, the forest, that sultry massed deepness of transpiring green, formed the theater of our play. We invented our boyhood as we grew along; but the forest—in which it was possible to get authentically lost—sustained our sense of awe and terror in ways that fantasy cannot.

Now I would not care to revisit those faraway scenes. That forest which seemed so vast to us was only a small thing after all, as the bulldozers, earth movers, and dragline shovels have proved. The woods we thought eternal have been logged by methods formerly considered too destructive, and the very mountainside on which the forest grew has been butchered by the strip miners into a shape of crude symmetry, with spoil banks and head walls and right-angled escarpments where even the running blackberry has a hard time finding a roothold. Stagnant water fills the raw gulches, and the creek below runs sulfur-yellow all year long.

Something like a shadow has fallen between present and past, an abyss wide as war that cannot be bridged by any tangible connection, so that memory is undermined and the image of our beginnings betrayed, dissolved, rendered not mythical but illusory. We have connived in the murder of our own origins. Little wonder that those who travel nowhere but in their own heads, reducing all existence to the space of one skull, maintain dreamily that only the pinpoint tip of the moment is real. They are right: A fanatical greed, an arrogant stupidity, has robbed them of the past and transformed their future into a nightmare. They deny the world because the only world they know has denied them.

Our cancerous industrialism, reducing all ideological differences to epiphenomena, has generated its own breed of witch doctor. These are men with a genius for control and organization, and the lust to administrate. They propose first to shrink our world to the dimensions of a global village, over which some technological crackpot will erect a geodesic dome to regulate air and light; at the same time the planetary superintendent of schools will feed our children via endless belt into reinforcement-training boxes where they will be conditioned for their functions in the anthill arcology of the future. The ideal robot, after all, is simply a properly processed human being.

The administrators laying out the blueprints for the technological totalitarianism of tomorrow like to think of the earth as a big space capsule, a machine for living. They are wrong: The earth is not a mechanism but an organism, a being with its own life and its own reasons, where the support and sustenance of the human animal is incidental. If man in his newfound power and vanity persists in the attempt to remake the planet in his own image, he will succeed only in destroying himself—not the planet. The earth will survive our most ingenious folly.

Meanwhile, though, the Big Woods is gone—or going fast. And the mountains, the rivers, the canyons, the seashores, the swamps, and the deserts. Even our own, the farms, the towns, the cities, all seem to lie helpless before the advance of the technoindustrial juggernaut. We have created an iron monster with which we wage war, not only on small peasant nations over the sea, but even on ourselves—a war against all forms of life, against life itself. In the name of Power and Growth. But the war is only beginning.

The Machine may seem omnipotent, but it is not. Human bodies and human wit, active here, there, everywhere, united in purpose, independent in action, can still face that machine and stop it and take it apart and reassemble it—if we wish—on lines entirely new. There is, after all, a better way to live. The poets and the prophets have been trying to tell us about it for three thousand years.

22

Freedom and Wilderness, Wilderness and Freedom

When I lived in Hoboken, just across the lacquered Hudson from Manhattan, we had all the wilderness we needed. There was the waterfront with its decaying piers and abandoned warehouses, the jungle of bars along River Street and Hudson Street, the houseboats, the old ferry slips, the mildew-green cathedral of the Erie-Lackawanna Railway terminal. That was back in 1964–65: then came Urban Renewal, which ruined everything left lovable in Hoboken, New Jersey.

What else was there? I loved the fens, those tawny

marshes full of waterbirds, mosquitoes, muskrats, and opossums that intervened among the black basaltic rocks between Jersey City and Newark, and somewhere back of Union City on the way to gay, exotic, sausage-packing, garbage-rich Secaucus. I loved also and finally and absolutely, as a writer must love any vision of eschatological ultimates, the view by twilight from the Pulaski Skyway (Stop for Emergency Repairs Only) of the Seventh Circle of Hell. Those melancholy chemical plants, ancient as acid, sick as cyanide, rising beyond the cattails and tules; the gleam of oily waters in the refineries' red glare; the desolation of the endless, incomprehensible uninhabitable (but inhabited) slums of Harrison, Newark, Elizabeth; the haunting and sinister odors on the wind. Rust and iron and sunflowers in the tangled tracks, the great grimy sunsets beyond the saturated sky. . . . It will all be made, someday, a national park of the mind, a rigid celebration of industrialism's finest frenzy.

We tried north too, up once into the Catskills, once again to the fringe of the Adirondacks. All I saw were Private Property Keep Out This Means You signs. I live in a different country now. Those days of longing, that experiment in exile, are all past. The far-ranging cat returns at last to his natural, native habitat. But what wilderness there was in those bitter days I learned to treasure. Foggy nights in greasy Hoboken alleyways kept my soul alert, healthy and aggressive, on edge with delight.

The other kind of wilderness is also useful. I mean now the hardwood forests of upper Appalachia, the overrated mountains of Colorado, the burnt sienna hills of South Dakota, the raw umber of Kansas, the mysterious swamps of Arkansas, the porphyritic mountains of purple Arizona, the mystic desert of my own four-cornered country—this and 347 other good, clean, dangerous places I could name.

Science is not sufficient. "Ecology" is a word I first read in H. G. Wells twenty years ago and I still don't know what it means. Or seriously much care. Nor am I primarily concerned with nature as living museum, the preservation of spontaneous plants and wild animals. The wildest animal I know is you, gentle reader, with this helpless book clutched in your claws. No, there are better reasons for keeping the wild wild, the wilderness open, the trees up and the rivers free, and the canyons uncluttered with dams.

We need wilderness because we are wild animals. Every man needs a place where he can go to go crazy in peace. Every Boy Scout troop deserves a forest to get lost, miserable, and starving in. Even the maddest murderer of the sweetest wife should get a chance for a run to the sanctuary of the hills. If only for the sport of it. For the terror, freedom, and delirium. Because we need brutality and raw adventure, because men and women first learned to love in, under, and all around trees, because we need for every pair of feet and legs about ten leagues of naked nature, crags to leap from, mountains to measure by, deserts to finally die in when the heart fails.

The prisoners in Solzhenitsyn's labor camps looked out on the vast Siberian forests—within those shadowy depths lay the hope of escape, of refuge, of survival, of hope itself—but guns and barbed wire blocked the way. The citizens of our American cities enjoy a high relative degree of political, intellectual, and economic liberty; but if the entire nation is urbanized, industrialized, mechanized, and administered, then our liberties continue only at the sufferance of the technological megamachine that functions both as servant and master, and our freedoms depend on the pleasure of the privileged few who sit at the control consoles of that machine. What makes life in our cities at once still tolerable, exciting, and stimulating is the existence of an alternative option, whether exercised or not, whether even appreciated or not, of a radically different mode of being *out there*, in the forests, on the lakes and rivers, in the deserts, up in the mountains.

Who needs wilderness? Civilization needs wilderness. The idea of wilderness preservation is one of the fruits of civilization, like Bach's music, Tolstoy's novels, scientific medicine, novocaine, space travel, free love, the double martini, the secret ballot, the private home and private property, the public park and public property, freedom of travel, the Bill of Rights, peppermint toothpaste, beaches for nude bathing, the right to own and bear arms, the right not to own and bear arms, and a thousand other good things one could name, some of them trivial, most of them essential, all of them vital to that great, bubbling, disorderly, anarchic, unmanageable diversity of opinion, expression, and ways of living which free men and women love, which is their breath of life, and which the authoritarians of church and state and war and sometimes even art despise and always have despised. And feared.

The permissive society? What else? I love America because it *is* a confused, chaotic mess—and I hope we can keep it this way for at least another thousand years. The permissive society is the free society, the open society. Who gave us permission to live this way? Nobody did. *We* did. And that's the way it should be—only more so. The best cure for the ills of democracy is more democracy.

The boundary around a wilderness area may well be an artificial, self-imposed, sophisticated construction, but once inside that line you discover the artificiality beginning to drop away; and the deeper you go, the longer you stay, the more interesting things get—sometimes fatally interesting. And that too is what we want: Wilderness is and should be a place where, as in Central Park, New York City, you have a fair chance of being mugged and buggered by a shaggy fellow in a fur coat—one of Pooh Bear's big brothers. To be alive is to take risks; to be always safe and secure is death.

Enough of these banalities—no less true anyhow—which most of us embrace. But before getting into the practical applications of this theme, I want to revive one more argument for the preservation of wilderness, one seldom heard but always present, in my own mind at least, and that is the political argument.

Democracy has always been a rare and fragile institution in human history. Never was it more in danger than now, in the dying decades of this most dangerous of centuries. Within the past few years alone we have seen two more relatively open societies succumb to dictatorship and police rule—Chile and India. In all of Asia there is not a single free country except Israel—which, as the Arabs say, is really a transplanted piece of Europe. In Africa, obviously going the way of Latin America, there are none. Half of Europe stagnates under one-man or one-party domination. Only Western Europe and Britain, Australia and New Zealand, perhaps Japan, and North America can still be called more or less free, open, democratic societies.

As I see it, our own nation is not free from the danger of dictatorship. And I refer to internal as well as external threats to our liberties. As social conflict tends to become more severe in this country—and it will unless we strive for social justice—there will inevitably be a tendency on the part of the authoritarian element—always present in our history—to suppress individual freedoms, to utilize the refined techniques of police surveillance (not exluding torture, of course) in order to preserve—not wilderness!—but the status quo, the privileged positions of those who now so largely control the economic and governmental institutions of the United States.

If this fantasy should become reality—and fantasies becoming realities are the story of the twentieth century—then some of us may need what little wilderness remains as a place of refuge, as a hideout, as a base from which to carry on guerrilla warfare against the totalitarianism of my nightmares. I hope it does not happen; I believe we will prevent it from happening; but if it should, then I, for one, intend to light out at once for the nearest national forest, where I've been hiding cases of peanut butter, home-brew, ammunition, and C-rations for the last ten years. I haven't the slightest doubt that the FBI, the NSA, the CIA, and the local cops have dossiers on me a yard thick. If they didn't, I'd be insulted. Could I survive in the wilderness? I don't know—but I do know I could never survive in prison.

Could we as a people survive without wilderness? To consider that question we might look at the history of modern Europe, and of other places. As the Europeans filled up their small continent, the more lively among them spread out over the entire planet, seeking fortune, empire, a new world, a new chance—but seeking most of all, I believe, for adventure, for the opportunity of self-testing. Those nations that were confined by geography, bottled up, tended to find their outlet for surplus energy through war on their neighbors; the Germans provide the best example of this thesis. Nations with plenty of room for expansion, such as the Russians, tended to be less aggressive toward their neighbors.

In Asia we can see the same human necessities at work in somewhat different forms. Japan might be likened to Germany; a small nation with a large, ever-growing, vigorous, and intelligent population. Confined by the sea, their open spaces long ago occupied and domesticated, the Japanese like the Germans turned to war upon their neighbors, particularly China, Korea, and Oriental Russia; and when that was not enough to fully engage their surplus energies, they became an oceanic power, which soon brought them into conflict with two other oceanic powers—Britain and the United States. Defeated in war, the Japanese turned their undefeated energies into industry and commerce, becoming a world power through trade. But that kind of adventure is satisfactory for only a small part of the population; and when the newly prosperous Japanese middle class becomes bored with tourism, we shall probably see some kind of civil war or revolution in Japan—perhaps within the next twenty years.

Something of that sort may be said to have already happened in China. Powerless to wage war upon their neighbors, the Chinese waged war upon themselves, class against class, the result a triumphant revolution and the construction of a human society that may well become, unfortunately, the working model for all. I mean the thoroughly organized society, where all individual freedom is submerged to the needs of the social organism.

The global village and the technological termitorium. More nightmares! I do not believe that human beings would or could long tolerate such a world. The human animal is almost infinitely adaptable—but there must be limits to our adaptability, limits beyond which, if we can survive them at all, we would survive only by sacrificing those qualities that distinguish the human from that possible cousin of the future: the two-legged, flesh-skinned robot, his head, her head, its head wired by telepathic radio to a universal central control system.

One more example: What happened to India when its space was filled, its wilderness destroyed? Something curiously different from events in Europe, China, or Japan; unable to expand outward in physical space, unable or unwilling (so far) to seek solutions through civil war and revolution, the genius of India—its most subtle and sensitive minds—sought escape from unbearable reality by rocket flights of thought into the inner space of the soul, into a mysticism so deep and profound that a whole nation, a whole people, have been paralyzed for a thousand years by awe and adoration.

Now we see something similar happening in our own country. A tiny minority, the technological elite, blast off for the moon, continuing the traditional European drive for the conquest of physical space. But a far greater number, lacking the privileges and luck and abilities of the Glenns and the Armstrongs and their comrades, have attempted to imitate the way of India: When reality becomes intolerable, when the fantasies of nightmare become everyday experience, then deny that reality, obliterate it, and escape, escape, escape, through drugs, through trance and enchantment, through magic and madness, or through study and discipline. By whatever means, in some cases by *any* means, escape this crazy, unbearable, absurd playpen of the senses—this gross 3-D, grade-B, X-rated, porno flick thrust upon us by CBS News, *Time, Newsweek,* the *New York Times, Rolling Stone,* and the *Sierra Club Bulletin*—seeking refuge in a nicer universe just next door, around some corner of the mind and nervous system, deep in the coolest cells of the brain. If all is illusion then nothing matters, or matters much; and if nothing matters then peace, of a sort, is possible, striving becomes foolish, and we can finally relax, at last, into that bliss which passeth understanding, content as pigs on a warm manure pile. Until the man comes with the knife, to carry the analogy to its conclusion, until pig-sticking time rolls around again and the fires are lit under the scalding tubs.

You begin to see the outline of my obsessions. Every train of thought seems to lead to some concentration camp of nightmare. But I believe there are alternatives to the world of nightmare. I believe that there are better ways to live than the traditional European-American drive for power, conquest, domination; better ways than the horrifying busyness of the Japanese; better ways than the totalitarian communes of the Chinese; better ways than the passive pipe dreams of Hindu India, that sickliest of all nations.

I believe we can find models for a better way both in the past and the present. Imperfect models, to be sure, each with its grievous faults, but better all the same than most of what passes for necessity in the modern world. I allude to the independent city-states of classical Greece; to the free cities of medieval Europe; to the small towns of eighteenth- and nineteenth-century America; to the tribal life of the American Plains Indians; to the ancient Chinese villages recalled by Lao-tse in his book, *The Way.*

I believe it is possible to find and live a balanced way of life somewhere halfway between all-out industrialism on the one hand and a make-believe pastoral idyll on the other. I believe it possible to live an intelligent life in our cities—if we make them fit to live in—if we stop this trend toward joining city unto city until half the nation and half the planet becomes one smog-shrouded, desperate and sweating, insane and explosive urbanized concentration camp.

According to my basic thesis, if it's sound, we can avoid the disasters of war, the nightmare of the police state and totalitarianism, the drive to expand and conquer, if we return to this middle way and learn to live for a while, say at least a thousand years or so, just for the hell of it, just for the fi of it, in some sort of steady-state economy, some sort of fr democratic, wide-open society.

As we return to a happier equilibrium between industrialism and a rural-agrarian way of life, we will of course also encourage a gradual reduction of the human population of these states to something closer to the optimum: perhaps half the present number. This would be accomplished by humane social policies, naturally, by economic and taxation incentives encouraging birth control, the single-child family, the unmarried state, the community family. Much preferable to war, disease, revolution, nuclear poisoning, etc., as population control devices.

What has all this fantasizing to do with wilderness and freedom? We can have wilderness without freedom; we can have wilderness without human life at all; but we cannot have freedom without wilderness, we cannot have freedom without leagues of open space beyond the cities, where boys and girls, men and women, can live at least part of their lives under no control but their own desires and abilities, free from any and all direct administration by their fellow men. "A world without wilderness is a cage," as Dave Brower says.

I see the preservation of wilderness as one sector of the front in the war against the encroaching industrial state. Every square mile of range and desert saved from the strip miners, every river saved from the dam builders, every forest saved from the loggers, every swamp saved from the land speculators means another square mile saved for the play of human freedom.

All this may seem utopian, impossibly idealistic. No matter. There comes a point at every crisis in human affairs when the ideal must become the real—or nothing. It is my contention that if we wish to save what is good in our lives and give our children a taste of a good life, we must bring a halt to the ever-expanding economy and put the growth maniacs under medical care.

Let me tell you a story.

A couple of years ago I had a job. I worked for an outfit called Defenders of Fur Bearers (now known as Defenders of Wildlife). I was caretaker and head janitor of a 70,000-acre wildlife refuge in the vicinity of Aravaipa Canyon in southern Arizona. The Whittell Wildlife Preserve, as we called it, was a refuge for mountain lion, javelina, a few black bear, maybe a wolf or two, a herd of whitetail deer, and me, to name the principal fur bearers.

I was walking along Aravaipa Creek one afternoon when I noticed fresh mountain lion tracks leading ahead of me. Big tracks, the biggest lion tracks I've seen anywhere. Now I've lived most of my life in the Southwest, but I am sorry to admit that I had never seen a mountain lion in the wild. Naturally I was eager to get a glimpse of this one.

It was getting late in the day, the sun already down beyond the canyon wall, so I hurried along, hoping I might catch up to the lion and get one good look at him before I had to turn back and head home. But no matter how fast I walked and then jogged along, I couldn't seem to get any closer; those big tracks kept leading ahead of me, looking not five minutes old, but always disappearing around the next turn in the canyon.

Twilight settled in, visibility getting poor. I realized I'd have to call it quits. I stopped for a while, staring upstream into the gloom of the canyon. I could see the buzzards settling down for the evening in their favorite dead cottonwood. I heard the poor-wills and the spotted toads beginning to sing, but of that mountain lion I could neither hear nor see any living trace.

I turned around and started home. I'd walked maybe a mile when I thought I heard something odd behind me. I stopped and looked back—nothing; nothing but the canyon, the running water, the trees, the rocks, the willow thickets. I went on and soon I heard that noise again—the sound of footsteps.

I stopped. The noise stopped. Feeling a bit uncomfortable now—it was getting dark—with all the ancient superstitions of the night starting to crawl from the crannies of my soul, I looked back again.

And this time I saw him. About fifty yards behind me, poised on a sand bar, one front paw still lifted and waiting, stood this big cat, looking straight at me. I could see the gleam of the twilight in his eyes. I was startled as always by how small a cougar's head seems but how long and lean and powerful the body really is. To me, at that moment, he looked like the biggest cat in the world. He looked dangerous. Now I know very well that mountain lions are supposed almost never to attack human beings. I knew there was nothing to fear—but I couldn't help thinking maybe this lion is different from the others. Maybe he knows we're in a wildlife preserve, where lions can get away with anything. I was not unarmed; I had my Swiss army knife in my pocket with the built-in can opener, the corkscrew, the two-inch folding blade, the screwdriver. Rationally there was nothing to fear; all the same I felt fear.

And something else too: I felt what I always feel when I meet a large animal face to face in the wild: I felt a kind of affection and the crazy desire to communicate, to make some kind of emotional, even physical contact with the animal. After we'd stared at each other for maybe five seconds—it seemed at the time like five minutes—I held out one hand and took a step toward the big cat and said something ridiculous like, "Here, kitty, kitty." The cat paused there on three legs, one paw up as if he wanted to shake hands. But he didn't respond to my advance.

I took a second step toward the lion. Again the lion remained still, not moving a muscle, not blinking an eye. And I stopped and thought again and this time I understood that however the big cat might secretly feel, I myself was not yet quite ready to shake hands with a mountain lion. Maybe someday. But not yet. I retreated.

I turned and walked homeward again, pausing every few steps to look back over my shoulder. The cat had lowered his front paw but did not follow me. The last I saw of him, from the next bend of the canyon, he was still in the same place, watching me go. I hurried on through the evening, stopping now and then to look and listen, but if that cat followed me any further I could detect no sight or sound of it.

I haven't seen a mountain lion since that evening, but the experience remains shining in my memory. I want my children to have the opportunity for that kind of experience. I want my friends to have it. I want even our enemies to have it—they need it most. And someday, possibly, one of our children's children will discover how to get close enough to that mountain lion to shake paws with it, to embrace and caress it, maybe even teach it something, and to learn what the lion has to teach us.

23

Dust: A Movie

A desert ghost town—call it Pariah—in the sunlight. The
time is today, tomorrow, or a thousand years ago. A few
clouds drift across the brilliant sky. One dancing dervish of
red dust whirls down the street of the abandoned town. The
twister dances out across the crumbling slopes of the hills,
vanishes. The camera turns, fully around, to survey the entire scene, coming to rest finally upon the corner of a stone
wall, beyond which can be seen the glittering facets of a
small muddy stream, the tamarisk and willow, the hills of
clay, shale, and sandstone, a slice of blue space. The camera

meditates upon this simple prospect. Nothing happens. Almost nothing: The shadows lengthen, the gradual transformations of the light proceed through the seamless phases of their nature. Nothing happens. Perhaps a lizard appears on the wall, looks around, performs its routine business, disappears; perhaps not. There is no sound except the stir of air, the breathing of the earth. A chink of adobe drops from the wall. Four hours pass. The sun goes down (having no alternative), leaving a panorama of colored vapors spread like a stain across the sky. The bare clay hills glow in organic hues of liver maroon, lung-colored rose. The first stars reveal themselves, unblinking beyond the pellucid atmosphere. The camera, deliberately but slowly, turns toward the east to await the moonrise. A second camera continues to observe the effects of the setting sun. A third camera continues to record the quality of the light on the ancient rock wall in the foreground. A fourth camera picks up and follows the movements of a human couple, a man and a woman seen in the distance somewhere across the creek, silhouetted for a time against the yellow sky. They appear to be lovers; but perhaps not. All images from the four cameras are blended in montage. As are the sounds. The moon rises, silver and enormous, glowing from within like a paper lantern, above the rim of the sandstone cliffs. As it rises, bulging above the world's edge, we hear at the same time the tinkle of music from an out-of-tune piano. Sounds of laughter, clink of glass, quiet words, liquids pouring, blood dripping on a wooden floor, gunfire, neigh of a horse, squeak of a screen door, the quiet talk of lovers, more laughter, cry of a great horned owl, song of coyotes, a laughing man, a shod horse walking down a dusty street. All sounds cease. The street is empty. The lovers, beyond the creek, pace along the skyline, their forms dark against the smoldering sky. The moon floats higher. The moon pauses. Silence. All is silent. The water of the muddy creek, rippling over an array of stones, which gleam, makes no audible sound. The lovers vanish. Two hours pass. Three. Four. The moon drifts upward and

westward into a sea of luminous clouds. DISSOLVE. Dawn. A
single camera records the sunrise. Reverse illuminations on
the barren hills, on the isolated cottonwoods along the water,
on the rock walls, the wooden ruins, a broken-down water
wheel. The camera goes for a tour, prowling among the
ruins, inspecting at close range the texture of the stone, the
warped, splintered doorways, a clump of prickly pear growing from an earthen rooftop, the sand, the mud at the water's edge, the coppery skin of a willow's stem, the dust of
the street, hoofprints, tracks of coyote and kit fox and rep-
tile in the sand, the footprints of a pair of humans—man
and woman—which wander in aimless fashion, as it seems,
among the boulders and junipers on the far bank of the
stream. The sun rises higher. Hours pass. Pause. The small
desert river flows. Afternoon. Heat. Clouds form out of nowhere. Lightning flashes in the distance and, after an appro-
priate interval of time, we hear the mutter and rumble of
the thunder. The camera observes the approach of the
storm. Wind whistles through the derelict ruins of the town.
Startled birds rise in a flock. Sheen of rain on the hills. The
storm arrives. Lightning flickers in the gloom. The rain
comes driving down. The wind presses against old walls;
things loosen and fall—a sheet of tin, a rotten timber, a slab
of rock that once was the lintel of a doorway. The cottonwood trees by the river groan in the wind's embrace. The
sun glows dim red beyond an amber haze. Within the dull
boom and moan of the wind, we hear chords struck from a
harp, the tinkle of an untuned piano. The storm engulfs the
scene, blown to frenzy by the frantic winds. The camera's
bewildered eye revolves, gives us one glimpse as the lightning flashes again of a man and a woman sprawled and
broken on rock, their torn clothing soaked with rain and
blood, their eyes wide open, lifeless, mirroring the storm.
CUT. Under evening light and a sky the color of aluminum
the camera, now at rest, observes the passage of a massive
flood down the riverbed. Uprooted trees float by, drowned
animals, fragments from the wreckage of a wooden boat.

The water is blood red, flecked with foam. Grumble of mighty rocks beneath the surge, overborne and tumbling seaward. The camera's eye, seeing beyond the flood, contemplates the spectacle of the sunset over the western hills, the vermillion clouds floating across a hundred miles of radiant sky. Birds cry, the flood purls on like flowing oil, frogs croak and sing from the mud flats beside the swollen river. CUT. Night. Stars. Scattered clouds, the dim shapes of ruined buildings. We see the flight of an owl, silent as a moth, down upon its unseen prey. A small cry. CUT. The trees are leafless. The desert is covered with a thin layer of snow. The sun from a clear sky blazes down on fields of snow, dazzling as diamonds, and on the bones of a human skeleton. DISSOLVE. We see the ghost town reduced to sunken stone walls and mounds of earth. The snow is gone. We look at the scene through a scrim of shimmering heat waves. DISSOLVE. Bleached bones lie scattered on the rock. Rain; the hills erode before our eyes. DISSOLVE. The bones are carried by run-off water toward the creek, inching along in fits and starts within a thin swirl of liquid mud. DISSOLVE. Rocks crumble from the canyon wall. The final traces of the town, overgrown with brush and cactus, melt into the desert. DISSOLVE. Dark birds hover in the sky. The growing flare of dawn. Five, six, seven deer walk beside the water. One pauses to drink, the others gaze at the cliffs beyond. In the foreground, immediately before the eye of the camera, a lion rises from a ledge to watch the progress of the deer. A slight noise from above. Slowly, deliberately, the lion turns its head and stares with burning yellow eyes directly into the camera. The camera zooms in close, the eyes fill the screen, and we see in their golden depths the reflection of the sunrise, the soaring birds, the cliffs, the clouds, the sky, the earth, the human mind, the world beyond this world we love and hardly know at all . . . . DISSOLVE. This film goes on, it has no end . . . . DISSOLVE . . . DISSOLVE . . . . DISSOLVE . . . . .

Printed in the United States
by Baker & Taylor Publisher Services